International Studies

vol. 4

CLEMSON
UNIVERSITY
PRESS

Published by Clemson University Press in Clemson, South Carolina

To order copies, contact Clemson University Press at 116 Sigma Dr., Clemson, South Carolina, 29634 or order via our website: www.clemson.edu/press.

Contents

Volume 4, Issue 1

REVIEWS

Teaching "Problematic" Yeats: Relevance Without Recuperation

Carrie Preston

In the era of #MeToo and #SayHerName, internet "callout culture,"[1] Trump-ism, Brexit, and an unprecedented global crisis of forced displacement—all abundantly represented in various forms of media—many college students are endlessly tuned-in to the most recent culture wars. Why and how do we teach W. B. Yeats today? I studied Yeats's "Leda and the Swan" (1924) in col-lege as a poem about myth, centered on an epistemological question: "Did she put on his knowledge with his power[...]?" My students today consider it a "rape poem." We celebrate the centennial of Yeats's even-more-famous "The Second Coming" (1919), a poem I studied as a prophetic revision of the Chris-tian apocalypse for the post-World War I moment. My current students worry about Yeats being sacrilegious and exemplifying cultural appropriation with his use of stereotypical imagery of the Middle East. Did I even recognize that the poem was set in the Middle East when I was in college? I have long acknowl-edged that my students teach me as much as I teach them, and that literature's power and relevance become evident as it impacts subsequent generations in different ways.

In this essay, I encourage scholars and teachers of Yeats to look anew at those works that are relevant to contemporary challenges in ways that strike many as *problematic* (a word my students and I overuse, but which I nonethe-less embrace). The problematic category includes some of Yeats's most famous and frequently taught poems, including "Leda and the Swan" and "The Second Coming." Both can help us engage with students about contemporary concerns, particularly sexual misconduct, cultural appropriation, and migration. Yeats's poems offer opportunities for nuanced and complex conversations that recog-nize many of our current challenges have a relevant history. Such conversations are all too absent from callout culture, and are and not always encouraged by more so-called "politically correct" literary works. Our classroom conversa-tions will be more productive if we work to suppress, to a certain extent, our recuperative strategies and tendencies. That is, we should not focus on excus-ing ("we can't expect Yeats to adhere to our versions of political correctness"), historicizing ("it was a different time"), or sanitizing ("let's look for underlying subversive currents") Yeats. While such critical approaches are crucial for some analytical projects, they can feel disingenuous to students, and they effectively reduce the complexity of the classroom conversations about Yeats's relevance to the contemporary challenges that are of utmost concern to our students.

LEDA AND THE #MeToo MOVEMENT

> Because of its vast historical vision and agonizing pantomime of passion and conflict, "Leda and the Swan" can justifiably be considered the greatest poem of the twentieth century.
>
> —Camille Paglia, *Break Blow Burn* (2005)[2]

Camille Paglia's excellent reading of "Leda and the Swan" was published before President Barak Obama's administration provided guidance to universities regarding their enhanced Title IX responsibilities to fight sexual misconduct in a 2011 "Dear Colleague" memo.[3] When those guidelines were rescinded in 2017 by President Donald Trump's controversial Education Secretary, Betsy DeVos, protests from students erupted across the United States, especially on campuses wracked by high-profile sexual assault cases, including Michigan State University, Yale University, and Baylor University, among others. DeVos has been sued by Equal Rights Advocates and other groups working on behalf of American students. Paglia's claim that "Leda and the Swan" is the "greatest poem of the twentieth century" was also published before the #MeToo movement was sparked in 2017 by a tweet from American actress Alyssa Milano. Just twenty-four hours later, over 500,000 had tweeted "me too" to indicate they had been sexually harassed or assaulted; in the following year, the hashtag was used 18 million times, while a backlash against the movement also surfaced.[4] Discussing Yeats's highly erotic and sensual description of the rape of Leda by Zeus in the guise of a swan provokes some different questions in the #MeToo era: Is it "problematic" to consider a poem about a rape the "greatest" of its century? What standards of greatness are we applying? What are the erotic and gendered implications of the poem? Are we prepared to answer students' questions about why we are teaching "Leda and the Swan" when it might make some of our students uncomfortable or even be "triggering" to survivors of sexual assault?

I believe that teachers and scholars of Yeats can discuss these difficult questions openly with students, and that people might arrive at different answers. While the particular answer is less important than the process of discussion, my students are not generally satisfied by the logic that "Yeats is famous; the poem is famous; you need to know it if you wish to be a cultured, literate person, English major, Modernist, etc." A prevalent but easily disputed set of claims, this line of thinking does a disservice to the impact of humanistic inquiry; it fails to address the biases inherent in standards of "famous," "cultured," and "literate" as well as the presumptions underlying what any literate person "needs to know"—which has changed dramatically over time and is not consistent across contemporary cultures.

My answer to the question of why we study "Leda and the Swan" is that it can help us explore the problematic sexual politics of our time, including rape culture, as well as the role of myth and biased standards of greatness in creating those politics. I tell my students early in the semester that I believe learning is not, and should not, always be easy or comfortable, and that we need to have very uncomfortable conversations about topics such as rape if we wish to change our culture. In classroom conversation, I work to prepare students to read and discuss challenging texts, some of which should make them uncomfortable, and I explain why I do not include "trigger warnings" on my syllabi. Those campaigning for trigger warnings in higher education have suggested that students should not be held responsible for engaging with course materials they might find troubling or problematic, particularly representations of sexual violence. I believe that approach, however well-intentioned, actually contributes to the tendency to avoid confronting the huge problem of rape culture on college campuses. The term trigger warning, as it is used and debated in higher education, implies that professors could anticipate "triggering" content for every student, despite the diversity of college populations. Triggers are defined in behavioral health literature as "any sensory reminder of the traumatic event: a noise, smell, temperature, other physical sensation, or visual scene."[5] Highly individualized and specific to any traumatic experience, triggering stimuli are not often correlated to the *content* of a discussion or reading. Mental health professionals have suggested that the goal of healing is not advanced when survivors avoid conversations related to trauma, and studies have found that trigger warnings do not alleviate student discomfort.[6] Critics also point out that demands for trigger warnings focus on representations of rape and sexual misconduct but ignore other traumas, especially those attending race, poverty, and ethnicity or the damage done when the experiences of minorities are systematically avoided in classrooms.[7]

When I discuss "Leda and the Swan" with students in the #MeToo era, I begin by acknowledging that the poem is a literary representation of a mythic rape. I emphasize aspects of the poem that do not adhere to contemporary standards for discussing sexual assault, including the principle that Leda, as a survivor, should be represented with dignity and without complicity. I also share with students my impulse toward recuperative readings (probably a professional liability) and tell them I hope to avoid any simple version of recuperation. At the same time, I ask students to examine the multiple meanings and complexity of even the most "problematic" lines. Many of the images in the first two stanzas of the poem suggest the violence of the attack and the suffering of Leda, alongside the "pantomime of passion and conflict."[9] The "sudden blow" in the first line of the poem is an image of violence, a "blow" to Leda's body, as well as a reference to the blowing air from the "great wings beating still" (*VP*

441, *l* 1). The "dark webs" that "caressed" Leda's thighs refer to the webbed feet of the swan but also suggest a web of entrapment. The "nape" or back of her neck is "caught in his bill," and she is "helpless" (*l* 3–4). The two questions that compose the second stanza might be read both as rhetorical and literal:

> How can those terrified vague fingers push
> The feathered glory from her loosening thighs?
> And how can body, laid in that white rush,
> But feel the strange heart beating where it lies? (*VP* 441, *ll* 5–8)

The rhetorical reading of the first question implies that she could not have pushed away Zeus in the form of a swan, even if her "fingers" were less "vague" in response to the attack. Similarly, a rhetorical reading would suggest that she could in no way have *avoided feeling* his "strange heart." If we read the questions literally, they ask if Leda could have avoided the rape or could have avoided feeling the attack. Many survivors of rape question how they might have prevented the assault, and many feel numb or disassociated during and after the trauma. Many also feel confused and even guilty about the complex physical experiences of the trauma, characterized in this poem by references to "that white rush" and "strange heart beating." Classroom conversations must make space for students to discuss how certain lines of the poem present Leda as complicit ("loosening thighs") and glorify rape with reference to Zeus's "feathered glory," even if professors think that is not the main point of Yeats's "Leda and the Swan."

I encourage students to consider the ways the form of the poem troubles any seemingly simplistic celebration of the mythic rape. The true, simple, even mundane rhymes in the first stanza ("still" and "bill") give way, in the second stanza, to rhymes that are less true ("push" and "rush"). In the third stanza, the rhymed quatrain form breaks down into a sextet with a broken third line, an ABC/DABD rhyme scheme, and a closing off-rhyme in "up" and "drop." The simplicity of the opening stanza and its rhymes are gone, replaced by broken lines and rhymes, uncertainty before history, and more questions: "Did she put on his knowledge with his power/ Before the indifferent beak could let her drop?" (*VP* 441, *ll* 13–14). Beyond suggesting that Leda "put on" anything in the moment of assault, the knowledge that she might have gained from Zeus is that the rape "engenders" Leda's daughter Helen, and through her, the Trojan War that would leave "Agamemnon dead" and destroy Troy. As Yeats's "No Second Troy" (1912) indicates, one of the Helens he imagined was largely responsible for the devastating war between the Trojans and Greeks, removing blame from Paris, the Trojan prince who took her to Troy, Menelaus, her vengeful husband, or the Greek king Agamemnon, who may have used the flight/abduction of

Helen as an excuse to plunder Troy: "Why, what could she have done, being what she is? / Was there another Troy for her to burn?" (*VP* 256–57, *ll* 11–12). "No Second Troy" provides another example of Yeats's tendency to pair questions, the second one limiting the reading of the first to: "She" (widely believed to refer to Yeats's beloved Maude Gonne) did what she did because of "what she is," and she is the kind of woman who burns a kingdom. "Leda and the Swan" offers a very different interpretation of responsibility for (the Trojan) war. Leda was "mastered by the brute blood of the air," as Zeus is described, and he was "indifferent" both to her terror and to the future devastation his assault "engenders." The language of "mastery," in relation to rape, is undeniably problematic. But, in relation to a god as indifferent brute, the language in the later poem emphasizes Zeus's responsibility, partially through the assault on a mortal woman, for a long chain of suffering.

The reading of "Leda and the Swan" I learned—the one that considers the poem an exploration of the relationship between power, metaphorically represented by sexual power, and knowledge—is not wrong. With that reading in mind, the "rape poem" label could be considered misguided and ahistorical, in that it might appear to ignore the poem's broader mythic implications as well as the fact that rape has been defined differently throughout history and across cultures. Yet, if we discuss the rape poem framework with our students, as uncomfortable as it might be for all, we can use "Leda and the Swan" to facilitate an important and challenging conversation that may help students recognize how their historical moment and its conceptions of rape influence their reading—as well as the relevance of poetry to their lives. While Yeats's works will not advance the gender politics many prefer in the #MeToo era—and we cannot expect them to—we can recognize that our gender politics are just as widely contested as they were during Yeats's time. Yeats's poems, layered as they are with classical myths and autobiographical details, help us understand the pervasiveness of cultural tropes, like the raped woman who gains knowledge or insight from her powerful rapist, or the beautiful woman who cannot help but cause battles between men.

"SLOUCHES TOWARD" (INSERT ANY REGION OF THE GLOBE'S) REFUGEE CRISIS

"Is Germany Slouching Toward Weimar Again?: No. Today's immigration problem is much more limited than the social ills of the interwar period."
—Joseph Joffe, *Wall Street Journal* (Sep. 23, 2018)[9]

One hundred years after Yeats wrote "The Second Coming" (1919), it is one of the most widely-quoted poems in English, so widely quoted that its phrase, "slouches toward____," can apparently be used without attribution in discussions of recent political events.[10] The phrase has characterized the presidency of Donald Trump ("America is slouching toward autocracy"),[11] Great Britain's departure from the European Union ("Slouching Toward Brexit"),[12] and the refugee crisis impacting Europe and beyond ("Slouching Toward Ankara: The EU-Turkey Migration Deal").[13] Josef Joffe asked "Is Germany Slouching Toward Weimar Again?" after demonstrators brandished Nazi symbols in protest of the Merkel government's refugee policies, leaving one dead and many wounded in Chemnitz on August 27, 2018. With a resounding "No," Joffe pointed to dramatic differences between Weimar Germany in the 1920s and the current strength of the German democracy, which, he claims, "suffers from only one serious ailment: uncontrolled immigration through its porous borders."[14] Joffe is no friend to the right-wing neo-Nazi demonstrators with signs reading "Refugees Not Welcome," but he, like many others throughout history, lays all the blame on migrants and refugees. Ironically, by alluding to Yeats's "The Second Coming" (without attribution), Joffe implicitly connects our current moment to the birth of the doomed Weimar Republic in 1919 (a centennial the world is not celebrating), the year Yeats composed the poem.

Writing in the wake of the First World War, Yeats saw "loosed upon the world," as he writes, "Mere anarchy" and "The blood-dimmed tide" (*VP* 401–02, *ll* 4–5). The immediate context for "The Second Coming" was the 1919 Treaty of Versailles, which ended the war, imposed punishing sanctions on Germany, and doomed the fledgling Weimar Republic. The Irish War of Independence was ripping apart Yeats's native Ireland, the Russian Revolution put Lenin in power, and armed conflict raged in Greece, Syria, Turkey, Mexico, Poland, and Afghanistan, among other places. Assigning "The Second Coming" on college syllabi today will not produce calls for trigger warnings and will be less immediately alarming than "Leda and the Swan." To help students understand the international relevance of the poem, as well as its misinterpretations, I share articles like Joffe's "Is Germany Slouching Toward Weimar Again?" or most recently, Jeet Heer's "The Centrists Did Not Hold," a report on the Democratic primary debates on July 30, 2019 that concluded: "All in all, the debate evoked the reverse of the famous lines from W. B. Yeats's poem 'The Second Coming'; this time, the best were full of passionate intensity, while the worst lacked all conviction. The centrists did not hold."[15]

Some of my students describe "The Second Coming" as problematic for reasons that I initially found surprising: specifically, for its representations of Christianity and the Middle East. The poem's second stanza adapts the promise of the future return of Jesus Christ from the New Testament, particularly the Revelation to John and the Gospels (Matthew 24–25; Mark 13; Luke 21:5–26; John 14:25–29). In the book of Revelation, the second coming of Christ will give rise to a resurrection of the faithful or elect, and inaugurate a millennial Kingdom on earth. After the millennium, there will be full resurrection and last judgment, leading to the creation of a new heaven and Earth and a new Jerusalem. Expectations of an imminent second coming were common in early Christianity and have emerged again during cataclysmic times, such as wars, epidemics, or natural disasters—or 1919, in the view of Yeats. Believing that the city of Jerusalem will be the site of Christ's return and location of his kingdom, Christians have traveled to Palestine so as to be present for the second coming. Whether via Crusades, missions, immigration, or tourism, Christian journeys to Palestine have contributed to the suffering and exploitation of non-Christian, Arab, Muslim, and Jewish populations.

The second stanza of "The Second Coming" draws on this complex of Christian beliefs in the end-of-times, but instead of a Christly figure, Yeats invokes "A shape with lion body and the head of a man, / A gaze blank and pitiless as the sun" (*VP* 401–02, *ll* 14–15). Contrary to the many declarative invocations of "slouching toward [Brexit, autocracy, Ankara, etc.]," the famous final lines of the poem present a question: "And what rough beast, its hour come round at last, / Slouches towards Bethlehem to be born?" (*VP* 401–02, *ll* 21–22). Yeats does not give an answer, but the beast is certainly not establishing an earthly kingdom of the righteous and a New Jerusalem. Several of my students have worried that this treatment of biblical material is disrespectful, and offensive to Christians. Yeats's speaker claims to have realized, of the time since the birth of Jesus, "That twenty centuries of stony sleep / Were vexed to nightmare by a rocking cradle…" (*VP* 401, *ll* 19–20). Suggesting that the cradle belongs to Jesus and that Christian time is a "nightmare," or at best, "a stony sleep," Yeats presents a very bleak vision of Christianity that troubles some students—both those who identify as Christian and those who worry that Christians would be offended by this representation and revision of the second coming of Christ.

Similarly, some of my students have been concerned that Yeats commits "cultural appropriation" in his representation of the Middle East. They point to images that portray the region in a negative and stereotypical manner—and that academics might call "orientalist" with reference to Edward Said's famous formulation.[16] Yeats locates his "rough beast" in biblical Palestine/contemporary Israel with a direct reference to Bethlehem—the birthplace of Jesus, near the presumed location of the New Jerusalem. Images such as the "sands of the desert" and "desert birds," along with the "pitiless" sun, present the landscape as desertous, a stereotype of the Middle East belied by the fact that parts of the region feature a mild Mediterranean climate that supports agriculture, particularly the growth of olives, oranges, pomegranates, barley, wheat, and lentils. Jerusalem and Bethlehem are in the Judean Hills, which are cooler than the deserts of the south and the Dead Sea region. The bleak expanse of desert, "shadows," "darkness," and "nightmare," all suggest a negative representation of the Middle East, and the Sphinx-like "rough beast" can be read as a particularly Orientalist image. Although many cultures have imagined chimeric creatures, Yeats invokes Egypt and the Great Sphinx of Giza for most readers when he describes, "somewhere in sands of the desert / A shape with lion body and the head of a man." The line might suggest that one place in the vast and complex "Orient" (Palestine) is interchangeable for another (Egypt), a quintessentially problematic and common habit of thought in a field that imagines "the Orient" as a coherent and uniform object of study.

Yeats's poetry and plays regularly invoke other cultures, from ancient Greece to the Middle and Far East, in ways that seem problematic to students raised to identify and "callout" instances of cultural appropriation and misrepresentation. While I want to affirm my students' social consciousness and cultural sensitivity (which has advanced hugely since my college years), I also hope to complicate their assumptions, which can sometimes tip from sensitivity to a less productive piety and "gotcha" mentality. I encourage my students to recognize that myths, legends, and other cultural materials are constantly being adapted, translated, and rewritten by artists. Cultures are alive, changing, and incoherent, not static and sacrosanct. Considering "Leda and the Swan" alongside "The Second Coming" allows me to pose some challenging questions that point to the tensions and contradictions in our understanding of cultural appropriation: Why do we seem to be less concerned about Yeats's appropriation of Greek myth in "Leda and the Swan" than with his invocations of that other Mediterranean country and culture, Palestine, although it is typically considered more Middle Eastern than Mediterranean? Why are many of us concerned that the revision of Christian myth in "The Second Coming" is offensive, even as we want Yeats's treatment of Greek myth to be more overtly critical of the rape in "Leda and the Swan"? A crucial part of the answer to these questions is that Palestine and the Middle East more generally are the site of devastating conflicts and asymmetrical power relations with deep roots in European imperialism. For many students, the identity positions of authors are relevant to whether or not they have a "right" to represent, much less critique, a culture or religion. Yeats, as a white Anglo-Irish man, was part of the British colonial system that carved up the Middle East, brokered power between countries and non-governmental actors, and took advantage of the colonies' natural resources and native labor. Yet Yeats was also a member of a colonized population, born into a country that was under British rule and suffered a devastating war for independence, and a civil war that resulted in a partitioned Ireland. While from one perspective Yeats's European identity would not give him the authority to represent the Middle East, he is an example of how complicated identity politics can be. Born into a Protestant Irish family, Yeats might be considered to have a "right" to critique Christianity through his revision of the second coming. But Christianity, unlike Greek myth, is a contemporary, widely-practiced religion presented by some, particularly American conservatives, as "under attack" and therefore considered in need of protection. As few people worship the ancient Greek pantheon today, the myth of Zeus and Leda is thought to need no such deference.

Who ultimately "owns" a cultural tradition, and who has the right to adapt it? Are we satisfied with the judgment that only those born into a tradition may use or be inspired by it? This culture-of-birth-determinism poorly accommodates migrants, immigrants, refugees, adoptees, and other mobile and/or displaced persons. That includes a lot of people in our increasingly migratory world, where 70.8 million people have been forcibly displaced by wars and persecution, the highest levels of displacement ever recorded.[17] Yeats's "The Second Coming" has been hailed as "prophetic" of nearly every crisis and catastrophe since its publication. Paglia claims the poem "has gained in prophetic power with each decade of the twentieth and now twenty-first century, from the rise of fascism and nuclear warfare to the proliferation of international terrorism."[18] Today, I find "The Second Coming" prophetic in relation to the crisis of forced displacement and the political debates over immigration that are raging around the world.

One way to read "The Second Coming" in relation to the global crisis of forced displacement is to bring in data about the current municipality of Bethlehem, and to set that picture next to the biblical Bethlehem of Christ's birth and the early-twentieth-century Bethlehem at the time of Yeats's composition. Throughout history, Bethlehem has been both a refugee town and a site of pilgrimage. Jesus was born in a manger in Bethlehem, according to Luke 2:1, because Mary and Joseph had to travel there to be registered for a census. When Yeats was writing "The Second Coming," Bethlehem took in Armenians and other minorities who were fleeing genocidal violence at the birth of the state of Turkey—a country which now hosts the world's largest number of refugees, approximately 3.5 million displaced people.[19]

Today, the Bethlehem toward which Yeats's "rough beast" "slouches" has been described as an "open-air prison" for Palestinians displaced by the creation of the Israeli state.[20] Bethlehem has long been the site of an important aquifer that dispenses water to the roughly equal number of Israelis and Palestinians now living in the area. A wall separates Bethlehem from the Israeli settlements surrounding the town, and Palestinian workers wait behind bars at "Checkpoint 300" for passage to jobs on the other side.[21] There are three refugee camps in the municipality of Bethlehem—Aida, Beit Jibrin, and Dheisheh—that host over 19,000 of the approximately 5.4 million Palestinian refugees registered by the United Nations Relief and Works Agency (UNRWA).[22] Discussing this

data may be considered problematic by students and others who equate attention to Palestinian suffering with anti-Semitism, although the equation is not
logical. The controversy provides an opportunity for a challenging classroom
discussion about the relationship between protesting institutionalized rac-
ism—whether in Israel or the USA—and anti-Semitism or anti-Zionism, terms
which also require differentiation and careful definition.

If the second stanza of "The Second Coming" seems to prophesy the suffering of refugees in Bethlehem and around the world, the first stanza describes
polarizing political discourse, characteristic of the Israeli-Palestinian conflict as
well as global debates about immigration and the crisis of forced displacement:
"The best lack all conviction, while the worst / Are full of passionate intensity"
(*VP* 401, *ll* 7–8). Those who genuinely want to alleviate the suffering of refugees
and migrants "lack conviction" about how to do so, whereas the anti-migra-
tion messages are characterized by passion, "intensity," and often, bigotry. As
an example of the latter, I might bring to class discussion the recent "send her
back" chant that emerged at a rally for President Trump in North Carolina on
July 17, 2019, inspired by Trump's tweeted claim three days earlier that four
congresswomen of color should "go back" to their countries (three were born
in the USA, and all are US citizens).[23] Paglia writes of the heated political rhetoric, as described in "The Second Coming, "neither consensus nor compromise
is possible. Public debate shifts to the extremes or is overtaken by violence,
which blocks incremental movement toward reciprocity and conciliation."[24]
True as this may be for politics, Yeats's poem does not advocate for moderation
or centrist politics with its "rough beast" in the desert and its suggestion that
the "nightmare" of modern Christian time is coming to an end. Rather than
looking for political or social answers to the troubled historical moment it invokes in the first stanza, "The Second Coming" turns to the language of vision,
spiritualism ("*Spiritus Mundi*" means World Spirit), and apocalypse.

While some students might consider the lack of real-world solutions in
"The Second Coming" to be a problematic deferral, discussing the refugee crisis can also help them realize the complexity of global challenges and the lack
of obvious solutions, or even the necessity of imaginative approaches. Yeats's
images of "mere anarchy" and the "blood-dimmed tide" can be associated with
the lack of effective administration and deadly conditions faced by immigrants
and refugees. Media provide devastating images of drowned refugees, from the
body of Aylan Shenu, a three-year-old Syrian boy, washed up on a beach in
Bodrum, Turkey in 2015 to the photo from this past summer of the drowned
El Salvadoran father, Óscar Alberto Martínez Ramírez, and his 23-month-old
daughter, Valeria, floating near the bank of the Rio Grande on the US-Mexico
border:[25] "The ceremony of innocence is drowned." Using classroom discussions to bring these images and the refugee crisis more generally to a poem

written a hundred years ago, I risk a reading that is presentist and even ahistorical. Yet again, I believe it is possible to discuss with students both the historical context of the poem and its relevance to contemporary readers and events without reducing or recuperating the text.

Just as I acknowledge in class that "Leda and the Swan" can be read as a rape poem, I recognize that teaching "The Second Coming" in relation to the global challenge of forced displacement and alongside images of drowned refugees can make students uncomfortable. I want to be sensitive to the disturbing nature of this material and prepare students to receive it. As with "Leda," I would not use a so-called trigger warning, partially because, as I mentioned above, research has demonstrated that they do not alleviate student distress. Additionally, trigger warnings have become so closely associated with sexual misconduct that issuing them for the drowning of refugees or other violent images and content confuses students. Works of art that include a murder, suicide, and other violence will only be criticized for not offering a trigger warning about the rape, as if those affected by other forms of violence, say forms associated with race, ethnicity, poverty, and displacement, should be of less concern.[26] This is a problematic assumption that clarifies cultural biases and priorities.

Many of Yeats's works will strike students, and perhaps scholars and teachers of Yeats, as problematic in relation to contemporary social movements like #MeToo, concerns about representation and appropriation of cultures and religions, and global challenges like the crisis of forced displacement. The laudable social consciousness and cultural sensitivity of college students, as well as their version of identity politics, can sometimes make it feel that any choice professors make when constructing a syllabus is potentially problematic: Yeats might appear particularly out of step with our cultural moment as a white, male poet who was famously ambivalent about the Irish War of Independence, spent a good deal of time in London, served as a Senator in Ireland's first post-colonial government (1922–28) where he eloquently but unsuccessfully battled divorce and censorship bills, and was later drawn to fascism, amongst other political positions that are widely considered problematic today.[27] I choose to acknowledge and embrace the problematic Yeats in my classroom, openly discussing why I find works like "Leda and the Swan" and "The Second Coming" relevant to our contemporary moment. These poems help us discuss the historical foundations of systems of gender and geopolitics as well as the contradictions inherent in many of our perspectives today. The problematic, relevant, unrecuperated Yeats generates more questions than answers, calling attention to the many questions in his poems. By teaching the problematic Yeats, we help our students confront the complexity of challenges we can only hope they will, compared to previous generations, address more compassionately and effectively.

NOTES

1. Conor Friedersdor, "The Destructiveness of Call-Out Culture on Campus: Reflections from Undergraduates of the Social Media Era," *The Atlantic*, May 8, 2017, https://www.theatlantic.com/politics/archive/2017/05/call-out-culture-is-stressing-out-college-students/524679/; Julian Vigo, "Call-Out Culture: Technological-Made Intolerance," *Forbes*, Jan. 31, 2019, https://www.forbes.com/sites/julianvigo/2019/01/31/call-out-culture-technological-made-intolerance/#63f6e3947653.

2. Camille Paglia, *Break Blow Burn* (New York: Pantheon, 2005), 117.

3. Full letter available at https://www2.ed.gov/about/offices/list/ocr/letters/colleague-201104.html.

4, "Measuring the #MeToo Backlash," *The Economist*, Oct. 20, 2018, https://www.economist.com/united-states/2018/10/20/measuring-the-metoo-backlash.

5. US Substance Abuse and Mental Health Services Administration, *Trauma-Informed Care in Behavioral Health Sciences,* Treatment Improvement Protocol (TIP) series 57 (Rockville, Md.: HHS Publications, 2014), 68.

6. Mevagh Sanson, Deryn Strange, and Maryanne Garry, "Trigger Warnings Do Little to Reduce People's Distress, Research Shows," *Association for Psychological Science*, Mar. 19, 2019, https://www.psychologicalscience.org/news/releases/trigger-warnings-distress.html. Susan P. Robbins, "Sticks and Stones: Trigger Warnings, Microaggressions, and Political Correctness," *Journal of Social Work Education* 52, no. 1 (2016), https://www.tandfonline.com/doi/full/10.1080/10437797.2016.1116850?scroll=top&needAccess=true.

7. Jack Halberstam writes, "The trigger-happy folks, on the other hand, fail to account for vast discrepancies within and among student bodies, and they mark sexual violence in particular as the most damaging and the most common cause of trauma among students. Both sides ignore the differences between and among students, and all fail to account for the differences that race and class make to experiences with trauma, expectations around protection, and exposure to troubling materials" (539). Halberstam, "Trigger Happy: From Content Warnings to Censorship," *Signs: Journal of Women in Culture and Society* 42, no. 2 (Winter 2017): 535–42.

8. Paglia, *Break, Blow, Burn*, 117.

9. Joseph Joffe, "Is Germany Slouching Toward Weimar Again?: No. Today's Immigration Problem is Much More Limited than the Social ills of the Interwar Period," *Wall Street Journal*, September 23, 2018, https://www.wsj.com/articles/is-germany-slouching-toward-weimar-again-1537723883.

10. Nick Tabor tracks the history of allusions to and "misapplications" of "The Second Coming" in Tabor, "No Slouch," *The Paris Review*, Apr. 7, 2015, https://www.theparisreview.org/blog/2015/04/07/no-slouch/. See also Adam Cohen's claim, "'The Second Coming' is fast becoming the official poem of the Iraq war." Cohen, "What W. B. Yeats's 'Second Coming' Really Says About the Iraq War," *The New York Times*, Feb. 12, 2007, https://www.nytimes.com/2007/02/12/opinion/12mon4.html.

11. E. J. Dionne, Jr., "America is Slouching Toward Autocracy," *The Washington Post*, Aug. 19, 2018, https://www.washingtonpost.com/opinions/america-is-slouching-toward-autocracy/2018/08/19/52e9b1aa-a244-11e8-8e87-c869fe70a721_story.html?utm_term=.0c4abd790e62.

12. Philippe Legrain, "Slouching Toward Brexit," *Foreign Policy*, Nov. 3, 2015, https://foreignpolicy.com/2015/11/03/slouching-toward-brexit-britain-europe-eu/.

13. Silvia Colombo, "Slouching Toward Ankara: The EU-Turkey Migration Deal," Global Memos, Council of Councils, Apr. 29, 2016, https://councilofcouncils.cfr.org/global-memos/slouching-toward-ankara-eu-turkey-migration-deal.

14. Joffe, "Is Germany Slouching Toward Weimar Again."

15. Jeet Heer, "The Centrists Did Not Hold," *The Nation*, Aug. 1, 2019, https://www.thenation.com/article/john-delaney-retire/.

16. Edward Said defined "Orientalism" as "...a style of thought based upon ontological and epistemological distinctions made between 'the Orient' and... 'the Occident'" in Said, *Orientalism* (New York: Pantheon, 1978), 69.

17. "Figures at a Glance" United Nations High Commissioner for Refugees (UNHCR) USA, June 19, 2019, https://www.unhcr.org/en-us/figures-at-a-glance.html.

18. Paglia, *Break, Blow, Burn*, 113.

19. "Which Countries Host the Most Refugees?" Knowing Arabia Watching Arabia (KAWA), June 20, 2019, https://kawa-news.com/en/which-countries-host-the-most-refugees/.

20. Simon Worrall, "The Little Town of Bethlehem Has a Surprising History," *National Geographic*, Dec. 23, 2017), https://news.nationalgeographic.com/2017/12/bethlehem-christ-birth-blincoe/.

21. Peter Beaumont, "A Day in the Life of the West Bank Occupation," *The Guardian*, June 6, 2017, https://www.theguardian.com/world/2017/jun/06/a-day-in-the-life-of-the-west-bank-occupation.

22. "Where We Work," United Nations Relief and Works Agency for Palestine Refugees in the Near East (UNRWA), https://www.unrwa.org/where-we-work. According to The World Factbook, there are 846,465 Palestinian refugees in the entirety of the West Bank, including Bethlehem, and 1,421,282 refugees in the Gaza Strip. There are approximately 238,000 internally displaced persons in Gaza and the West Bank, including those displaced as long ago as 1967 and some displaced since 2014 when the Israeli-Palestinian conflict in Gaza intensified again. See "West Bank," The World Factbook, US Central Intelligence Agency (CIA), https://www.cia.gov/library/publications/the-world-factbook/geos/we.html and "Gaza Strip," The World Factbook, CIA, https://www.cia.gov/library/publications/the-world-factbook/geos/gz.html.

23. Conor Friedersdorf, "'Send Her Back': The Bigoted Rallying Cry of Trump 2020," *The Atlantic*, July 18, 2019), https://www.theatlantic.com/ideas/archive/2019/07/send-her-back/594253/; David Remnick, "A Racist in the White House," *The New Yorker*, July 15, 2019, https://www.newyorker.com/news/daily-comment/a-racist-in-the-white-house-donald-trump-tweets-ocasio-cortez-tlaib-omar-pressley.

24. Paglia, *Break, Blow, Burn*, 111.

25. Siobhán O'Grady and Rick Noack, "Photo of Drowned Migrant Child Recalls an Image that Shocked the World in 2015," *The Washington Post*, June 26, 2019, https://www.washingtonpost.com/world/2019/06/26/photo-drowned-migrant-child-recalls-an-image-that-shocked-world/?utm_term=.e0e0592948ad.

26. Trigger warnings related to, for example, murder, suicide, racial violence, racial microaggresions, or accidental death are rarely demanded, although these forms of violence are also ubiquitous in our culture and have an inordinate impact on people of color. This discrepant treatment of forms of violence is evident in a recent essay by Charlene Smith, which offers strategies for "Staging Sexual Assault Responsibly," HowlRound Theatre Commons, July 10, 2019, https://howlround.com/staging-sexual-assault-responsibly#block-comments). Smith discusses her remarkable "feminist version" of Thomas Middleton and William Rowley's *The Changeling*, a play from the 1620s in which the noblewoman Beatrice-Joanna hires a man to murder her fiancé after she falls in love with another man. The servant she hires "forces her to pay him with her virginity." Although murder and suicide are devastating forms of violence in the play, the essay does not discuss how to responsibly and ethically stage those scenes; nor does the "note about content" issued for the play warn about murder and suicide: "Thomas Middleton and William Rowley's *The Changeling*" Brave Spirits Theatre, Oct. 18–Nov. 18, 2018, http://www.bravespiritstheatre.com/portfolio/the-changeling/.

27. For Yeats's Senate speeches, see Donald R. Pearce, "The Senate Speeches of W. B. Yeats" (London: Faber and Faber, 1961). Conor Cruise O'Brien in 1965 gave his famous verdict that Yeats was "as near to being a Fascist as the conditions of his country permitted." O'Brien, "Passion and Cunning: An Essay on the Politics of W. B. Yeats," reprinted in O'Brien, *Passion and Cunning: Essays on Nationalism, Terrorism, and Revolution* (New York: Simon and Schuster, 1988), 8–61. Yeats followed different and conflicting political positions over his lifetime, and these positions do not easily translate into the centrist, liberal, and conservative designations operating today; any discussion of Yeats's politics must be rooted in a careful analysis of a particular text and its specific political moment. See also Peter Liebregts and Peter van de Kamp, eds., *Tumult of Image: Essays on W. B. Yeats and Politics* (Amsterdam: Rodopi, 1995) and Jonathan Allison, *Yeats's Political Identities: Selected Essays* (Ann Arbor: University of Michigan Press, 1996).

Yeats's Queer Dramaturgies: Oscar Wilde, Narcissus, and Melancholy Masculinities In Calvary

Zsuzsanna Balázs

"Have you noticed that the Greek androgynous statue is always the woman in man, never the man in woman? It was made for men who loved men first."
—W. B. Yeats (*L* 875)

David Cregan has called Frank McGuinness the first Irish playwright to apply a distinctively queer dramaturgical epistemology in his plays.[1] Yet it is less often acknowledged that Yeats's drama also took significant steps towards creating space for an anti-normative and anti-authoritarian queer dramaturgy, and thus intervened in normative constructs of sexuality and gender, indirectly joining the sexual liberation and women's emancipation movements of his time. This was predominantly the result of his collaborations with and inspirations from transgressive artists such as Florence Farr, Michio Itō, Sarah Bernhardt, Vaslav Nijinsky, and Loïe Fuller, as well as his manifold transcultural inspirations which defied sexual polarization and hyper-masculinity in favor of more illicit forms of *eros* and a gender-bending body ideal. These inspirations included the occult, ancient Greece, ancient India and Tantric philosophy, the Noh theater, the great New Women artists of the time, Percy Bysshe Shelley's poetry, Sergei Diaghilev's anti-(hetero)normative ballet movement,[2] London's queer activism of the 1890s,[3] and Oscar Wilde, on whom I will focus in this study.

I will argue that Yeats's drama, which is often seen as an anti-democratic and elitist space, is also able to foster a space of inclusion and visibility for people treated by the patriarchal state as invisible (no)bodies, who defy conventional categorizations. This includes powerful women who disrupt conventional notions of motherhood and marriage, but also effeminate men, dancers, actresses, gay people, and people with any sign of difference or excessive, recalcitrant temperaments. Judith Butler calls such unrecognized subjectivities ungrievable lives, which cannot be recognized as injured or lost by the mainstream political frameworks which guide society's interpretation of the world.[4] Yet Yeats's drama has the potential to open up the frameworks of recognition for marginalized subjectivities by representing their lives as grievable, by sympathizing with their pain, and by making visible the structures of insult and violence that aim to hurt them. This is a means of claiming political recognition and participation for unrecognized lives and stories, and deconstructing heterosexuality and masculinity as the main presumptive frameworks.

So far, the transgressive and anti-normative aspects of Yeats's works have been addressed mainly by Elizabeth Cullingford, Susan Cannon Harris, Alexandra Poulain, Ben Levitas, Cassandra Laity, and Jason Edwards from various angles, and I wish to join their discussions here. I aim to highlight the often-muted queer sensibilities in *Calvary* (1920) in the context of Yeats's public sympathy for Wilde. I wish to open up this play for new contemporary interpretations and demonstrate how it can resonate with ideas proposed by contemporary queer theorists, mainly with Judith Halberstam's and Leo Bersani's ideas of failure, betrayal, male bonding, and death drive, Dider Eribon's ideas of solitude and melancholy, and Eve Kosofsky Sedgwick's thoughts on performativity and the closet.

I begin with a discussion of the queer aesthetic of Yeats's theater and his feminist and queer networks, which is followed by a section on Wilde, Christ, and Narcissus. The final section addresses the queer dramaturgical strategies in *Calvary*. I mainly discuss representations of queer subjectivities here, but I also embrace a more expansive notion of queer as strangeness and "as a force of disruption"[5] which is able to reveal the anxieties repressed in the normative world.

YEATS'S QUEER AESTHETIC

Due to Yeats's position as a white, male, middle-class Protestant citizen of the British Empire and his controversial responses to the rise of authoritarian politics, Yeats and his works could be seen as representatives of the dominant literary tradition and the mainstream patriarchal political discourse, as Cullingford has explained.[6] Even in his position as an Irish nationalist, Yeats was expected to represent tradition and masculinity. Hence, most readings and productions of Yeats's plays tend to stress only the normative and heteronormative aspects of his dramaturgy, even though his plays, especially the later ones, abound in transgressive characters and anti-normative masculinities and femininities. Cullingford also pointed out, using Hélène Cixous's words, that Yeats was one of those artists who frequently "let something different from tradition get through."[7]

Portraying sexual dissidence and illicit desires was part of this endeavor. Cullingford identified two main types of transgression in Yeats's poetry: the woman in man, "and the more socially transgressive man in woman."[8] This is true for Yeats's plays as well, where the characters displaying sexual dissidence are usually dancers associated with the wind or the waves. Both the waves and the wind represent potential, dissidence, movement, fluidity, plasticity, and the wavering of identity—a state of ungraspability—all of which inherently resist homogenizing efforts.[9] An example of this is Yeats's *The Land of Heart's Desire*, where the queer young girl, while seducing Mary Bruin, describes their kind as the ones who ride the winds and run on the waves.

Transgressive women are usually associated with the wind in Yeats's works, and thus also with the fierce, shape-changing women of the Sidhe and the figure of Salomé. The transgressive and effeminate male characters, on the other hand, are usually connected to the waves (represented, for instance, by male dancers in *Fighting the Waves*) and sometimes to the wind as well. In his introduction to Fighting the Waves, Yeats describes the changing philosophy of Europe in which man has become "a swimmer, or rather the waves themselves" (*VPL* 569). In his notes to "The Hosting of the Sidhe" (1893), Yeats also draws the connection between Salomé, the Sidhe, and the wind: "Sidhe is also Gaelic for wind, and certainly the Sidhe have much to do with the wind. They journey in whirling wind, the winds that were called the dance of the daughters of Herodias in the Middle Ages" (*VP* 800).

In her book *Irish Drama and the Other Revolutions* (2017), Susan Harris stresses that the emerging Irish aesthetic in the 1890s was already remarkably queer. Irish playwrights, including Yeats, began to dramatize the embodiment of sexual and social politics thanks to the influence of London's queer socialism, Shelley's radical *eros*, and the independent, educated New Women of the time.[10] Harris's book is also very enlightening because it gives justice to Florence Farr's political and social importance as a queer woman and as "an English feminist turned actress"[11] whose contribution to avant-garde drama is much more significant than it has been accounted for. Besides Farr[12], Yeats's New Women influences included Sarah Bernhardt,[13] Mrs. Patrick Campbell, Eleonora Duse, and the dancers Isadora Duncan and Loïe Fuller, who were all powerful figures in the performing arts and encouraged ways of being other than the dominant modes.

The rich relationship between queerness and modern Irish drama is well established, but it is less often acknowledged how Yeats's theater contributed to and, in fact, inaugurated this queer aesthetic with the performance of his play *The Land of Heart's Desire* in 1894, in the milieu of London's turn-of-the-century queer activism. Harris explains that Yeats's play was staged as part of the season of avant-garde drama organized by Farr in the Avenue Theatre along with John Todhunter's *A Comedy of Sighs*. Despite London's very active queer socialist atmosphere, both Yeats's and Todhunter's plays failed because of their portrayal of transgressive women.[14] More specifically, *The Land of Heart's Desire* displays the desire between a young girl (fairy child) and an older, newly wed woman named Mary Bruin. It includes some moments of intimate physical touch between the two characters, hence Harris called the play "unambiguously queer-positive and feminist."[15] More importantly, both Yeats's and Todhunter's plays fused the "two fundamental anxieties evoked by the New Woman: the fear that she would reject motherhood, and the fear that she would reject heterosexuality."[16] The representation of lesbian desire is still very limited in Irish theater, but it needs to be highlighted that Yeats's *The Land of Heart's Desire* and Todhunter's *A Comedy of Sighs* were the first Irish plays which staged desire between women that was encoded in the framework of the supernatural, which could "obscure the more troubling aspects of female desire."[17]

In "The Catastrophe," Yeats mentions that Wilde overwhelmed him with compliments after the first performance of *The Land of Heart's Desire* (*Au* 287), encouraging him to follow this transgressive path in his art despite the huge failure of the plays and G. B. Shaw's vicious reaction—not only to the two plays but to Farr's androgynous, "sexless" stage presence. Shaw described Farr in her role in Todhunter's play as "a nightmare, a Medusa, a cold, loathly, terrifying, grey, callous, sexless devil."[18] As Harris explains, Yeats also felt resentment about the success of Shaw's play *Arms and the Man* in 1894, and saw it as the victory of a pugilistic masculinity,[19] because Shaw rewrote it to stress masculinity after the failure of Yeats's and Todhunter's plays: "To save himself from similar punishment, Shaw revised *Arms and the Man* and replaced Farr with a more gender-conforming actress."[20] Yet Harris's discussion makes it clear that Farr made a very significant contribution to making Yeats's drama more inclusive of a wide range of gender and sexual possibilities. What is more, the founding of the Irish Literary Theatre in 1897, after Yeats's negative experience with London audiences, "was, in part, Yeats's attempt to continue Farr's experiment in a more hospitable environment."[21]

Creating such a theatrical aesthetic and drawing inspiration from these artists was an important political statement in itself, in the context of emerging authoritarian and totalitarian nationalist political ideologies which built on the concepts of respectability and normalcy, refused ambiguity in every field of life, and looked at dancers and actresses with growing suspicion and scorn.[22] It was important within the Irish political context as well, in which Republican soldiers and Black and Tans (the early manifestations of fascism) broke into houses during the Irish War of Independence and humiliated women by shaving their heads.[23] In addition, W. T. Cosgrave's Free State Ireland drew heavily on the Italian fascist model and engaged in censorship,[24] while in the 1930s Éamon de De Valera's Ireland consolidated its regressive sexual politics.[25]

This queer aesthetic was predominantly the result of Yeats's pervasive, rich queer and feminist networks, which included dancers, activists, suffragists, New Women, poets, and other artists from whom he drew much inspiration—both directly and indirectly—and who shaped his drama in considerable ways. Besides Wilde, Farr, and Bernhardt, these cultural networks included, most notably, his lesbian friends Edith Shakleton Heald, Hilda Matheson, and Lady Dorothy Wellesley, but also the artists Aubrey Beardsley and Edmund Dulac, Gate Theatre dramatists Micheál MacLiammóir, Hilton Edwards, Lennox Robinson,[26] and Madame Bannard-Cogley—also known as Toto, who (with Edwards and MacLiammóir) organized cabaret performances in Dublin. Michael Patrick Lapointe has also pointed out that Yeats expressed his concerns about the anguish he sensed in his colleague Edward Martyn. He felt sympathy for the desires Martyn had to repress and the vicissitudes he had to endure because of social pressure and because of his own conservative views and religious caution, which Yeats referred to in *The Cat and the Moon* too.[27] The women of the Irish Revolution should also be mentioned here, many of whom were lesbians. Yeats's friendship with Constance Markievicz and Eva Gore-Booth is well known, but few have emphasized Gore-Booth's role as the founder of Ireland's first feminist periodical *Urania* in 1916, which published the works of lesbian artists and whose articles stressed that sex is only an accident.[28] Ninette de Valois and Michio Itō brought Sergei Diaghilev's anti-(hetero)normative ballet movement to Yeats's attention; Diaghilev deliberately countered the classical ballet (*ballet blanc*) tradition by working with effeminate dancers like Vaslav Nijinsky and tall, boyish dancers like Ida Rubinstein, whose body and movements were labelled as unwomanly and disproportionate by most critics.[29] More precisely, Itō's art had been shaped by Nijinsky's performances before Itō began his collaboration with Yeats on *At the Hawk's Well*, in which Itō played the Hawk-Woman.[30]

In *The Death of Cuchulain*, Yeats also expresses his disagreement with the classical ballet tradition, which strengthens idealized notions of femininity and portrays women as fragile and weak: "I spit upon the dancers painted by Degas. I spit upon their short bodices, their stiff stays, their toes whereon they spin like peg-tops, above all upon the chambermaid face" (*VPL* 1052). Yeats was also influenced by two Italian avant-garde playwrights, Luigi Pirandello and Gabriele D'Annunzio, who had controversial affiliations with fascism, yet whose plays featured the most powerful New Women of the time and provided a scathing criticism of the sexual/gender polarization, the desexualization of bodies, and patriarchal rule that constituted some of the main pillars of fascist rule.[31]

Even though Yeats's turn to the drama was originally a search for what he called "more of manful energy" (*VP* 849), his experimentation with dramatic form and multiple identities, and his use of non-linear, more and more fluid, and anti-mimetic dramaturgical structures also allowed for a dramaturgy that resisted repressive and exclusive normative frames. As Cormac O'Brien explains, the fragmented dramaturgical strategies which characterize anti-realism "disavow realist narrative drama in favor of free-flowing theatrical form"[32] and are able to challenge "the very concept of norms, and systems of theatrical and social normalizing;"[33] "the queerer the form, the queerer the possibilities for masculine identities."[34]

Yeats gradually moved towards dance and movement-based plays featuring more and more physical touch, embodiment/disembodiment processes, spectral characters, strangers and strangeness, as well as dream elements, all of which challenge the patriarchal authority and mastery of language and discourse. This is especially true for the figure of the male dancer, as dance itself has always represented the threat of the feminine and the erotic for patriarchal, anti-erotic societies which fear the power of *eros*.[35] As Gabriele Brandstetter explains, "[a]round the turn of the century, the body-image of dance reflected contemporary patterns of femininity that were (largely) based on two key models: the model of ancient Greece and the model of the exotic."[36] It is not by accident that experimental avant-garde theater was regarded as a constant threat to political power because of its tendency to break away from normative sexuality and tradition, creating queer alliances and thus a conspiracy against the status quo. Harris has also pointed out that the sexual liberation movement held "that freedom from the heterosexual family unit was inseparable from freedom from economic oppression and political tyranny."[37]

What is queer in Yeats is often not immediately graspable, comprehensible, or visible: "The thing, the 'queer' is what emerges among, across, and between,"[38] and "it is how the elements rub, collide, and comingle."[39] James Flannery also stated that Yeats was in many ways a twenty-first century writer, whose plays try to convey many vital messages through text and dramaturgy—yet most of them remain entrapped or hidden in the dramatic text and in subtext, which the audience cannot see and often cannot understand.[40] Dissident and transgressive spectacle in Yeats's plays often takes place offstage, described by other characters, but once they are depicted, the plays' queer potential can also increase. Yeats's plays include several moments when the audience can be queerly moved because the spectacle, dance, or image transgresses traditional borders of authority, language, and representation, which feel like "a queerly transitory suspension of the regular rules of society."[41]

Totalizing and homogenizing systems—such as patriarchy, imperialism, (ultra)nationalism, and heteronormativity—see difference, disorder, and ambiguity as their major enemies. They build on concepts of unified national identity, security, compulsory heterosexuality, traditional family values, politics of hope and optimism, moral and sexual prudery, hierarchy, clear separation of gender roles, virility, female modesty, respectability, segregation, and classification of people into transparent categories. Yeats's drama, however, is queer because it reveals the destructive mechanism of these systems by representing the tension between the oppressive normative discourse and the non-normative subjectivities it tries to silence. Yeats's plays abound in obscurity, disunity, ambiguity, and fluidity of meaning. They portray a constant shifting between identities, inversion of gender roles and heroism, various forms of failure, non-hierarchical characterizations, and potent hybrid and shape-changing bodies—like the Sidhe and bird-women, and bodies separated from their voices. They also display explicit expressions of eroticism, solitude as a form of protest, sexually ambiguous diction, same-sex and other illicit desires, powerful women, strong feminist voices, and characters who disobey patriarchal figures and refuse categorization. This way, Yeats's drama gave visibility to subjectivities and subcultures that the normative discourse wanted to hide from the public eye and thus engaged contemporary debates about the feminist, gender non-conforming New Woman, and homosexuality. This tension between the queer and the normative, the authoritarian and the recalcitrant is also the main reason why Yeats's plays can be queered, and his portrayal of the pressure that the normative discourse puts on stigmatized individuals is what makes his drama so relevant for queer and feminist research today.

In Yeats's plays, the pressure sometimes comes from the representative of the state (like in *The King's Threshold*, *The Player Queen* and *The King of the Great Clock Tower*) or family members (like in *The Land of Heart's Desire*), but more frequently from a family patriarch or some other, often invisible, patriarchal figure (as in *Calvary* and *The Cat and the Moon*). Yet the oppressive performative utterances of the normative characters are countered with another set of performative speech acts and gestures coming from the characters who are perceived as strange and disruptive. What is more, as Yeats himself acknowledged, New Women actresses like Farr were perceived by bourgeois nationalist audiences as insults on public morality and were proximate to violence against the state and the nation. He described *The Land of Heart's Desire* as "a wild mystical thing carefully arranged to be an insult to the regular theatre goer who is hated by both of us. All the plays [Florence Farr] is arranging for are studied insults. Next year she might go to Dublin as all her playwrights by a curious chance are Irish" (*L* 384).

I also contend that the queer moments of Yeats's drama are not restricted to explicitly articulated same-sex desire. Queer moments also include unfulfilled spiritual, emotional, or physical yearning for members of the same sex or some other unavailable love; more expanded notions of female/male friendship and love; sexually ambiguous diction, bodily discomfort, and sense of displacement as symptoms of unarticulated desires; and forces of disruption that are also sources of attraction. Most of these appear in various forms in *The Land of Heart's Desire*, *The Countess Cathleen*, *The Dreaming of the Bones*, *Calvary*, *The Cat and the Moon*, *The Resurrection*, *A Full Moon in March*, and *The King of the Great Clock Tower* as well. Yeats's plays often portray attraction between "womanly" men and "manly" women. This is a returning pattern in the Cuchulain plays and *A Full Moon in March* and characterizes Yeats's own desires as well. He also inverts traditional notions of heroism by replacing male heroes with female heroes (as in *Deirdre* and *The Only Jealousy of Emer*), portraying women who turn their diminishment into power and oppress the oppressor (as Decima in *The Player Queen*), or representing heroes who leave hyper-masculinity behind and opt for a non-competitive, more tender masculine identity (as *Christ in Calvary*, or Cuchulain in *The Death of Cuchulain* and in the poem "Cuchulain Comforted"). Sinn Féin's unsigned review of an Edward Martyn play from 1912 nicely illustrates contemporary reactions to such inverted gender representations: "We tire ... of Mr. Martyn's weak men and strong women ... Martyn can do large things in drama, and does not do them because he lets a little devil compounded of perversity and sentimentality run away with him."[42]

There is also a lot of nonverbal discursive hiatus in Yeats's play texts, which can provide opportunity for a queer ambiguity, especially the dance scenes which have the potential to disturb the patriarchal authority of language. Some of these dramaturgical strategies are mentioned in recent essay collections, such as *Queer Dance* (2015) and *Queer Dramaturgies* (2016), as the main components of contemporary queer performance, but these works can also help us see where Yeats's plays can lead queer. It should also be emphasized that a theatre which takes pleasure in escaping enclosure and fixed meaning, moving between multiple identities, layers of reality, and closeted identities and desires, is also a queer theatre that disrupts social and theatrical norms. Hence, I believe that a more comprehensive queer re-evaluation of Yeats's drama is in order now.

The Gate and Druid Theatres recognized and demonstrated some of these potentialities of Yeats's plays in performance: the character of Aleel in *The Countess Cathleen* was first played by Farr, but in its 1953 production, Micheál MacLiammóir took on the role: he was wearing heavy makeup and his lips were painted, recalling drag performance and also the spectacle of the male Dionysian dancers of *The Resurrection* (1931), who are dressed up as women and whose lips are painted vermilion. In 1987, Garry Hynes also directed Sophocles's *Oedipus* in Yeats's version in the Druid Lane Theater in Galway, and in this production, Oedipus King of Thebes was played by Marie Mullen, resulting in a similar drag spectacle.[43] Besides MacLiammóir and Hynes, Yukio Mishima, a gay Japanese poet and playwright, also recognized the queer potential of Yeats's plays. Mishima translated many of Yeats's Noh plays into Japanese and admired their aesthetic pessimism.[44] Mishima applied this aesthetic pessimism in his own Noh plays as well, in his descriptions of the painful beauty of Saint Sebastian's pierced, naked body which bears affinities with the melancholy figure of Christ in Yeats's *Calvary*. Interestingly, it was this spectacle that raised Mishima's first same-sex desire, as described in his *Confessions of a Mask* (1949): "It is not pain that hovers about his straining chest, his tense abdomen, his slightly contorted hips, but some flicker of melancholy pleasure like music."[45]

In the following two sections, I illustrate how the use of the unhappy Lazarus motif and the implicit references to Narcissus in *Calvary* work to provide a discourse of legitimation for gay masculinities and same-sex love.[46] My focus is on melancholy, self-doubting masculinities and dramaturgies of exclusion and inclusion, for as Didier Eribon explains, any representation of an effeminate or melancholy/contemplative man implies "male homosexuality—all of them—even when one knows this has no basis in reality"[47] and "[a]nytime one speaks of homosexuality, then, it can only be heard as an attempt to affirm it, to flaunt it, it can only be seen as a provocative gesture or a militant act."[48] Halberstam also stresses that signs of effeminacy (including contemplative, solitary, and melancholy men) have always been condemned by masculine societies as a threat to the politics of virility and as a betrayal of patriarchal fraternity.[49] While male bonding and homoerotic fraternity can be more easily worked into patriarchal social structures and narratives, the real threat is the refusal of these bonds—rejecting masculine mastery and choosing solitude instead, settling for a "non-suicidal disappearance of the subject,"[50] as the unhappy Lazarus aims to achieve in Yeats's *Calvary*.

I also find it striking that Yeats's plays defy conventional capitalist notions of success and heroism, deploying various processes of unbecoming, undoing social relations, disruption, confusion, failure, absence, silence, solitude, forgetting, unknowing, sorrow, dissidence, negativity, and refusal. Halberstam discusses these forms of negativity in relation to shadow or counterintuitive feminism, which arises from queer, postcolonial, and black feminisms and stresses that this kind of aesthetic pessimism is able to counter imperialist and nationalist projects of hope, which do not tolerate sorrow and negativity and which enforce happiness and optimism.[51] Halberstam stresses that connecting queerness to death drive and failure works "to propose a relentless form of negativity in place of the forward-looking, reproductive, and heteronormative politics of hope that animates all too many political projects."[52] In fact, Yeats also claimed that he positioned himself against the mainstream political discourse to instead represent defeated, marginalized voices: "Why must I think the victorious cause the better? [...] I am satisfied [...] to find but drama. I prefer that the defeated cause should be more vividly described than that which has the advertisement of victory" (*VPL* 935). This aesthetic pessimism is not about nihilism, but about tracing the struggles of alternative ways of life, turning away from the restrictive normative ways to find and propose alternatives to traditional notions of authority, desire, social relations, and heroism. Halberstam calls this low theory[53] and compares it to Antonio Gramsci's counterhegemony, which is the circulation of another, competing set of ideas to change society, or, in other words, it is "a detour en route to something else."[54]

"Some Boy Of Fine Temperament:"
Oscar Wilde, Narcissus, And Christ As Counter-Heroes

One of the means of defying the (hetero)normative discourse is the creation of counter-heroes through a performance of effeminacy as authority, which appears both in Yeats's plays and in his writings about Wilde. In *A Vision*, Yeats mentions Wilde in Phase 19, along with the equally transgressive figures of Gabriele D'Annunzio, Lord Byron, and a certain actress (possibly referring to the great New Women actresses of his time). This is the phase of the disunity of being, where "the being is compelled to live in a fragment of itself and to dramatize the fragment" (*AVB* 110). Yeats claims that these people's thoughts express an exciting personality which is "always an open attack; or a sudden emphasis, an extravagance, or an impassioned declamation of some general idea, which is a more veiled attack" (*AVB* 111). Yeats's comment on Wilde is also striking: "I find in Wilde, too, something pretty, feminine, and insincere, derived from his admiration for writers of the 17th and earlier phases, and much that is violent, arbitrary and insolent, derived from his desire to escape" (*AVB* 112). Here the disunity of being and the extravagant personality are not necessarily negative. This phase and the people belonging to it seem to signify the performative turn, which is able to attack the discourse through a counter-performance of excess and difference. In fact, as Cullingford put it, Yeats too "had considerable trouble becoming a man"[55] and his sexual identity was indefinite; "[w]omen who loved women also loved Yeats."[56]

As Eribon explains, Wilde's "name quickly became the symbol both of gay culture and of the repression it inevitably calls down on itself whenever it goes too far in the direction of making itself public."[57] Jason Edwards also holds that "Wilde's death in 1900 made Yeats more determined to use his work as a vehicle to increase public sympathy for homosexual men,"[58] mostly on behalf of Wilde and Roger Casement. For instance, in 1901, in his review of John Eglington's *Two Essays on the Remnant*, Yeats seizes the occasion to criticize the Irish state for airbrushing people like Wilde from the frameworks of recognition (*CW10* 53–59). Edwards also refers to an unpublished letter of Yeats written to John Quinn in 1914, in which Yeats expresses his sympathy for "the generation of the green carnation," a flower which became symbolic of Wilde and homosexual recognition.[59] In "The Catastrophe," Yeats also describes how his contemporaries responded to Wilde's arrest and lamented that "[t]he World is getting more manly!" (*Au* 284).

As to Greek mythology, Eribon highlights the use of Greek love and ancient Greece in literature, which have long been seen as "a locus of legitimation for loves between members of the same sex,"[60] and allowed gay people "to provide

themselves with a set of references that justified what Christian culture, social prej-
udices, and even the law condemned to silence."[61] David M. Halperin also believes
that references to classical Greece and Greek love have become equal to references
to same-sex love.[62] Yeats refers to this in a letter to Lady Dorothy Wellesley in 1936:

> Your lines have the magnificent swing of your boyish body. I wish I could be a girl
> of nineteen for certain hours that I might feel it even more acutely. [...] Have you
> noticed that the Greek androgynous statue is always the woman in man, never the
> man in woman? It was made for men who loved men first (*L* 875).

Yeats also associated Greek sculpture with power, movement, and dance:
"Those riders upon the Parthenon had all the world's power in their moving
bodies and in a movement that seemed, so were the hearts of man and beast
set upon it, that of a dance" (*AVB* 201). Moreover, Yeats's first experience of
Farr's powerful queer stage presence in Todhunter's *A Sicilian Idyll* (1890) was
also in a Greek context, as she played "a brazen Hellenistic New Woman with a
hint of lesbianism."[63] As Laity explains, Yeats was fascinated with her grace and
power, with her boyish beauty, and described her as "Greek and arrogant."[64]
In fact, the use of Greek, Roman, and Celtic mythologies along with Oriental
themes and biblical frameworks in literature and theater have always been able
to represent repressed subcultures and forbidden desires in code, thanks to
their mainstream cultural position.

Yeats's admiration for ancient Greek drama through his readings of Fried-
rich Nietzsche and his use of the Apollonian-Dionysian dichotomy in his plays
is well known,[65] yet his interest in ancient Greece also included the myth of
Narcissus.[66] Hedwig Schwall has written about Yeats's frequent use of the story
of Narcissus and the nymph Echo in his poems to articulate the Poet-Muse relationship,[67] yet I believe that the same-sex aspects of the Narcissus story also
feature in Yeats's works, especially because the effeminate Narcissus staring at
his own image was associated with Oscar Wilde at the time. Thomas Nast created a caricature of Wilde-as-Narcissus, and Wilde himself wrote a tale about
Narcissus entitled "The Disciple," in which the pool admits that he was also in
love with Narcissus, as he saw his own image and beauty reflected in Narcissus's loving eyes. Wilde also often compared Lord Alfred Douglas to Narcissus
and Hyacinth. In a letter to Robert Ross, Wilde writes: "He is quite like narcissus—so white and gold. [...] Bosie is so tired: he lies like a hyacinth on the
sofa, and I worship him."[68] Another important link here is Nijinsky's famous
1911 performance of Narcissus in Paris, in Mikhail Fokine's ballet *Narcisse*,
which encouraged same-sex love and effeminacy. Nijinsky's relationship with
Diaghilev, the founder of the *Ballets Russes* movement, furthered the connection between Nikinsky, Narcissus, and homosexuality.[69]

Yeats, in his introductions to *Fighting the Waves* and *The Resurrection*, makes recurring references to a new type of love that is yet to be acknowledged and which "neither hate nor despair can destroy" (*VPL* 571); he also refers to the imminence of an age which includes, not excludes. Yeats seems to advocate for tolerance and acceptance here, stressing the importance of making rejected forms of life recognizable: "[o]ur civilization was about to reverse itself, or some new civilization about to be born from all that our age had rejected" (*VPL* 932) and "[p]erhaps we shall learn to accept even innumerable lives with happy humility" (*VPL* 935). Ben Levitas has also implied that, in fact, Yeats's attempt to create the theater's anti-self was also an attempt to create an anti-normative theater: a theater that is "more sensitive to an instinct of alienation, a dissentient unease adrift in consensus."[70] Levitas demonstrates this in Yeats's *The Land of Heart's Desire*, where "'the stranger' [the fairy child who seduces the newly wed Mary Bruin] is also a 'strangeness': the unfamiliar, or de-familiarising, form that intrudes into the house of realist narrative and carries with it the power to disrupt the normative materialism of domesticity."[71]

Yeats also identified himself with a female dancer, Herodiade, and described himself as someone who, in his effort to create an art that goes against accepted sureties and norms, is dancing alone in her luminous circles: "I am certain that there was something in myself compelling me to attempt creation of an art as separate from everything heterogenous and casual, from all character and circumstances, as some Herodiade of our theatre, dancing seemingly alone in her narrow moving luminous circle" (*Au* 247). This image can also recall Fuller's famously transgressive Serpentine/Butterfly dances; she played Salomé as well as Herodiade, and Yeats mentions her in "Nineteen Hundred and Nineteen," as her fluid movements seemed to "whirl out new right and wrong" (*VP* 430).

More pressingly, in "At Stratford-on-Avon" (1901), Yeats expressed his sympathy for young effeminate boys who prefer contemplation to physical activity, and condemned the toxic performance of hyper-masculinity. Yeats compares Shakespeare's Richard II and Henry V and sides with Richard II, who had always been looked upon as a sentimental, melancholy, and weak king. He warns against the idealization of the hypermasculine Henry V, who was so good at performing power, and had a "a resounding rhetoric that move[d] men" (*E&I* 108). Although Richard II was expected to lead with "rough energy" (*E&I* 106), he had "nothing to give but some contemplative virtue" (*E&I* 106). Yeats continues that Shakespeare scholars:

> took the same delight in abasing Richard II that school-boys do in persecuting some boy of fine temperament, who has weak muscles and a distaste for

school game. And they had the admiration for Henry that school-boys have for the sailor or soldier hero of a romance in some boys' papers. (*E&I* 104)

Yeats concludes that Shakespeare did not celebrate such hypermasculine heroes, but presented them with tragic irony. According to Edwards, Yeats in his defense of Richard II "eulogised Wilde,"[72] as Richard "shared Wilde's tragic destiny in being born in a masculine age antithetical to his own tender personality."[73]

Eribon explains the peculiar relation between gay men and art, and how this contemplative inner life can become a transformative energy, using an example from Marcel Proust's *Cities of the Plain* (*Sodome et Gomorrhe*), in which Proust evokes a young boy mocked by the other boys, because he "walks alone for hours on the beach, sitting on boulders and questioning the blue sea with a melancholy eye, an eye already full of worry and persistence."[74] In his essays about Wilde, Yeats associates Wilde's life experience with insult and melancholy, and connects Wilde to Christ as well as to a Lazarus-like figure who cries because Christ healed him.[75] When everyone urged Wilde to run away from the insults, Yeats praised Wilde's strength in not running away: "he has resolved to stay to face it, to stand the music like Christ" (*Au* 288). Yeats also associates Wilde's name with performativity and to the Greeks, and compares his storytelling style to Homer's and to "a dance [Yeats] once saw in a great house" (*Au* 133). Wilde also identified himself with the figure of Christ in *De Profundis* (1897), in which he mentions Christ's name more than sixty times and sees him as a contemplative artist and writer like himself.[76]

After detailing how Wilde had been trussed up, dragged up and down, been "hooted in the streets of various towns" (*Au* 132), and scorned by newspapers, Yeats mentions Wilde's obsession with a tale about Christ, which made a lasting impact on Yeats's imagination as well:

> One day he began, "I have been inventing a Christian heresy," and he told a detailed story, in the style of some early Father, of how Christ recovered after the Crucifixion, and escaping from the tomb, lived on for many years, the one man upon earth who knew the falsehood of Christianity (*Au* 136).

In the "The Catastrophe," Yeats yet again mentions Wilde's tale about Christ, which seemed to reflect Wilde's difficulties as a gay man, and which Wilde repeated to himself when he was in deep melancholy. In this story, Christ meets three people who are unhappy because he healed them. Christ's meeting with an old man grasped Yeats's attention the most: "At last in the middle of the city He saw an old man crouching, weeping upon the ground, and when He asked why he wept, the old man answered, 'Lord, I was dead and You raised me into life, what else can I do but weep?'" (*Au* 286).

In his introduction to Wilde's *The Happy Prince*, Yeats recalls this tale once again and claims that it "adds something new to the imagination of the world" (*CW6* 150). Here Yeats more explicitly connects Wilde's life experience and melancholy with that of the weeping old man who tells Christ, "Lord, I was dead and you raised me into life, what else can I do but weep?" (*CW6* 150) This line is important as it can also describe the difficult life of people who face a precarious existence and stigma, people whom the heteronormative world either wants to exclude or "heal"—including them in its repressive, homogenizing narrative only to mark them as deviant, strange, emotional, and overly melancholy. It also implies that melancholy is part of this stigmatized life, which can cast a dark shadow even on the moments of greatest triumph, as Eribon also points out: "This 'melancholy' arises from the unending, unfinishable mourning of the loss homosexuality causes to homosexuals, that is to say, the loss of heterosexual ways of life, ways that are refused and rejected (or that you are obliged to reject because they reject you)."[77]

Thomas Carlyle's name should also be mentioned in this context. Carlyle's book on heroism asserted that authority was strictly masculine; history was about great men, and greatness entailed a combination of aesthetic leadership and segregation. Hence, *On Heroes, Hero-Worship, and The Heroic in History* (1840) became a major point of reference for Fascist and nationalist visualities.[78] Carlyle was a major influence on Standish O'Grady and even on Wilde, but as Geraldine Higgins points out, Yeats was never really interested in Carlyle "except to disparage his prose style."[79] Wilde built on Carlyle's ideas on the hero, but only to challenge them by posing as an effeminate hero which "created a clear sense of gender and sexual difference."[80] As Mirzoeff explains, this was a countervisual claim to autonomy, staged against Carlyle's reality: "If his being Irish could not be posed as Heroic aristocracy because of his perceived embodied difference, Wilde repositioned it as a form of Heroic resistance to tyranny that nonetheless endorsed the continuance of a decentralized British empire."[81] For Mirzoeff, this countervisual claim is always performative, always goes against the masculine authority of visuality, and represents trans, queer, and feminist projects: it "is the means by which one tries to make sense of the unreality created by the visuality of authority while at the same time proposing a real alternative."[82]

Yeats also made a countervisual claim for Wilde: at a time when everyone saw Wilde as the exact opposite of a man of action, Yeats detailed Wilde's tenderness and kindness, claiming that he "considered him essentially a man of action, [...] and [Wilde] would have been more important as a soldier or politician; and [Yeats] was certain that, guilty or not guilty, he would prove himself a man" (*Au* 285). Here Yeats deconstructs the normative and gendered views of manliness, heroism, and authority as the opposite of tenderness, kindness, and effeminacy. This is similar to the example Mirzoeff uses in his book about Sojourner Truth, who presented herself as a hero of the US abolitionist movement that also "challenged the gendering of heroism as inevitably masculine."[83] Yeats also recalls that Wilde created a counter-hero of himself through his performance of effeminacy as authority: "I had met a man who had found him in a barber's shop in Venice, and heard him explain, 'I am having my hair curled that I may resemble Nero'" (*Au* 285–86).

"TAKE BUT HIS LOVE AWAY:"
QUEER LOVE AND CLOSETEDNESS IN *CALVARY*

Calvary is usually interpreted in the context of the Easter Rising, and in fact it offers several layers of meaning. Here my focus is on the relationship between the male characters of the play, in light of Wilde's legacy. *Calvary* features an emotionally loaded quarrel and breakup between Christ, who appears to represent patriarchal authority, and the disillusioned Lazarus and Judas. The two rebel against Christ's and his invisible Father's authoritative efforts, which are introduced by the image of a contemplative white heron staring at himself, refusing to act in any way. Yeats's subtle allusions to Narcissus, and his focus on the eroticism of male friendships through the story of the raising of Lazarus in the subtext, can serve to legitimize the discourse about the strong emotional bond and love between men, as this episode of the Gospel of John (Jn 11–12) highlights the profound love and friendship between Christ and Lazarus. The crowd tells Jesus, "Lord, he whom you love is ill,"[84] as a result of which he stays two days longer in the place where he is. This episode also shows the figure of Christ in great despair, weeping because of the possibility of losing the man he loves so much, and when the crowd sees him weeping, they exclaim, "See how he loved him!"[85]

The choice of Christ's figure as the central character could serve to stress the themes of eros, anti-authoritarianism, and melancholy masculinities in the play. According to the song of Isaiah, he was "despised and rejected of men, a man of sorrows and acquainted with grief: and we hid as it were our faces from him."[86] Christ was also seen by Wilde as "the supreme romantic type"[87] thanks to his imaginative nature and romantic temperament, and he had "all the colour-elements of life: mystery, strangeness, pathos, suggestion, ecstasy, love."[88] After Flannery's production of Calvary in 1965, MacLiammóir also paid a tribute to Yeats by claiming that he was a "free mind dealing with the greatest and most romantic figure in the world."[89] For Wilde, Christ was also against laws and was inherently anti-authoritarian: "He would not hear of life being sacrificed to any system of thought or morals."[90] Portraying Lazarus as an unhappy rebel who turns against patriarchal authority—similar to Sylvia Plath's "Lady Lazarus"—could further reinforce the play's anti-authoritarianism and queer aesthetic.

Calvary was written in 1920 and published in 1921, but it was never performed during Yeats's lifetime. The various productions of the play after Yeats's death have never explicitly built on the queer sensibilities of the play, yet I believe Calvary can convey important messages about queerness today, once the more muted aspects of the play are highlighted. These include the physical touch between same-sex characters, the non-hierarchical characterization, and the rejection of unifying, homogenizing narratives and physical force in favor of contemplation. O'Brien includes in his description of queer dramaturgical strategies the questioning of fixed ideas of manhood, symbolic scenography, meta-commentary, and a sense of masculinity entrapped in the wrong body or the self-doubting, sometimes unhappy masculinities,[91] all of which feature in *Calvary*. There is also a palpable tension between voices of exclusion and voices of inclusion in this play. On the one hand, it features a vocabulary of exclusion and insult along with a performance of hypermasculine authority, which work to ban emancipatory efforts; on the other hand, recalcitrant temperaments, self-consolation, self-sufficiency, and solitude are performed by the excluded characters to claim emancipation, visibility, and voice for themselves.

Calvary challenges our expectations; with every line, speech, and action it disrupts, changes, and fragments the linearity and orthodoxy of the biblical narrative to convey messages about the fluidity of performances of power, masculinity, and difference. Yeats goes against tradition here in many different ways, which is discussed in detail by Alexandra Poulain in *Irish Drama, Modernity and the Passion Play*. Poulain argues that in *Calvary*, Yeats distances himself from the traditional ritual of the Passion and neutralizes its performative efficiency; he also forces the Passion narrative into the alien theatrical form of the Noh, which it also challenges.[92] Her analysis outlines the two major readings of the characters: one that reads Judas, Lazarus, the Roman soldiers, and the white heron as marginalized figures, who do not wish to ask anything from Christ and who claim freedom from the totalizing narrative of the Rising. At the same time, Christ can also be read as the marginalized character who cannot identify with the narrative of the Rising and the physical force it promotes.[93]

But the play inevitably invites another reading as well, in which Lazarus, Judas, Christ, and the white heron belong to the same marginalized category, as against the totalizing force of Christ's Father, the mocking crowd, and soldiers, who represent the world which operates with the semblance of inclusion, only to exclude those who do not wish to belong to its totalizing narrative. Poulain also argues that Yeats rewrote the Easter Rising as an ironic Passion play in *Calvary* to show that the rebels' sacrifice "fails to include the whole nation within a single emancipatory narrative."[94] Yet the play's ambivalence and complexity, as well its implicit links to Wilde and Narcissus, make a space for a queer reading as well. *Calvary* clearly points out how the system fails to include certain stories and individuals in its main discourse—but by stressing this lack of inclusion and the structures of exclusion, it also fosters a narrative of recognition for those who feel stigmatized, questioning the masculine Carlylian and normative views of heroism. Radio Eireann scriptwriter Warren O'Connell also claimed that he saw the play as a "hymn of freedom of which Sartre or Beckett would have approved."[95]

But *Calvary* is also a hymn of dissidence and solitude, and in fact, the refusal of inclusion and assimilation constitutes a seminal part of its queer dramaturgy. In *A Cultural Politics of Emotion*, Sara Ahmed explains that "[h]eteronormativity functions as a form of public comfort by allowing bodies to extend into spaces that have already taken their shape."[96] She calls this heterosexualization, which generates a feeling of discomfort and displacement in queer subjects whose bodies cannot sink into this space.[97] *Calvary* is full of male bodies perceiving such feelings of discomfort: the resurrected Lazarus who is longing for death and solitude, Christ standing completely vulnerable and exposed to the mocking crowd, and the famished heron who cannot fulfil his "conventional" duty to take action and eat. Ahmed's main argument is that the maintenance of this feeling of discomfort is an indispensable part of rejecting the homogenizing efforts, violence, and traps of heteronormativity, which either explicitly refuse queer subjects or want to assimilate them and create homonormativity.[98] Queer subjects reject normative ways of life because those norms reject them; therefore their resistance operates as a necessary shield and a counterattack.

Calvary can also be interpreted as a drama about closetedness, where the explicit expression of the word "love" to describe the relationship between men has performative power. I do not suggest that these characters should be read as ones with a queer subjectivity, but the play attempts to legitimize male lightness, tenderness, and expressions of affection between men. For Eve Kosofsky Sedgwick, "closetedness itself is a performance initiated as such by the speech act of a silence […] in relation to the discourse that surrounds and differentially constitutes it."[99] Thus whenever the word love is used to describe the relationship between two men it becomes a performative act, which can also function as a claim for the right to look: "The right to look is not about seeing. It begins at a personal level with the look into someone's eyes to express friendship, solidarity, or love. […] The right to look claims autonomy, not individualism or voyeurism, but the claim to a political subjectivity and collectivity."[100] This subjectivity can arrange the visible and the sayable, and in this play the expression of love between men becomes visible and sayable through the framework of the Lazarus-Christ and Judas-Christ relationships. Wilde also refers to the Lazarus-Christ and Judas-Christ bonds in his *Ballad of Reading Gaol*:

> And there, till Christ call forth the dead,
> In silence let him lie:
> No need to waste the foolish tear,
> Or heave the windy sigh:
> The man had killed the thing he loved,
> And so he had to die.
>
> And all men kill the thing they love,
> By all let this be heard,
> Some do it with a bitter look,
> Some with a flattering word,
> The coward does it with a kiss,
> The brave man with a sword![101]

The quarrel between Christ, Lazarus, and Judas is introduced by the image of a passive, contemplative white heron that should be fishing in the stream. Yet the heron is not able to do anything but stare at his own reflection, "upon the glittering image of a heron" (*VPL* 781), and eventually dies because he is so dumbfounded by his own image that he forgets to eat and drowns in the water. It is usually this white heron that causes confusion for the audience and the readers, as the heron is the key symbol of the play, and thus the play's meaning depends on how we interpret the heron's role. This is an image which does not immediately make sense, which is one of the play's queer dramaturgical elements. If we consider the more hidden same-sex references and moments of the play, this heron could be read as a Narcissus-like figure, which not only implies self-love but love of the same sex, especially because neither the heron nor Narcissus were aware that they were fascinated with their own reflections. [102]

According to Ovid, a young boy named Ameinias fell in love with Narcissus, who did nothing but scorn the nymphs and the company of young people. Thus Ameinias cursed him, saying "May he himself fall in love with another, as we have done with him! May he too be unable to gain his loved one!"[103] In fact, what we call narcissism today is better characterized by Narcissus before he fell in love with his own reflection, when he still mocked people for their feelings and desires for him. Once he fell in love with his reflection (not knowing it was his own image), the other became more important to him than his own self, representing the absolute collapse of self-centered, arrogant narcissism.

Ovid's description of Narcissus features similar keywords to the ones we find in Yeats's play: dream, contemplation, whiteness, and motionlessness. And the solution to this complicated desire is death, transformation, and then re-birth as a flower. Ovid writes:

[w]hile [Narcissus] sought to quench his thirst, another thirst grew in him, and as he drank, he was enchanted by the beautiful reflection that he saw. He fell in love with an insubstantial hope, mistaking a mere shadow for a real body. Spellbound by his own self, he remained there motionless, with fixed gaze, like a statue carved from Parian marble. As he lay on the bank, he gazed at the twin stars that were his eyes, at his flowing locks, worthy of Bacchus or Apollo, his smooth cheeks, his ivory neck, his lovely face where a rosy flush stained the snowy whiteness of his complexion, admiring all the features for which he himself was admired.[104]

Like Narcissus, the white heron in *Calvary* is also

"Motionless under the moon-beam,
Up to his feathers in the stream;
Although fish leap, the white heron
Shivers in a dumbfounded dream.
[…]
Although half famished he'll not dare
Dip or do anything but stare
Upon the glittering image of a heron,
That now is lost and now is there.
[…]
But that the full is shortly gone
And after that is crescent moon,
It's certain that the moon-crazed heron
Would be but fishes' diet soon. (*VPL* 780–81)

The meta-commentary on the white heron provided by the three Musicians serves to express a discourse of exclusion, and also to challenge that discourse. One of the key phrases in *Calvary* is the repetition of "God has not died for the white heron" (*VPL* 780) three times at the beginning of the play and "God has not appeared to the birds" (*VPL* 787) at the end, after the crucifixion. Both lines are uttered by the Second Musician, and the birds are constantly associated with the three male characters in the play. The First and Third Musicians speak for Christ, the heron, Judas, and Lazarus, creating for them a countervisual claim to autonomy which refuses segregation and categorization, and which claims the right to existence.[105] The Second Musician, however, seems to represent the world which defines itself only by excluding others, like heteronormativity and patriarchy. Thus, the function of this repetitive phrase is to exclude the solitary white heron, the birds, Judas, and Lazarus from the realm of normalcy, here represented by the invisible Father figure. It operates with the performative power of insult, whose aim is to mark the consciousness of those whom it excludes. The repeated phrase represents the visuality of authority which separates, segregates, classifies whom it visualizes, counters desire, and refuses all emancipatory efforts.[106]

When Lazarus and then Judas appear in the play, both terrify the crowds and represent the appearance of strangeness which has no place in the normative narrative—and the crowd turns and flees from this strangeness. In his notes to *Calvary*, Yeats also connects the solitary, contemplative birds to the subjective age which includes the individual, as opposed to the objective one which oppresses and excludes them: "such lonely birds as the heron, hawk, eagle, and swan, are the natural symbols of subjectivity, especially when floating upon the wind alone or alighting upon some pool or river" (*VPL* 789). The song for the folding and unfolding of the cloth at the end of the play continues this solitary bird imagery. The Second Musician insists on excluding these birds by claiming that "God has not appeared to the birds" (*VPL* 787), but the First and Third Musicians celebrate the lonely birds who have chosen their part and who are content with their savage hearts. The First Musician then portrays two swans flying next to each other, which in the context of the play's theme of strong male friendships, appears like an image of same-sex alliance: "why do they fling / White wing out white wing? / What can a swan need but a swan?" (VPL 788).

The reference to birds also carries a queer undertone today, since in literature and the arts birds are often used as synonyms for queer people, effeminate gay men, and forbidden desires, as in Yeats's *The Land of Heart's Desire* or in Tennessee Williams's *Orpheus Descending*.[107] Yeats's famous collaborator Edmund Dulac's painting, *Charles Ricketts and Charles Shannon as Medieval Saints* (1920), is also a good example of the fusion of bird symbolism, Christianity, and queer undertones, as the saints are holding a kingfisher and a peacock feather in their hands. Interestingly, Julian Carter in Queer Dance mentions bird-women and swans as symbols of queer resistance and queer becoming, as "feathers do not lend themselves to conventional argumentative trajectories."[108]

Just like Narcissus, Christ becomes both the violator and the victim in this play, as he seems to represent patriarchal authority and wants to seem "all-powerful" (*VPL* 784). But masculinity is entrapped in the wrong body here, as Christ fails to perform the role of conventional patriarchal authority. Poulain claims that Christ's "own power, a mere extension of his autocratic Father's, is the power of the Word with which he handles his creatures like mere puppets."[109] Christ tries to explain his authoritarianism with statements like "[m]y Father put all men into my hands" (*VPL* 784) and "I do my Father's will"

(*VPL* 783). Instead of physical force, he uses emotional arguments to impose his power on Lazarus and Judas and make them feel uncomfortable, emphasizing how generous he has been to them; therefore they should never complain. This is like the "self-authorizing of authority"[110] which makes certain forms of violence and insult appear legal and benign.

Yet Christ is also contemplative, vulnerable, and self-doubting; before his quarrel with Lazarus, he "dreams His passion through" (*VPL* 781) and "[h]e stands amid a mocking crowd, / Heavily breathing" (*VPL* 781). He is presented as someone who is the opposite of conventional images of masculinity, as "[h]e climbs up hither but as a dreamer climbs" (*VPL* 781) and he "wears away His strength"(*VPL* 781). Poulain claims that Christ's figure also challenges the traditional Noh structure, in which Christ should be the shite (the one who acts). Yet here he is the passive *waki* instead, who fulfils the role of spectator: "he is the passive, visionary dreamer who conjures the shadows of the past onto the stage and hears their grievances."[111] The words "mockery," "mock," and "mockers" are mentioned only with reference to Christ, who must endure this derision to obey his Father. Lazarus points this out, indicating that Christ is performing a role that was forced on him: when Christ defends himself "I do my Father's will," (*VPL* 783), Lazarus reproaches him "[a]nd not your own" (*VPL* 783). This resonates with Mario Mieli's idea that stigmatized and oppressed subjectivities sometimes internalize the figure of the oppressor in order to resist and reject centuries of victimhood,[112] which is in fact similar not only to what Christ and Lazarus do in the play, but also to Wilde's wish to resemble Nero, and pose as a Carlylian hero only to subvert these conventional power images.

Christ experiences exclusion and mockery because he is different: he sings as First Musician, "O, but the mockers' cry / Makes my heart afraid, / As though a flute of bone / Taken from a heron's thigh, / A heron crazed by the moon, / Were cleverly, softly played" (*VPL* 781–82) The fact that these characters can be read as both antagonists and protagonists also contributes to the non-hierarchical, more dialectical dramaturgical structure which is part of the play's queer dramaturgy. The crowd's mocking reaction to Lazarus, Judas, and Christ positions all three characters in a lower dramaturgical position as the embodiments of strangeness and disruption. Yet Yeats gives voice to the stories and grievances of all three of them, so that we can understand why Lazarus and Judas have to turn away from Christ, while at the same time sympathizing with Christ's pain.

Christ's grievance is that he feels betrayed by the two men with whom he shared a strong emotional bond, and who abandon him here because of his performance of patriarchal authority. This is very similar to Narcissus's tragedy, who cried out at his own image: "Whoever you are, come out to me! Oh boy beyond compare, why do you elude me? Where do you go, when I try to reach you? [...] Where are you fleeing? Cruel creature, stay, do not desert the one who loves you!"[113] Leo Bersani argues that homosexuality is often seen by the normative discourse as congenital to betrayal, which is manifested in refusing to identify with other men as a group.[114] This is a kind of strangely heroic act of unbecoming that refuses to surrender to a higher phallic order, which is an interesting idea to consider in the context of the Lazarus-Christ and Judas-Christ relationships in the play.

Lazarus's grievance is that Christ "dragged [him] to the light" (*VPL* 782) despite his will to lay dead in "an old mountain cavern" (*VPL* 782). Lazarus laments that Christ "disturb[ed] that corner / Where [he] had thought [he] might lie safe for ever" (*VPL* 783), and he also suggests that their fate is the same, in that both are travelling towards death.

> *Lazarus.* You took my death, give me your death instead.
> *Christ.* I gave you life.
> *Lazarus.* But death is what I ask.
> Alive I never could escape your love,
> And when I sickened towards my death I thought,
> 'I'll to the desert, or chuckle in a corner,
> Mere ghost, a solitary thing.' I died
> And saw no more until I saw you stand
> In the opening of the tomb; 'Come out!' you called;
> You dragged me to the light as boys drag out
> A rabbit when they have dug its hole away;
> And now with all the shouting at your heels
> You travel towards the death I am denied. (*VPL* 782–83)

The way Lazarus describes Christ's "benign" violence here is evocative of the ways discourse forces queer people to talk about their sexuality, to escape from the safety of the closet only to categorize them as abnormal and prove the healthiness of normalcy, which Foucault calls the "formidable trap"[115] of discourse. This is how power wants to hide itself beneath the mask of tolerance. Foucault also asserts that "power in the West is what displays itself the most, and thus hides itself the best."[116] Dragging Lazarus to the light was an act of visualizing him despite his will, and as Mirzoeff explains, this kind of visualization is "part of the labor of being analyzed."[117] But Lazarus refuses this action and demands a way for himself to find safety and solitude, again among solitary birds; he commands Christ to take his controlling eyes off him.

After Flannery's production of *Calvary*, an audience member asked Ma-cLiammóir why he thought Lazarus was so unhappy about being brought back from the dead, and MacLiammóir answered with a question: "Madam, wouldn't you?"[118] This was similar to Oscar Wilde's tale in which the old man turned to Christ: "Lord, I was dead and you raised me into life, what else can I do but weep?" (*CW6* 150)

The above quarrel between Christ and Lazarus also illustrates one of the main queer aesthetic elements of the play, namely, the combination of and tension between the death drive (*Thanatos*) and the life drive (*eros*).[119] The connection between the death drive and queer aesthetics is well established, but Gordon Elliot Walker associates the combination of life and death instincts with queer aesthetics in his study of Jean Cocteau's Orpheus trilogy, in which Cocteau dramatized the meeting of Orpheus and Narcissus and created the character of Orpheus Narcissus, who exists at the intersection between desire and death. As Herbert Marcuse explains in *Eros and Civilization*, Narcissus is usually seen as representing contemplation, beauty, and death drive—like Lazarus, who is not afraid of death, the only thing for which he asks—while the Orphic Eros masters death through liberation.

Yet, as Walker demonstrates, this also works the other way round, with Narcissus representing the life drive and Orpheus standing for the death drive, travelling constantly towards death. This interchangeability demonstrates the coexistence of the two instincts in these figures; just like Yeats in *Calvary*, Jean Cocteau combines these two instincts in the character of Orpheus Narcissus to generate a queer aesthetic.[120] Marcuse also asserts:

> "[t]he classical tradition associates Orpheus with the introduction of homo-sexuality. Like Narcissus, he rejects the normal Eros, not for an ascetic ideal, but for a fuller Eros. Like Narcissus, he protests against the repressive order of procreative sexuality. The Orphic and Narcissistic Eros is to the end the negation of this order—the Great Refusal.[121]

Marcuse further details that both Orpheus and Narcissus are akin to Dionysus—who, in the Orphic mythology is also often identified with Narcissus—and represent aestheticism and contemplation. Thus, they become the exact antithesis of Prometheus, the voice which commands and who represents conventional masculinity and the performance principle, like the invisible Father/God figure in *Calvary*. Orpheus himself is akin to Narcissus, as according to Ovid's description, he abstained from the love of women and offered his love to young and tender boys, as a result of which the Ciconian women mocked him and threw stones at him while he sang.

The quarrel between Judas and Christ in *Calvary* is introduced by the First Musician, who sings about the love between the two men: "Take but His love away, / Their love becomes a feather / Of eagle, swan or gull, / Or a drowned heron's feather / Tossed hither and thither / Upon the bitter spray / And the moon at the full" (*VPL* 784). Even though this passage could refer to the love of God, its dramaturgical position—it comes right after Lazarus leaves the stage and just before Judas appears—makes it an ambiguous reference that can also imply the profound love between Christ, Lazarus, and Judas. Judas also wants to break away from the patriarchal authority represented by Christ and his Father: "I have betrayed you / Because you seemed all powerful. [...] And is there not one man / In the wide world that is not in your power?" (*VPL* 784). Judas continues: "I could not bear to think you had but to whistle / And I must do; but after that I thought, / 'Whatever man betrays Him will be free'; And life grew bearable again" (*VPL* 785). He kisses Christ, after which Christ is crucified, mocked, and danced around by Roman soldiers/gamblers. It is also worth mentioning that Yeats used the *eros* as a political weapon and the crucifixion was often equivalent to sexuality: in the Free State years, "Yeats constructed the erotic in opposition to the Catholic sexual ethic, and to censorship."[122] The Roman soldiers dancing around the crucified body of Christ also recall Yeats's closing image of his essay "The Catastrophe," in which harlots begin a mocking dance at the news of Wilde's condemnation: "When the verdict was announced the harlots in the streets outside danced upon the pavement" (*Au* 291).

After these emotional quarrels and the recalcitrance of Lazarus and Judas, Christ's reaction is not rage or violence, as would be expected from an oppressive patriarchal authority, but sadness and a painful renunciation of the love of his two companions. Instead of blaming Judas or Lazarus, Christ's perception of his Father changes, and he seems to realize that it was his Father who betrayed him by forcing on him this performance of masculine authority. While lying on the cross surrounded by dancing men, he cries out: "My Father, why hast Thou forsaken Me?" (*VPL* 787).

The Roman soldiers not only dance around him, but they talk about quarrels and friendship between men. They are holding hands, which is a spectacle of male same-sex alliance, and also an ironic commentary on the main action, which mocks and insults Christ because he was unable to settle the quarrels and keep the love of the two men: "In the dance / We quarrel for a while, but settle it / By throwing dice, and after that, being friends, / Join hand to hand and wheel about the cross" (*VPL* 787). The stage direction makes it clear that unlike Lazarus, Judas stays and helps place Christ's body on the cross. Even though there are no details regarding the movements of the characters here, this scene must include some sort of physical contact between Christ's body and Judas, followed by the dancing gamblers holding hands.

The Resurrection (1931) can also help us interpret Yeats's *Calvary*; in this play, the figure of Christ appears as a strangeness disturbing the world of reason and science, represented by the Greek man. Here Christ is also associated with Dionysus and his worshippers, who consist of men dressed up as women, dancing with one another in a trance: "What a spectacle! In Alexandria a few men paint their lips vermilion. They imitate women that they may attain in worship a woman's self-abandonment" (*VPL* 915). The appearance of Christ at the end of the play forces the Greek man to confront this strangeness by touching Christ's body. Clare Croft also emphasizes that queerness exists and arises very much from the realm of the affection of touch, and stresses the great power of the press of bodies in queer performance, which has a potential to teach new ways of looking.[123] The Greek man expects the body to be disembodied, but he suddenly feels Christ's body and screams. This is "the shock of a man of science" (*VPL* 98), but also a kind of male homosexual panic which "became the normal condition of male heterosexual entitlement."[124] In Flannery's production the dancers were placed onstage, and he claimed that male dancers performing an ecstatic dance in the moment when the Greek man touched Christ's breast reinforced the play's main action.[125]

In *The Secret Rose* (1897) Yeats included a story, "The Crucifixion of the Outcast," which also resonates with the vicissitudes of Wilde's life after his incarceration for sodomy and gross indecency in 1895. This story appears like an early draft of *Calvary*. Yeats mentions in "The Catastrophe" that Wilde found this story "sublime, wonderful, wonderful" (*Au* 287). Its protagonist, Cumhal, is an artist, and Yeats's description of him evokes Wilde: a man with a thin brown hair and a pale face, who wore a short, parti-colored doublet and pointed shoes. Just as in *Calvary*, the crucifixion provides the framework here: it happens in Cumhal's mind's eye at the beginning of the story, and becomes reality at the end. Cumhal sees the crosses and thinks that "just such another vagabond like himself was hanged on one of them" (*CWVP7* 7). The traces of violence towards people like him suddenly causes him bodily discomfort, and he begins shivering and sweating at this vision. In his search for a place to sleep, he is exiled to a cold outbuilding; when he raises his voice against this condition, he is ignored. Nevertheless his response is not anger but art, and he begins singing.

The men of the town become enraged by the strange, effeminate singing man. They panic; fearing that his behavior will spread to the children, they decide to silence him. The crosses are full, which indicates a mass murder of people these men have found deviant in some way: "Then we must make another cross. If we do not make an end of him another will, for who can eat and sleep in peace when *men like him* are going about the world?" (*CWVP7* 13; my emphasis). When they are ready to crucify Cumhal, the townsmen continue to verbally humiliate him, making it clear that they are normal and respectable, while his kind is abnormal; they compare him to the wind. Cumhal, however, speaks in his own defense and expresses pride in being like the wind: "'Friend,' answered the glee man, 'my soul is indeed like the wind, and it blows me to and fro, and up and down, a lid puts many things in my mind and out of my mind, and therefore am I called the Swift, Wild Horse" (*CWVP7* 15). The final image is very similar to that of *Calvary*: beggars, wolves, and birds surround him ready to tear his body apart, but he calls them outcasts too, and cries out at their betrayal just like Christ in *Calvary*: "'Outcasts,' he moaned, 'have you also turned against the outcast?'" (*CWVP7* 19).

Calvary has been interpreted in different ways, but given the pervasive presence of Wilde's influence in Yeats's theater, the play also examines the repressive power and patriarchal authority of normalcy and insult on queer love. *Calvary* attempts to acknowledge the hurts and experiences of exclusion that stigmatized people have to endure, but it also demonstrates the transformative energies that this journey entails. If staged today at one of the gay theater festivals, Yeats's *Calvary* would fit in perfectly, as many contemporary gay/queer theater productions build on biblical frameworks and Greek mythology to portray melancholy masculinities, thus challenging today's homogenizing gay aesthetic which wants to create homonormativity and see happy gay people assimilated into heteronormative social structures. In its own historical context, *Calvary* was an unconventional play, featuring insecure, contemplative anti-Carlylian characters who embraced failure and difference at a time when the mainstream political and religious discourses condemned men who lived in sadness and showed too much tenderness.[126] Even today, a play like Calvary would be unusual as it displays a "move towards a fuller understating of the non-mainstream gay men who face the challenges of precarious existence, incumbent stigma and disability, and are yet politically involved,"[127] as O'Brien put it with regard to contemporary queer dramaturgies. Yeats's drama is, therefore, able to call the normative frames into question and create countervisuality for those who are left outside, thus making visible lives that are "exceeding the normative conditions of recognizability."[128]

NOTES

1. David Cregan, "Coming Out: Frank McGuinness's Dramaturgy and Queer Resistance," *Irish University Review* 40, no. 1 (2010): 46.
2. See Judit Nényei, *Thought Outdanced: The Motif of Dancing in Yeats and Joyce* (Budapest: Akadémiai Kiadó, 2002) and Sylvia C. Ellis, *The Plays of W. B. Yeats: Yeats and the Dancer* (London: Palgrave Macmillan, 1999).
3. See Susan Cannon Harris, *Irish Drama and the Other Revolutions: Playwrights, Sexual Politics and the International Left, 1892–1964* (Edinburgh: Edinburgh University Press, 2017).
4. Judith Butler, *Frames of War: When is Life Grievable?* (London and New York: Verso, 2009), 1–3.
5. Clare Croft, "Introduction," in *Queer Dance: Meanings and Makings*, ed. Clare Croft (Oxford: Oxford University Press, 2017), 1–37, 2.

6. Elizabeth Cullingford, *Gender and History in Yeats's Love Poetry* (Cambridge: Cambridge University Press, 1993), 6.
7. Hélène Cixous, quoted in Cullingford, *Gender*, 20.
8. Cullingford, *Gender*, 269.
9. Isadora Duncan writes about the affinities between dance, the Greeks, freedom, and the movement of waves and the wind in *The Art of Dance* (New York: Theatre Arts Books, 1928).
10. Harris, *Irish Drama*, 19.
11. Harris, *Irish Drama*, 16.
12. See Cassandra Laity, "W. B. Yeats and Florence Farr: The Influence of the 'New Woman' Actress on Yeats's Changing Images of Women," *Modern Drama*, 28, no. 4 (1985): 620–37.
13. Bernhardt was famous for her provocative en travesti roles. Among many other characters, she played Pelléas in Maeterlinck's *Pelléas et Mélisande* (1904) in London, and Yeats was amazed by the spectacle of Bernhardt and Mrs. Patrick Campbell as lovers in that production. See Katherine Worth, *The Irish Drama of Europe from Yeats to Beckett* (London: Bloomsbury, 2013), 39.
14. Harris, *Irish Drama*, 12.
15. Harris, *Irish Drama*, 50.
16. Harris, *Irish Drama*, 48.
17. Harris, *Irish Drama*, 48.
18. G. B. Shaw quoted in Harris, *Irish Drama*, 50.
19. Harris, *Irish Drama*, 53.
20. Harris, *Irish Drama*, 12.
21. Harris, *Irish Drama*, 54.
22. See George L. Mosse, *Nationalism and Sexuality: Respectability and Abnormal Sexuality in Modern Europe* (New York: H. Fertig, 1985).
23. See Linda Connolly, "Towards a Further Understanding of the Violence Experienced by Women in the Irish Revolution," Maynooth University Social Sciences Institute Working Paper Series, No. 7 (2019) and Gemma Clarke, *Everyday Violence in the Irish Civil War* (Cambridge: Cambridge University Press, 2014).
24. See Mark Phelan, "Irish Responses to Fascist Italy, 1919–1932" (PhD thesis, National University of Ireland Galway, 2013) and Caitríona Beaumont, "Women, citizenship, and Catholicism in the Irish free state, 1922/1948," *Women's History Review* 6, no. 4 (December 1997): 563–85.
25. For more details see Susan Cannon Harris, *Gender and Modern Irish Drama* (Bloomington and Indianapolis: Indiana University Press, 2002).
26. Colm Tóibín refers to the alleged homosexuality of Lennox Robinson and his close friendship with George and W. B. Yeats in Tóibín, *New Ways to Kills Your Mother: Writers and Their Families* (New York: Scribner, 2012), 69.
27. Lapointe, "Edward Martyn's Theatrical Hieratic Homoeroticism," 76.
28. See Sonja Tiernan, "Tabloid Sensationalism or Revolutionary Feminism?: The First-Wave Feminist Movement in an Irish Women's Periodical," *Irish Communication Review* 12, no. 1, (2010): 77–87.
29. See Jennifer L. Campbell, "Dancing Marines and Pumping Gasoline: Coded Queerness in Depression-Era American Ballet," in *Queer Dance: Meanings and Makings*, ed. Clare Croft (Oxford: Oxford University Press, 2017), 126–27. See also Peter Stoneley, A Queer History of the Ballet (London and New York: Routledge, 2007).
30. See Terri A. Mester, *Movement and Modernism: Yeats, Eliot, Lawrence, Williams, and Early Twentieth-Century Dance* (Fayetteville: University of Arkansas Press, 1997), 73.

31. For Pirandello's and D'Annunzio's collaboration with New Women artists and their resulting feminist and queer theater see, for instance, Lucia Re's articles on D'Annunzio, "Eleonora Duse and Women: Performing Desire, Power and Knowledge." *Italian Studies*. 70, no. 30 (2015): 347–63 and "D'Annunzio, Duse, Wilde, Bernhardt: il rapporto autore/attrice fra decadentismo e modernità." *MLN* 117, no. 1, Italian Issue (January 2002): 115–52, and also James Jason Hartford's discussion of D'Annunzio's *Le Martyre de Saint Sébastien* (1911) in *Sexuality, Iconography, and Fiction in French: Queering the Martyr*. Oxford, UK: Palgrave Macmillan, 2018. For *Pirandello, see Daniela Bini, Pirandello and His Muse: The Plays for Marta Abba* (Gainesville, FL: University Press of Florida, 1998) and John Champagne, *Aesthetic Modernism and Masculinity in Fascist Italy* (London and New York: Routledge, 2013).
32. Cormac O'Brien, "Gay Masculinities in Performance: Towards a Queer Dramaturgy," *Irish Theatre International* 3 no. 1 (2014): 76.
33. O'Brien, "Gay Masculinities," 81.
34. O'Brien, "Gay Masculinities," 83.
35. Audre Lorde explains that anti-erotic, patriarchal societies fear the erotic and relegate it to the bedroom alone because the erotic helps recognise the power of one's own body and a joy which is not achieved with marriage or belief in God. Lorde, "The Power of the Erotic," in *The Master's Tools Will Never Dismantle the Master's House*, Penguin Modern 23 (London: Penguin Books, 2018), 13.
36. Gabriele Brandstetter, *Poetics of Dance: Body, Image, and Space in Historical Avant-gardes* (Oxford: Oxford University Press, 2015), 89.
37. Harris, *Irish Drama*, 4.
38. Croft, *Queer Dance*, 3.
39. Croft, *Queer Dance*, 7.
40. James W. Flannery, "Action and Reaction at the Dublin Theatre Festival," *Educational Theatre Journal* 19, no. 1 (March 1967): 80.
41. Alyson Campbell and Stephen Farrier, eds., *Queer Dramaturgies: International Perspectives on Where Performance Leads Queer* (London: Palgrave Macmillan, 2016), 3.
42. Quoted in Michael Patrick Lapointe, "Edward Martyn's Theatrical Hieratic Homoeroticism," In *Deviant Acts: Essays on Queer Performance*, ed. David Cregan, Dublin: Carysfort Press, 2009, 82.
43. Photographs, reviews and other details of these performances are available in the digitized Gate Theatre Archive and Druid Archive of the National University of Ireland, Galway.
44. John K. Gillespie, "Beyond Byzantium: Aesthetic Pessimism in Mishima's Modern Noh Plays," *Monumenta Nipponica* 37, no.1 (Spring 1982): 29–39.
45. Yukio Mishima, *Confessions of a Mask*, transl. Meredith Weatherby (New Directions Publishing, 1958), 27.
46. Dider Eribon discusses the use of classical mythology and Oriental themes as a means of legitimizing the discourse about same-sex love in Eribon, *Insult and the Making of the Gay Self* (Durham, NC: Duke University Press, 2004).
47. Eribon, *Insult*, 71.
48. Eribon, *Insult*, 16.
49. Judith Halberstam, *The Queer Art of Failure* (Durham, NC and London: Duke University Press, 2011), 160.
50. Leo Bersani, quoted in Halberstam, *The Queer Art of Failure*, 150.
51. Halberstam, *The Queer Art of Failure*, 106.
52. Halberstam, *The Queer Art of Failure*, 106.
53. Halberstam, *The Queer Art of Failure*, 15.
54. Stuart Hall quoted in Halberstam, *The Queer Art of Failure*, 15.
55. Cullingford, *Gender*, 5,

56. Cullingford, *Gender*, 269.

57. Eribon, *Insult*, 145.

58. Jason Edwards, "'The Generation of the Green Carnation': Sexual Degeneration, The Representation of Male Homosexuality, and the Limits of Yeats's Sympathy," in *Modernist Sexualities*, eds. Hugh Stevens and Caroline Howlett (Manchester and New York: Manchester University Press, 2000), 45.

59. Edwards, "'The Generation of the Green Carnation,'" 54.

60. Eribon, *Insult*, 155.

61. Eribon, *Insult*, 156.

62. David M. Halperin, *One Hundred Years of Homosexuality: And Other Essays on Greek Love* (New York and London: Routledge, 1990).

63. Laity, "W. B. Yeats and Florence Farr," 622.

64. W. B. Yeats quoted in Laity, "W. B. Yeats and Florence Farr," 623.

65. See Susan Jones, "Nietzsche, Modernism, and Dance: Dionysian or Apollonian?" in *Literature, Modernism, and Dance* (Oxford: Oxford University Press, 2013), 44–70.

66. Brian Arkins discusses Yeats's use of Greek mythology in Arkins, *Builders of My Soul: Greek and Roman Themes in Yeats* (Savage, Md.: Barnes and Noble Books, 1990); see also Elizabeth Muller, "Defining Beauty: The Paterian Yeats," *International Yeats Studies* 2, no. 1 (November 2017): 24–45.

67. Hedwig Schwall, "Allegories of Writing: Figurations of Narcissus and Echo in W. B. Yeats's Work," in *Writing Modern Ireland*, ed. Catherine E. Paul (Liverpool: Liverpool University Press, 2015), 24.

68. Oscar Wilde, *The Complete Letters of Oscar Wilde*, eds. Merlin Holland and Rupert Hart-Davis (London: Fourth Estate, 2000), 526.

69. Mester, *Movement and Modernism*, 73.

70. Ben Levitas, "The Dancer and the Heart's Desire: W. B. Yeats and the Theatre of Modernity," *The Yeats Journal of Korea* 56 (2018): 112.

71. Levitas, "The Dancer and the Heart's Desire," 120.

72. Edwards, "'The Generation of the Green Carnation,'" 46

73. Edwards, "'The Generation of the Green Carnation,'" 40.

74. Marcel Proust quoted in Eribon, *Insult*, 30.

75. Yeats tended to associate effeminate men with the figure of Christ, and he made a comparison between Christ and the sexually transgressive Mohini Chatterjee as well, who was always described by men (including Wilde) as beautiful and attractive. See Rajbir Singh Judge, "Dusky Countenances: Ambivalent Bodies and Desires in the Theosophical Society," *Journal of the History of Sexuality* 27, no. 2 (May 2018): 264–93.

76. Oscar Wilde, *De Profundis and Other Prison Writings*, ed. Colm Tóibín (London: Penguin Books, 2013), 122.

77. Eribon, *Insult*, 37.

78. See Nicholas Mirzoeff, *The Right to Look: A Counterhistory of Visuality* (Durham, NC & London: Duke University Press, 2011), 17.

79. Geraldine Higgins, *Heroic Revivals from Carlyle to Yeats* (New York: Palgrave Macmillan, 2012), 12.

80. Mirzoeff, *The Right to Look*, 151.

81. Mirzoeff, *The Right to Look*, 152.

82. Nicholas Mirzoeff, "The Right to Look," *Critical Inquiry* 37, no. 3 (Spring 2011): 485.

83. Mirzoeff, *The Right to Look*, 147.

84. Michael D. Coogan, ed., *The New Oxford Annotated Bible: New Revised Standard Version with the Apocrypha*, 4th ed. (Oxford: Oxford University Press, 2010), 167.

85. Coogan, *The New Oxford Annotated Bible*, 168.

86. Wilde, *De Profundis*, 121.
87. Wilde, *De Profundis*, 125.
88. Wilde, *De Profundis*, 123.
89. Micheál MacLiammóir quoted in Flannery, "Action and Reaction," 72.
90. Wilde, *De Profundis*, 127.
91. O'Brien, "Gay Masculinities," 85–86.
92. Alexandra Poulain, *Irish Drama, Modernity and the Passion Play* (London: Palgrave Macmillan, 2016), 56.
93. Poulain, *Irish Drama*, 54–55.
94. Poulain, *Irish Drama*, 61.
95. Quoted in Flannery, "Action and Reaction," 78.
96. Ahmed, 148.
97. Ahmed, *The Cultural Politics of Emotion* (New York and London: Routledge, 2004), 148.
98. Ahmed, *The Cultural Politics of Emotion*, 149.
99. Eve Kosofsky Sedgwick, *Epistemology of the Closet* (London: Harvester Wheatsheaf, 1991), 3.
100. Mirzoeff, *The Right to Look*, 1.
101. Wilde, *De Profundis*, 232.
102. Herbert Marcuse, *Eros and Civilization: A Philosophical Inquiry into Freud* (London: Routledge, 1956), 167.
103. Ovid, *The Metamorphoses of Ovid*, transl. Mary M. Innes (Baltimore, Md.: Penguin Books, 1955), 92.
104. Ovid, *The Metamorphoses*, 92.
105. Mirzoeff, *The Right to Look*, 4.
106. Mirzoeff, *The Right to Look*, 3.
107. George E. Haggerty, *Gay Histories and Cultures* (New York and London: Garland Publishing, 2000), 516.
108. Julian B. Carter, "Chasing Feathers: Jérôme Bel, *Swan Lake*, and the Alternative Futures of Re-Enacted Dance," in Queer Dance, 109.
109. Poulain, *Irish Drama*, 58–59.
110. Mirzoeff, *The Right to Look*, 7.
111. Poulain, *Irish Drama*, 60.
112. Mario Mieli, *Elementi di critica omosessuale* (Milano: Feltrinelli, 2017), 131.
113. Ovid, *The Metamorphoses*, 92–93.
114. Halberstam, *The Queer Art of Failure*, 151.
115. Michael Foucault, *Politics, Philosophy, Culture: Interviews and Other Writings: 1977–1987*, transl. A. Sheridan, ed. L. D. Kritzman (New York and London: Routledge, 1990), 114.
116. Foucault, *Politics*, 118.
117. Mirzoeff, *The Right to Look*, 10.
118. Micheál MacLiammóir, quoted in Flannery, "Action and Reaction," 79.
119. Freud introduced these concepts in *Beyond the Pleasure Principle* (1920).
120. Gordon Elliot Walker, "Jean Cocteau: Orpheus Narcissus" (MA thesis, Louisiana State University, 2015), 13.
121. Marcuse, *Eros*, 171.
122. Cullingford, *Gender*, 8.
123. Croft, *Queer Dance*, 14.
124. Sedgwick, *Epistemology of the Closet*, 185.
125. Flannery, "Action and Reaction," 74.
126. Wilde, *De Profundis*, 107.
127. O'Brien, "Gay Masculinities," 85.
128. Butler, *Frames of War*, 4.

Yeats And Digital Pedagogy

Rob Doggett

As people who love and admire Yeats, we need to reckon with the fact that digital technology is profoundly transforming the ways that readers encounter and thus experience his poetry. I'll begin on a mostly pessimistic note, arguing that digital media tends to encourage a mode of reading that is oriented toward the acquisition of practical knowledge and, in so doing, works to undercut the type of aesthetic experience that many of us traditionally associate with reading poetry. Next, I'll briefly mention the lessons that we can learn from Yeats's own efforts to use a new mass communication technology, radio, to encourage the public to see poetry as a living and communal form of art—which for him meant teaching people to appreciate those aural aesthetic qualities that are most apparent when a poem is chanted, sung, or read aloud. Finally, I'll return to the relationship between Yeats's poetry and digital technology in the present, offering a more hopeful take in which I'll sketch out some of the ways that teachers can use digital tools to foster a mode of reading that, instead of fixating on practical knowledge, opens students up to the types of profound questions that this art form can evoke. Building on Marjorie Perloff's work, this is a form of aesthetically-engaged reading that begins with the recognition "that a poem …is a made thing—contrived, constructed, chosen—and that its reading is also a construction on the part of the audience."[1]

Not too long ago I was teaching an undergraduate seminar on Yeats, and I called on a student to read "The Second Coming" aloud. As the young man started in on the "widening gyre" and the inept falconer, I noticed that he was reading—not from the edition of Yeats's *Collected Poems* that I'd ordered for the class—but from his mobile phone. I admit that I am not, instinctively, a digital guy. I prefer actual, material books, which are what we use in my classes. But I let it slide, figuring that my students had already heard enough from cranky middle-aged professors decrying the evils of mobile phones and, anyway, it probably is, as Yeats once put it among a different generation of school children, "Better to smile on all that smile, and show / There is a comfortable kind of old scarecrow" (*VP* 443–46, *ll* 31–32). I did, however, ask for the link to the site so that I could take the version he'd found and display it on a screen in front of the class. What I got can be seen in Figures 1 and 2.[2]

At that point, I stopped smiling. I began scrolling up and down through the site, taking in all of the hot links and flashing advertisements while muttering something about Yeats and the apocalypse. I turned to my students and asked with a mix of incredulity and growing horror: "Do most of you actually read

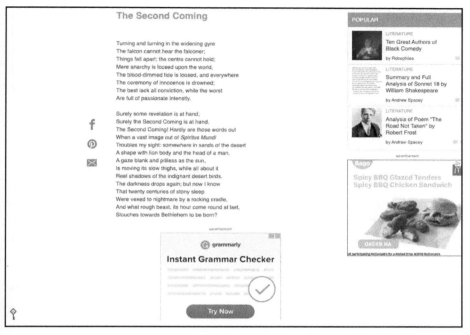

Figure 1 : "The Second Coming"

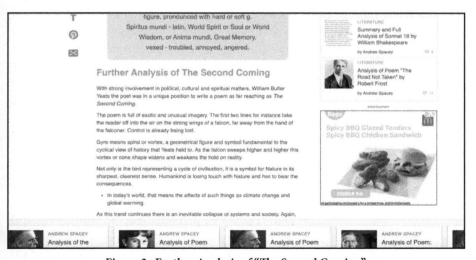

Figure 2 : Further Analysis of "The Second Coming"

poetry like this—on a phone? On the internet?? On this kind of site???" They looked at me with genuine pity, as if I'd asked whether or not they'd ever heard of Facebook or Instagram—the way that I used to look at my father, years ago, when he couldn't figure out how to program the VCR to record his favorite television shows. And it struck me that something fundamental, something I had always taken for granted about the way we encounter and study poetry, had changed.

Think about what happens when we pick up a book and start reading "The Second Coming." Even if we're sitting in a crowded café, we enter into quiet solitude as we immediately register, through physical contact, what textual theorists such as Jerome McGann and George Bornstein refer to as a work's bibliographical codes, those features of books—cover design, layout, spacing, arrangement, ordering, dedications, table of contents, introductions, and even copyright pages—that are part of any poem's publishing history.[3] The November 1920 edition of *The Dial*, where we get "a waste of desert sand" instead of "somewhere in the sands of the desert;" the Cuala Press edition, where the design recalls Yeats's connection to the nineteenth-century arts and crafts movement; and the section of *Michael Robartes and the Dancer* from 1922's *Later Poems*, which, like all of Yeats's publications, was carefully arranged, so that by the time we encounter "The Second Coming" late in the volume we have already been taught to think in the terms and symbols of his nascent occult visionary system.[4] On most poetry websites, if a user clicks on the "more poems" link, she ends up at the next title in alphabetical order (the much earlier poem "The Secret Rose"), but if a reader continues through the 1952 Macmillan *Collected Poems*, she arrives at "A Prayer for My Daughter," which moves the reader from a broad-based vision of historical transformation to a more personal meditation on how that transformation might impact the poet's own family. In this case, the connection between the poems is signaled by the clause "*once more* the storm is howling," and by the "rocking cradle" transforming into "the cradle-hood" under which the speaker's "child sleeps on." (*VP* 403, *ll* 1–2).

The physical book, in short, prompts us to read the poem in the material context that the book has established, as much because of what the material text excludes—think of all those flashing advertisements—as because of what it incorporates. Added to this, readers immediately begin to draw upon our own more general contextual knowledge—about world history, literary history, culture, philosophy, religion, poetry in general, Yeats in particular, and so much more. A reader of the material text proceeds through the poem in a linear manner. Because the reader is holding a book of poems instead of, say, an instruction manual for programing a DVD player, he is not in a cognitive mode that privileges the poem's instrumental, communicative function.

Instead, readers are attuned to what formalist critics define as a poem's "literariness," those qualities of language—imagery and metaphor, tone and point of view, rhythm and meter, syntax and punctuation—that constitute not just what a poem can plausibly mean but *how* a poem means. And, finally, because we are dealing with art, readers expect that the poem will elicit a broader intellectual or emotional response that cannot be reduced to any one summary statement—some snippet of what I referred to before as practical information. All this is to say that, at a basic level, the material text allows us to enter into a mindset that approaches the poem as a work of art.

Using "The Second Coming" as an example, readers move from the title into the poem itself and can begin to identify patterns that spark broader associations: the widening gyre and the flight of the falcon set against the falconer, who serves as the marker of a center that "cannot hold;" chaos expanding in the face of a failing social order, "the blood-dimed tide" overwhelming "the ceremony of innocence"—a state of affairs that is aptly summarized in the first stanza's concluding two lines, which are memorable partly because of the clauses' parallel syntax. The second stanza begins with the kind of grand rhetorical declaration that we often find Yeats's late poems, as if the societal disintegration envisioned in the first stanza portends the return of Christ, yet we immediately pick up on the irony by noting the repetition of "surely," as we now contemplate a nightmare vision of cataclysmic transformation. The images, which echo and expand upon the opening juxtaposition of flux and stability, invite us to try to assemble the associational patterns into some fixed statement of meaning that we cannot quite reach—that moment of aesthetic contemplation that Kant characterizes as "purposiveness without purpose," when the aesthetic object exceeds our cognitive judgement.[5] The poem ends with a prophecy framed as a question, and a question framed as a prophecy—a striking combination of the interrogative and the imperative forms that gestures toward some metaphysical structure constituted by eternal transformation that can be evoked and partially apprehended through images, but that cannot be fully comprehend by the rational mind.[6] As a reader's eyes pass over the final question mark and into the blank space between poems, she or he is left pondering this inscrutable something. Like Stephen Dedalus at the start of *Ulysses*, trying to recall his previous night's dream, readers are left "almosting it."[7]

I realize that this kind of reading speaks to a very specific type of aesthetic experience—one that occurs in quiet solitude, begins with sustained concentration and, ideally, ends with contemplation, as certainty gives way to uncertainty. I'm not suggesting that it's a universal experience, but at the very least, it's the kind of aesthetic experience that many scholars have had, generally value, and often model for their students. And for good reason: the invention of the printing press, followed later by the mass distribution of easily portable books, produced, at a material level, a cognitive mode designed to generate precisely this type of aesthetic experience.[8] Literary theorist Katherine Hayles defines this cognitive mode as "close reading," distinguishing it from other modes that have emerged in the digital age.[9]

Another mode that Hayles identifies is "hyper reading." It involves engaging simultaneously with multiple texts and information streams, shifting quickly among diverse modalities—texts, still images, moving images, sound, etc.—and it ultimately aims for the rapid acquisition of content knowledge, most of which, if recent studies in cognitive neuroscience are accurate, is quickly forgotten. What struck me in my classroom, and what continues to give me pause, is that my students frequently encounter poetry in a technological medium that, because it makes hyper reading seem intuitive, is perfectly engineered to undercut the very aesthetic experience, born out of close reading, that I took to be the foundation of literary studies.

Consider the digital version of "The Second Coming" my student was using (Figure 3).[10] A summary precedes the poem. The poem is bracketed by links to analytical essays on other Yeats works; there are also embedded links to themes, key terms, video commentaries, audio clips of famous people reading the poem, biographical information, more Yeats poems and, of course, advertisements. It's made for hyper reading, which means that it is difficult for even those trained in the mode of close reading to engage the poem itself with anything like sustained concentration, let alone contemplation. If, as Keats famously wrote, the ideal poet "is capable of being in uncertainties, Mysteries, doubts, without any irritable reaching after fact & reason,"[11] this particular site

Figure 3 : Summary of "The Second Coming"

demands that we continually reach for additional facts and additional information. According to the philosopher Malcolm Budd, "The value of a poem as a poem does not consist in the significance of the thoughts it expresses, … for if it did, the poem could be put aside once the thoughts it expresses are grasped."[12] This website, however, encourages us to see the value of the poem precisely in the thoughts that are expressed—the supposedly true meaning of the poem's content neatly summarized at the outset, and then developed in all of those additional interpretative essays. For the Russian formalist Viktor Shklovsky, the crucial difference between literary language and ordinary language is that the former is impractical, in the sense that literary language impedes the efficient transferal of information.[13] When we're in the digital realm, though, the technology is expressly designed to enable the efficient acquisition of knowledge—think about the mindset you enter into when doing a Google search. Thus the technology in general, and certainly this poetry website in particular, alters the rhetorical context to such an extent that a poem which is clearly intended to be received primarily as aesthetic discourse is now received, like everything else on the page, as pragmatic discourse. It's as if the poem were designed to communicate practical information and just happens to feature line breaks, unusual syntax, striking images, and cryptic metaphors.

Media historians generally agree that there are four ages of literature: the oral age, when poems were recited from memory and plays were performed at festivals before live audiences; the chirographic age, when literature was produced in the form of hand-written manuscripts; the print age, which introduced mechanical reproduction and eventually the mass dissemination of literature; and our own digital age, where online technology has made literature more widely available than ever before. Each of these ages has been marked by a fundamental shift in the medium within which literature is encountered. We are now living through one of those instances of profound transformation, the first in over 500 years. As I've been pointing out, the digital medium effectively collapses the distinction between aesthetic and pragmatic discursive modes, to the point that it encourages us to understand poems not as art but as vehicles for information transmission. All of which is to say that teacher-scholars need to reckon with this moment of profound technological change. Even if we continue to value books as material objects, for more and more people hyper reading will become the default mode, which will change the way that material texts are read. In his polemical 2008 article for the *Atlantic*, "Is Google Making Us Stupid," Nicholas Carr gives us a taste of how this could play out:

> What the Net seems to be doing is chipping away my capacity for concentration and contemplation. […] My mind now expects to take in information the way the Net distributes it: in a swiftly moving stream of particles. […]

Immersing myself in a book [...] used to be easy, [but now] my concentration often starts to drift after two or three pages. I get fidgety, lose the thread, begin looking for something else to do. I feel as if I'm always dragging my wayward brain back to the text. The deep reading that used to come naturally has become a struggle.[14]

Whether or not we feel the same way, we need to begin answering the question: how might we use digital technology to enable new generations of readers to engage with Yeats's poetry *as* poetry? How might we encourage them to become close readers—capable of "being in uncertainties"—without simply telling them to turn off their mobile phones? I'm going to sketch out some ways to answer these questions, but first I need to introduce one important caveat.

Although my focus has been on a specific type of aesthetic response—one that brings together elements from Enlightenment philosophy, Romanticism, and formalist literary criticism—the fact of the matter is that, regardless of how we frame the issue, there is no hard and fast line between aesthetic and pragmatic discourse, between emotional and rational thought, between knowledge and contemplation. Reading poetry always combines a bit of both, so that when we read Yeats's poetry in an aesthetic mode, we nevertheless draw upon prior information about his life, his writings, his theories, the work of other scholars, historical and political contexts, and much more. The expert does this more intuitively, the novice often through research, but both have traditionally been reliant on those institutions—publishing houses, libraries, and universities—that control the flow of scholarly information. With digital technology, those barriers have mostly fallen away, to the point that a vast storehouse of "prior knowledge"—drafts, editions, letters, biographies, allusions, interpretations—are often just a click away. This is generally a good thing, even if we aren't entirely sanguine about the quality of frequently unvetted information out there. What this means, in any case, is that we have a technology that has vast potential to assist people in reading and thinking about Yeats's poetry, even as the medium itself often serves to undercut the kinds of aesthetic responses to his poetry that, for many of us, are the reason that we value his writings in the first place. As readers, admirers, and teachers of Yeats, we have a pedagogical responsibility to engage with that technology in creative ways so that a new generation of readers, confronting this vast storehouse of information, will learned to pause, embrace uncertainty, and come to value his poetry in all of its aesthetic complexity.

As Yeats's work on the radio suggests, the temptation—which is always the case when any transformative media technology comes on the scene—is to engineer the technology in such a way that it will replicate the kinds of experiences people had prior to the advent of that technology. For Yeats, that meant trying to re-create, on radio, the intimate communal experience of a live poetry reading, a country pub sing along, or a literary salon.[15] For us, it might mean creating websites featuring Yeats's poetry that duplicate and expand upon best practices in editing and book publication, thereby replicating what happens when someone who needs a bit of help with contextual knowledge to get going encounters his work in a skillfully annotated edition of the poems. As early as 1996 William O'Donnell and Emily Thrush, in their article, "Designing a Hypertext Edition of a Modern Poem," show how a hypertext version of "Lapis Lazuli" can offer not only "a direct translation of the conventional methods of a printed edition" but can do so in a way that will smoothly incorporate notes, commentaries, and bibliographical information that will "be helpful to any (rather than most) of a wide range of readers. If the structure of the annotation is effectively designed," they continue, "the expert can pursue topics of interest that would be arcane to most readers, while at the same time the nonexpert is free to pursue topics that would be annoyingly tiresome to experts."[16] In their version from the mid-1990s, readers can hide these comments (so that they simply have the poem standing alone on the screen); they can display them (so that they have access to a wealth of background information); and they can turn on the "text history" feature (so that they see individual lines as they appeared in drafts and early editions). This site remains a terrific model for how digital technology can help readers of all levels to understand and interpret Yeats's poetry. What is noteworthy in O'Donnell and Thrush's article is that the focus remains on accessing content knowledge, the kind of information that is useful for formulating arguments about the communicative meaning of Yeats's poetry. Or, to put in the terms I've outlined, no matter how well we engineer the technology, we're still operating in and encouraging readers to operate in a hyper reading cognitive mode. By contrast, helping people attend to the literariness of a poem—the formal density of language—is, I strongly believe, still best achieved through interactive pedagogy of the classroom, since habits of mind and aesthetic sensibilities develop slowly over time and through guided practice.

But how can we encourage these habits of mind among our students in the digital age? The key, it seems to me, is to help student recognize that a poem is not this stable, autonomous art object that they are tasked with decoding. Instead, in thinking about a poem as "a made thing," I aim for my students to see poetry as a collaborative or interactive aesthetic experience that depends upon their own close reading.

I was thinking about all this roughly a year ago when I began putting together an upper-level undergraduate seminar on Yeats, and it occurred to me that the moment when I was most conscious of that sense of poetry as collaboration was when I'd had the opportunity to prepare an edition of Yeats's early writings. Editing Yeats makes one acutely aware of his attention to craft and to audience reception, of the way that every published edition alters the bibliographical codes and thus changes how we encounter his writings, and of the fact that his poems, which he revised again and again, are not stable monuments but dynamic, living utterances. What struck me in that pedagogical project is that digital technology could help my students experience precisely that sense of collaboration. By creating websites focused on the drafts of individual poems, the publishing history of a volume, a theme that connects his poems across several periods, and the design of one individual work, my students—I know this sounds idealistic but I think it's true—would actually *be re-creating art with Yeats*. The point, I want to stress, is not the product (what they produce) but the process (the act of production). By attending to Yeats's poetry and his volumes as made things, which they would then re-create in a new medium, my students could develop those close reading skills that will open them up to the kinds of aesthetic experiences that many of us—schooled in quiet solitude, concentration, and contemplation—take for granted.

The students produced four websites, hosted on a private university server to comply with copyright legislation. The first site deals with "Sailing to Byzantium" and "Byzantium" (Figure 4).[17] After an overview of the Cornell Yeats Series, which features drafts of individual poems, and the *Variorum* edition of Yeats's poems, my students used a tool called a "Versioning Machine" to create a website in which readers can explore Yeats's drafting process of these two poems in a format that allows for easy side-by-side comparison of individual lines (Figure 5). The site is an example of what might be produced as an alternative for scholars who do not have ready access to the expensive Cornell Series, or who prefer seeing the drafts visually presented in this way.

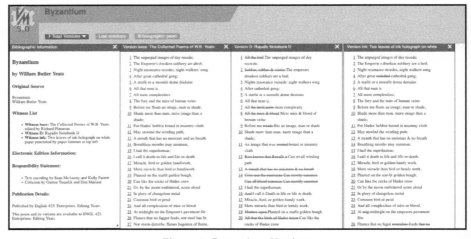

Figure 4 : Byzantium Versions

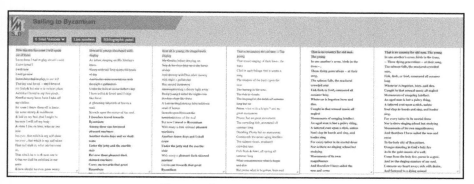

Figure 5 : Byzantium Versions

After the students created the site, I asked them to reflect in writing on Yeats's revision strategies. What immediately became clear is that they had developed a real understanding of the poems' formal qualities—especially of the way that Yeats's alternations are often about rhythm, meter, and other aural qualities. They had, in other words, shifted their attention from poetry's communicative function to its formal, material aural qualities—its "music."

Something similar happened with another site that focused on *The Tower* (Figure 6).[18] A group of students charted out the publishing history of the individual poems; by clicking on the "poems" drop-down menu, users can see how each poem appears in the 1928 version, but then they can move through the poem's publishing history, with the students supplying commentary on the versions that appeared in *The Exile, October Blast, The Stories of Red Hanrahan*, and *The Secret Rose*. Users can also go from the home page to each of these volumes directly, which allows for an easy comparison of Yeats's arrangement strategies. In their written reflection, students were, unsurprisingly, very attentive to each publication's bibliographical and contextual codes, which meant that the process of creating this digital site actually pushed them toward—and not, as might be expected, away from—a real engagement with these texts as material objects. It defamiliarized the process of reading poetry for them, in the sense that it prompted them to ask questions about how different contexts produce different experiences of the poem, as opposed to the usual method of ferreting out the supposedly secret meaning of a given poem.

In the third website the group examined a thematic connection, as they assembled poems that referenced Maud Gonne and provided background on her life and relationship to Yeats. Their research on Gonne prompted them to reflect self-consciously on the types of questions that editors face when they incorporate annotations (Figure 7): how much biographical detail should they supply?[19] Does it make sense to claim that a particular poem is about Maud Gonne? What about those moments when Yeats's poetic representations of his

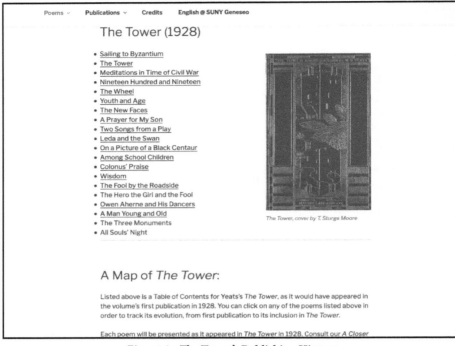

Figure 6 : The Tower's Publishing History

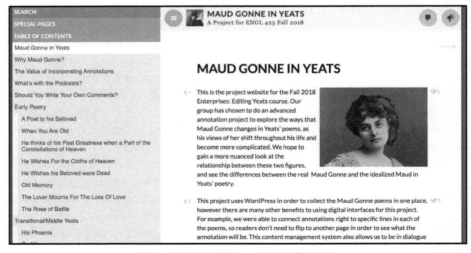

Figure 7 : Maud Gonne in Yeats's Poetry

ideal beloved do not square with what historical accounts indicate? In creating this site and having to puzzle through these types of questions, my students became acutely aware of how editorial decisions about something that initially seemed pretty simple—offering background information—can have a profound impact on how readers experience a poem. They came to realize that information, which we tend to amass rapidly in hyper reading, is not neutral, and that the contextual apparatus is always a kind of argument about the poem—one that starts by defining which information is relevant and which is not. I hope that this exercise has made my students more attentive readers of poetry in general and, when it comes to digital versions of poetry, that they will be less likely to immediately click through links hunting for the supposedly true meaning of poem. I hope they will also be more cognizant of the interactive, collaborative relationship between reader and text.

The last site focused on *In The Seven Woods* and was in many ways the most ambitious part of the project. After conducting research on the Dun Emer Press and the role of Yeats's sisters in creating volumes of his poetry, the students set out to make a new, digital version of *In The Seven Woods*—one that would allow the reader to experience the work in an entirely new way (Figure 8).[20] The homepage features a map of the seven woods of Coole Park, with each poem tagged by location and by a flower, whose color corresponds to one of the four seasons. The idea is that readers would undertake a temporal and spatial journey, charting their own path through the woods, where the poems would evoke place and seasonal associations. A journey through the spring begins with "In the Seven Woods," goes to "Under the Moon," and ends at "The Players Ask for a Blessing," whereas, autumn takes users to "Never Give All the Heart," "The Folly of Being Comforted," and "The Old Men Admiring Themselves in

Figure 8 : Digital **In the Seven Woods**

the Water." Readers could spend a lot of time debating how well the poems fit within these groupings—for me, they often do, at least in terms mood and imagery—but the key point is that the students have taken the original version of the volume and re-made it so that it can signify in new, unexpected, and aesthetically meaningful ways.

The undergraduate students involved in this project collaborated with Yeats, and in so doing, they made decisions that required them to see the poetry not as some static art object, cold and distant, but as something that is alive. We cannot force students to abandon their mobile devices in favor of books, and we cannot impose the exact kind of aesthetic response to poetry that many of us value, but we can develop a form of digital pedagogy—creative, collaborative, and built on active engagements with poetry's richness and difficulty—that will foster a mindset that is more attentive to the aesthetic than the pragmatic, art over information, the formal density of language over its prosaic communicative function.

NOTES

Thanks to the SUNY Geneseo students who created the projects featured in this article: Matthew Albanese, Kira Baran, Nicole Callahan, Cindy Castillo, Leah Christman, Hannah Fahy, Jennifer Galvao, John Lathrop, Daniel Mariani, Sean McAneny, Hannah McSorley, Emma Medina, Kelly Parrett, and Gaston Touafek.

1. Marjorie Perloff, *Radical Artifice: Writing Poetry in the Age of the Media* (Chicago: University of Chicago Press, 1991), 27–28.

2. Figures 1–3: "Summary and Analysis of the Poem 'The Second Coming' by William Butler Yeats," Owlcation, Updated March 5, 2019, https://owlcation.com/humanities/Summary-and-Analysis-of-Poem-The-Second-Coming-by-William-Butler-Yeats.

3. See Jerome McGann, *The Textual Condition* (Princeton, NJ: Princeton University Press, 1991) and George Bornstein, *Material Modernism: The Politics of the Page* (Cambridge: Cambridge University Press, 2001).

4. For the differences in editions, see *VP* 401–02.

5. Immanuel Kant, *Critique of Judgement*, trans. James Creed Meredith (Oxford: Oxford University Press, 2009), 57–59.

6. Seamus Deane, *Strange Country: Modernity and Nationhood in Irish Writing Since 1790* (Oxford: Oxford University Press, 2006), 174.

7. James Joyce, *Ulysses* (New York: Vintage International, 1990), 47.

8. For an excellent overview of the issues at stake in current debates about reading habits in the digital age, see Adam Hammond, *Literature in the Digital Age: An Introduction* (New York: Cambridge University Press, 2016).

9. N. Katherine Hayles, *How We Think: Digital Media and Contemporary Technogenesis* (Chicago: Chicago University Press, 2012), 11–12.

10. Figure 3: Andrew Spacey, "Summary and Analysis of the Poem 'The Second Coming' by William Butler Yeats," Owlcation, Updated March 5, 2019, https://owlcation.com/humanities/Summary-and-Analysis-of-Poem-The-Second-Coming-by-William-Butler-Yeats.

11. John Keats to George and Tom Keats, December 21, 27 (?), 1817, in *The Letters of John Keats 1814-1821*, vol. 1, ed. Hyder Edward Rollins (Cambridge: Harvard University Press, 1958), 193.

12. Malcolm Budd, *Values of Art: Pictures, Poetry and Music* (London: Allen Lande, 1995), 83–85.

13. Viktor Shklovsky "Art, as Device," trans. and intd. Alexandra Berlina, *Poetics Today* 36, no. 3 (September 2015): 161–63.

14. Nicholas Carr, "Is Google Making Us Stupid," *The Atlantic* (July/August 2008), https://www.theatlantic.com/magazine/archive/2008/07/is-google-making-us-stupid/306868/

15. See Emily Bloom, *The Wireless Past: Anglo-Irish Writers and the BBC* (Oxford: Oxford University Press, 2016); see also the special issue on Yeats and mass communications edited by Emilie Morin and David Dwan, *International Yeats Studies* 3 (2018), https://tigerprints.clemson.edu/iys/vol3/iss1/1.

16. William O'Donnell and Emily A. Thrush, "Designing a Hypertext Edition of a Modern Poem," in *The Literary Text in the Digital Age*, ed. Richard J. Finneran (Ann Arbor: University of Michigan Press, 1996), 200.

17. Figures 4 and 5: Sean McAneny, Daniel Mariani, Kelly Parrett, and Gaston Touafek, "Byzantium Versions," SUNY Geneseo, December 2018.

18. Figure 6: Matthew Albanese, Cindy Castillo, and Jennifer Galvao, "*The Tower's* Publishing History," SUNY Geneseo, December 2018.

19. Figure 7: Nicole Callahan, Hannah McSorley, and Leah Christman, "Maud Gonne in Yeats's Poetry," SUNY Geneseo, December 2018.
   Figure 8: Kira Baran, Hannah Fahy, John Lathrop, and Emma Medina, "Digital *In the Seven Woods*," SUNY Geneseo, December 2018.

W. B. Yeats And The End Of The World

Justin Quinn

I

It's hard to find good rhymes for "world." For instance, "furled" is an older usage that conjures officer parades and imperial trumpets. Both "swirled" and "whirled" seem too decorative, as though they are trying hard to be poetic; one thinks of the bleached curlicues of Jugendstil art and architecture. And good luck trying to get a word like "pearled" or "skirled" into a twenty-first century poem. "Hurled" is not bad, but because it describes such a specific kind of movement the rhymer is immediately locked into a particular kind of scene, and possibly tone, if they choose to employ it. In this respect "curled" is similar: quite acceptable, but a difficulty arises if it is constantly combined with such a useful, all-purpose word as "world." It becomes awkward as, for instance, the combination of "child" and "mild." Can you call an infant "mild?" I don't think you can, but bludgeoned by annual repetition we've become inured to the infant Jesus referred to as "tender and mild" in "Silent Night." This is a problem, as "world" is simply so useful. It denotes a fundamental concept of human conversation and culture. It can briefly imply vastness. For most poets, it's a dangerous word to use in a poem (like "history" or "geography"). Possibly it should be banned from poetry for a few decades (along with history and geography). In these two respects it's a bit like the word "sky" or "sea," though these two are easy to rhyme.

W. B. Yeats liked using the word. Here are some examples from his work:

> Rose of all Roses, Rose of all the World!
> The tall thought-woven sails, that flap unfurled [...]
> —"The Rose Of Battle" (*CW1* 34, *ll* 1–2)

> Rose of all Roses, Rose of all the World!
> You, too, have come where the dim tides are hurled [...]
> —"The Rose Of Battle" (*CW1* 34, *ll* 25–26)

> But O, sick children of the world,
> Of all the many changing things
> In dreary dancing past us whirled,
> To the cracked tune that Chronos sings [...]
> —"The Song Of The Happy Shepherd" (*CW1* 19, *ll* 6–9)

That has long faded from the world;
The jewelled crowns that kings have hurled [...]
—"He Remembers Forgotten Beauty" (*CW1* 46, *l* 4)

Yeats doesn't do particularly well with the rhymes, but there are two mitigating factors here: first, as I said, it's hard; and second, all of these examples are from early in his career. Just as he is entranced to the point of ridiculousness with the word "dim" up to the end of the 1890s, so too is he overly enamored of the force of the word "world." Why?

In this period, Yeats is interested in Irish material, whether from mythology or folk tradition. For instance, you have a man who's standing in Dromahaire, who dreams of a "world-forgotten isle" (*CW1* 37, *l* 8). Here he means what we might call "the Great World"—the zone of worldly things and worldly wiles; fairyland is represented in contrast to it. This is an important binary in his early work. Another binary we find clustered around "world" is that of the local and the universal. Often, his poems are involved with small-town stuff, i.e., what's going on in Dromahaire, Peter Gilligan's parish, Innisfree, Knocknarea, Knocknashee, Tiraragh, Ballinafad, Glencar, etc. It may seem obvious to say that Yeats is not a local or regional poet, but it bears repeating that he immersed himself in local detail in order to re-present it for readers beyond these rural Irish communities. This takes a particular form in the poems themselves, as he frequently invokes the distant horizon of the "world" by way, again, of contrast. Observe the opening of "The Song of the Happy Shepherd:"

The woods of Arcady are dead,
And over is their antique joy;
Of old the world on dreaming fed;
Grey Truth is now her painted toy;
Yet still she turns her restless head:
But O, sick children of the world,
Of all the many changing things
In dreary dancing past us whirled,
To the cracked tune that Chronos sings,
Words alone are certain good.
Where are now the warring kings,
Word be-mockers?—By the Rood
Where are now the warring kings?
An idle word is now their glory,
By the stammering schoolboy said,
Reading some entangled story:
The kings of the old time are dead;
The wandering earth herself may be
Only a sudden flaming word

In clanging space a moment heard,
Troubling the endless reverie. (*CW1* 19, *ll* 1–21)

With a curt gesture, Yeats stretches the horizon of the world behind the speaker of the poem by referencing the "sick children of the world." Clearly, this is not the limited world of the Shepherd's community (more on that in a moment), nor is it the world of getting and doing—the Great World—mentioned above. Rather it would seem to be the globe. We are, I think, to imagine all of the children throughout the world who are sick.

But where is this Shepherd from? Not Dromahaire or Knocknarea, nor, it would seem, any particular Irish village. He knows about Arcady, yet he doesn't speak ancient Greek. He is a generic shepherd dreamed up out of translations of Greek and Roman pastorals, as mediated through anglophone poetry in the preceding centuries, thus giving him an English shading as well. Yet the poem rubs shoulders with others that have particularly Irish settings. It is a cosmopolitan imagination of an earlier age, one that's more regionally and linguistically restricted. Shepherds, by nature of their occupation, are very unglobalized, so the footloose nature of this one is noteworthy. One of the things he imagines is the word—that near-rhyme for world—wandering over the earth. "World" requires a rhyme, and throughout his early work Yeats searches for this work. This global vision also encourages the young poet to produce a poetry that can range over the world's expanses, as prefigured in this poem. And to do so, in the first place, requires a new type of mobile language.

II

In his recent book, *W. B. Yeats and World Literature: The Subject of Poetry* (2016), Barry Shiels examines Yeats's work and "the effects of money, trade and globalisation."[1] He attends especially to what he refers to as the "international mobility of reference" in Yeats's poetry, some of which we see in the poem above, and more generally in his wide-ranging cultural references, especially in the late poetry.[2] He examines how this relates both to his ideas of the Irish nation and to the inchoate issue of "global assimilation associated with accelerated means of cultural exchange and the extended dominion of English language literature."[3] We have become accustomed to discussions of culture and globalization, but literary studies for the most part attend to the contemporary period, considering, say, how the novels of Mohsin Hamid, Kamila Shamsie, or Mohammed Hanif attempt—as they flit between time-zones, languages, cultures—to represent the phenomenon of globalism. But Shiels shows that globalized literature and its idiom did not emerge in just the last twenty years or so, but has a major antecedent in Yeats. For instance, he argues that Yeats's dealings with Irish antiquarian material and (since he could neither speak nor read Irish) his distance from Irish-language material allowed him "to invent a 'common' English applicable to no particular locale—and spoken by no particular person."[4] Of course, certain clear markers of Irishness—both thematic and linguistic—are laid down in the poems, but these are small in number and strategically placed so as not to disturb (in the first places) British and US readers. This "common English," Shiels argues, has more generally served to found a global literary lingua franca. He remarks that:

> For a monoglot Yeats notched-up a surprising number of important translation credits. As well as the Irish folklore considered in the last chapter, and two late translations (of translations) of the Oedipus plays, he worked to improve Rabindranath Tagore's translation of *Gitanjali* (1912), offered advice to Ezra Pound on the Ernest Fenollosa manuscript for the twin 1916 publications *Certain Noble Plays of Japan* and *Noh or Accomplishment: A Study of the Classical Stage of Japan*, and "[p]ut into English" a new abridged version of the *Upanishads* with Shri Purohit Swāmi (1937).[5]

In relation to the last-mentioned text he continues:

> What distinguishes the Yeats and Shri Purohit version [...] is its presumptuousness. Showing no need for parenthetical explanation and with a clear emphasis on brevity and simplicity, their edition compresses the scholarly apparatus which we might expect to accompany such a technical feat of translation. Theirs is not a translation into English from another language, but an original production of world English.[6]

This "world English" would seem to have the great advantage of begetting a global literary traffic (as Shiels says, "foreign Genius transmitted over great distances").[7] Such an emphasis moves us beyond not only the national context for studying Yeats's work, but also the postcolonial (despite India's status at the time). Two good examples of this are his readings of "Lapis Lazuli" and "The Statues," when Shiels refers to the ways that Yeats's "poems allude to and associate between multiple and diverse materials without providing much or any explanation of their provenance or historical context." In relation to the latter he remarks that it "reduces historical particulars to the single movement of modernity which, in disaffected mood, the poet calls 'the filthy modern tide.'"[9]

Shiels illuminates a fundamental aspect of Yeats's poetry that has not been addressed by nationalist, revisionist, or postcolonial readings. It especially illuminates the work of the 1920s and 1930s, which has always exceeded those theoretical frameworks, and by default has fallen into an amorphous idea of great works of the European tradition. Shiels also helps us read an early poem like "The Song of the Happy Shepherd," as we observe how its production of a generic pastoral mode slots easily into this idea of a "world English" poetry, especially when such a poem is contiguous with "Anashuya and Vijaya," set as it is in an Indian temple in the Golden Age, or the ones which follow, "The Indian Upon God" and "The Indian to His Love."

Critics have shown how British imperialism, and its later US incarnation, informs a world literature that is transported by "this 'common' English applicable to no particular locale." Aamir R. Mufti says that "the history of world literature is inseparable from the rise of English as global literary vernacular and is in fact to some extent *predicated* on the latter."[10] The idea of world literature might originally been Goethe's—at least that's the anecdote that is routinely deployed in World Literature theory—but German was left behind a long time ago, along with French:

> If English is now incontestably the lingua franca of neoliberal capitalism, the language, for instance, in which individuals in a wide range of professions and in various sectors of industry and finance can most reliably expect to be able to communicate with their counterparts from across the world, then we might say that this book is concerned with the subset of that global linguistic reality, namely, the situation of English as a *global literary vernacular*—English not merely as a language of literary expression but as a cultural system with global reach, not simply a transparent medium but an assemblage and apparatus for the assimilation and domestication of diverse practices of writing (and life-worlds) on a world scale.[11]

Mufti's book, *Forget English! Orientalisms and World Literature* (2016), is concerned with those moments when other languages/cultures impinge on the edge of English, whether it's Agha Shahid Ali's use of Urdu poetry in English or the recent rise of Pakistani novelists writing in English. He examines the distortions, omissions, and gains that occur along the border between anglophone culture and smaller, less globally prestigious cultures. But he is on the critical *qui vive* when it comes to anglophone culture, suspicious of the stealthy and insidious ways imperialism can reimpose itself in culture.

This is a debate which is now only beginning: Emily Apter harmonizes with Mufti, criticizing the desolation of a world literature that is mediated predominantly through English. Gayatri Spivak and Tim Parks agree.[12] Alexander Beecroft is more sanguine:

> [G]lobal literature represents a rupture not only with the identification of the literature with its nation of origin but also with postcolonial literatures as such. By this argument, a "postcolonial literature" such as Indian literature in English represents an attempt to create a narrative for a national literature in

English out of the colonial experience, where a Global English literature (if such a thing yet exists) instead constructs a community of English speakers (or English readers) through a myth of origin that foregrounds interconnection rather than subjugation.[13]

Beecroft ends his *Ecology of World Literature* (2015) with a chapter on global literature, but again for the most part he sees this as a feature of the contemporary period; Shiels allows us to understand that global literature has longer antecedents, one of which is Yeats. Viewed in this manner, the past begins to stretch back further from the present. The future, however, is possibly very brief, as the world may soon end.

III

So far, then, we have Yeats standing at the beginning of an incipient world literature in English, as one of its co-creators. As he reaches over a great distance to, say, Tagore, and brings him into English, problems arise with this new poetic idiom that Yeats didn't take into consideration: although he is the poet of a nation that is trying to establish itself in opposition to Empire, he's using a medium that is, in Mufti's phrase, *predicated* on Empire. This was the mainspring of a lot of postcolonial criticism, but here I want to consider a different issue. For while Yeats's practice did indeed open this new idiom in anglophone poetry, the one that Shiels describes so thoroughly while also providing an excellent rebuttal to Tim Parks's view that global literature in English is monotonous and dull, Yeats himself for the most part is thinking about the *end* of the world.[14] While, say, social democrats were working out how to transform Europe and the world in the 1920s and 1930s, Yeats scorned all such attempts at amelioration, viewing them as a betrayal of aristocratic value and probably a perversion of human nature. For the "world," as it appears in his poetry and plays, has the attributes I mentioned above (the place of business, wiles, etc., a zone that's exceeded by spiritual vision, or which contrasts with the local by virtue of its vastness; a place to wander homeless), but the other repeated associations convey that the world is something that can end, and also something that can be destroyed—indeed, that seems to bring forth the desire in humans to destroy it. In other words, "The blood-dimmed tide is loosed" (*CW1* 107, *l* 5).

The end of the world has forever been nigh. As Frank Kermode reminds us, there have always been excellent reasons for thinking that it's all going to end:

[i]t is commonplace to talk about our historical situation as uniquely terrible and in a way privileged, a cardinal point of time. But can it really be so? It

seems doubtful that our crisis, our relation to the future and the past, is one of the important differences between us and predecessors. Many of them felt as we do. If the evidence looks good to us, so it did to them.[15]

Kermode and his readers' "crisis," when he gave these lectures in 1965, is not straightforwardly "ours" anymore—though we still face nuclear annihilation. Here I'm interested in Yeats facing the prospect of the end of the world, and what this can tell us about his practice as a poet. What's the connection—is there a connection?—between this desire for, his relish and his anticipation of, the end of the world, and the formal choices of rhyme in his poetry? What are the implications of this for our own culture?

First, though, what is the nature of our present ideas of apocalypse, and how do they affect culture? In his work, the Romantic critic and philosopher Timothy Morton attempts to make the connection between Last Things and culture. He arrives with an original description of our particular apocalypse, and he argues that it enables a particular new type of art, which might be called *un*modernist, though decidedly not *post*modernist. For him, the end of the world is ecological disaster, especially global warming. He calls this a *hyperobject*. That is, it is not an object in the sense in which a table or a continent or a cloud is an object, rather it is a set of relations between objects, or phenomena. In Morton's descriptions, it has several features. First, it is viscous. The means that it cannot be studied at arm's length or beneath a microscope (that would mean it was merely an object):

> The mirror of science melts and sticks to our hand. The very tools we were using to objectify things, to cover Earth's surface with shrink wrap, become a blowtorch that burns away the glass screen separating humans from Earth, since every measurement is now known as an alteration, as quantum-scale measurements make clear.[16]

This no doubt comes, at least in part, from a Latourian idea of science, but the speculative fiction writer Jeff VanderMeer is more helpful in illustrating this. In *Annihilation* (2014), a group of scientists enter a zone where strange things occur. Toward the end of the book, the narrator is trying to make sense of the bizarre events that have occurred, and she pulls out her microscope, the instrument that above all others signifies scientific precision:

> I set up my microscope on the rickety table, which I suppose the surveyor had found already so damaged it did not require her further attention. The cells of the psychologist, both from her unaffected shoulder and her wound, appeared to be normal human cells. So did the cells I examined from my own sample. This was impossible. I checked the samples over and over, even

childishly pretending I had no interest in looking at them before swooping down with an eagle eye.

I was convinced that when I wasn't looking at them, these cells became something else, that the very act of observation changed everything.[17]

The narrator's suspicion that the cells have agency eventually leads her to conclude that the entire zone is a "complex, unique, intricate, awe-inspiring, dangerous organism. It might be inexplicable. It might be beyond the limits of my senses to capture—or my science or my intellect—but I still believed I was in the presence of some kind of living creature, one that practiced mimicry using my own thoughts" (VanderMeer, *Annihilation*, 119). Viscosity is no longer only feature of the examined phenomena, but of the instruments and indeed the examiners themselves.

A second quality of Morton's hyperobject is that it is nonlocal, or massively distributed in space. We only see bits of it here and there, and have to learn to see the connections. From disparate phenomena we have to infer a larger whole. Another aspect is phasing. If the hyperobject's nonlocality refers mainly to geographical dispersion, then phasing is about distribution over time: "Hyperobjects seem to phase in and out of the human world. [...] they occupy a high-dimensional phase space that makes them impossible to see as a whole on a regular three-dimensional human-scale basis. We can only see pieces of hyperobjects at a time."[18]

The final characteristic I'll mention here is interobjectivity, which means that we can only intuit the presence of hyperobjects by the marks that they leave on objects. This is connected with the idea of nonlocality, and also with viscosity, insofar as it decentralizes human agency and consciousness, locating it instead along a spectrum of consciousness, conceivably stretching even as far as mycorrhizal webs of communication in old forests (though Morton doesn't mention these). Humans have realized "that they are not running the show," even though now they find themselves "at the very moment of their most powerful technical mastery on a planetary scale."[19] Rather than living in a world that we can control and direct, "we have discovered that we are already falling inside the abyss, which is not pure empty space, but instead the fiery interior of a hyperobject."[20]

Morton's global warming hyperobject is useful for us here as it throws into relief Yeats's apocalypse. Yeats is not as analytic, sufficing himself with images of tides of global bloodshed and anarchy being loosed upon the world. Morton's idea of what awaits us is more detailed:

What exists outside the charmed circles of Nature and life is a charnel ground, a place of life and death, of death-in-life and life-in-death, an undead place of zombies, viroids, junk DNA, ghosts, silicates, cyanide, radiation, demonic forces, and pollution. My resistance to ecological awareness is a resistance to the charnel ground. It is the calling of the shaman to enter the charnel ground and to try to stay there, to pitch a tent there and live there, for as long as possible. Since there are no charnel grounds to speak of in the West, the best analogy, used by some Tibetan Buddhists (from whom the image derives), is the emergency room of a busy hospital. People are dying everywhere. There is blood and noise, equipment rushing around, screams. When the charm of *world* is dispelled, we find ourselves in the emergency room of ecological coexistence.[21]

This is an image of a place where infrastructure has broken down, without even the alternative structure of a war-zone. It is a generalized image of panic, emergency, chaos.

Morton's image of the charnel ground riffs off ubiquitous imagery of ecological disaster brought on by global warming. And while his idea of the hyperobject is suggestive, his analysis itself—that is, the way be breaks down its features—is not well defined. Routinely, theorists in this mode respond that sharp definitions are the purview of modernist control of materials, and those days are gone. Yes, of course—but then why the travesty of analysis (the numbered breakdown of characteristics)?

IV

What comes next in Morton's book *Hyperobjects* is clear: a new aesthetic. After describing the hyperobject of global warming, he then considers what kind of art is appropriate for the era. He requires what he calls an "attunement to the non-human" that entails the forswearing of aesthetics that claim mastery over their materials.[22] We must abandon the Prospero model of the artist whose "complex machines [...] upgrade the subject."[23] Actual landscape was not previously admissible as art, but having been processed in, say, Wordsworth's "complex machines" of poetic technique, suddenly they are. Once the older model of art is abandoned, we supposedly can open ourselves to things, materials, and ultimately to hyperobjects. Here is Morton's description of one work:

Consider Robert Ashley's *She Was a Visitor*. Ashley intones the phrase "She was a visitor" into a microphone. The audience begins to pronounce whatever phoneme of the phrase an individual chooses. The piece becomes a massively distributed pronunciation of "She was a visitor," split into sonic chunks. It spine chillingly captures the alien presence of the strange stranger, the notion of entities as irreducibly uncanny. There is an echo of the Greek tragic chorus and the protagonist, as Ashley's voice speaks over the hissing, clicking ocean

> of syllables. "She was a visitor" becomes strange. Perhaps she was a visitor to my house. Perhaps she was a visitor to the concert hall. Perhaps she was a visitor from another planet. She gives us a glimpse of the futural essence of a thing. Likewise, the phrase itself becomes a "visitor," an alien being that rustles like a rainforest around Ashley. In the mouths of the audience, the phrase becomes a hyperobject—distributed, yet there [...][24]

This is the same effect as achieved by mantras in, say, meditation. Zen Buddhism also wishes to decenter the human ego and bring a similar "attunement to the non-human." More importantly, Morton's assumes that the time of hyperobjects requires artworks that are themselves hyperobjects.

This seems to be a repetition of the Modernist aesthetic fallacy. In 1915, Ezra Pound wrote: "One discards rhyme, not because one is incapable of rhyming neat, fleet, sweet, meet, treat, eat, feet but because there are certain emotions or energies which are not represented by the over-familiar devices or patterns."[25] Thus artists, faced with what Eliot called "the immense panorama of futility and anarchy which is contemporary history," must find a way to embody that panorama in their works.[26] The artwork in its content and method must resemble its object. Artists themselves must be weak and lame. Of a poem by Brenda Hillman, Morton remarks that "[f]ar from foregrounding the human subject's supposed priority to things, this inversion of normal lineation truly makes the poem a response, in the deep sense of *tuning*."[27] This is, in Morton's view, different from Modernism, which wished to construct objects that embodied these forces; artworks now, on the other hand, must rather resemble manuals of disintegration, must themselves be disintegrating.

Morton is committing the same error of many critical theorists when they descend to look for examples of art that fit their ideas. Are we talking about hyperobjects? Then artworks that respond to these must have the same features as hyperobjects. It repeats the implication of Pound's remark above that old poetic techniques cannot adequately deal with new phenomena. Those older conventional techniques (rhyme, meter, stanza), as used in Romantic lyrics, are "complex machines that upgrade the subject." This characterization is slick: because these techniques are machine-like that makes them somehow nonorganic; because they are complex, they are almost like computers; "upgrade" embeds them in a consumer economy. By implication, it attributes a greater organicity, authenticity, and nonconsumerism to, say, works by Hillman and Young. Now, Morton would hate this implication; but he's in denial: like many other critical theorists, he cannot accept that there can be a *variety* of aesthetic strategies in response to what his theory describes.

Which returns us to Yeats, who, when faced with apocalypse, chose *sprezzatura*: "such men as come / Proud, open-eyed and laughing to the tomb" (*CW1*

139, part III, *ll* 15–16). Within that laughter we find an allegiance to the traditional forms of poetry as a stance, a gait, a set of moves in the face of chaos. This may seem distinctly unZen, as it implies a maintenance of mastery, a strengthening of the ego rather than its dissolution in the waves of the nonhuman.

But this old connection between traditional poetic form and domination is a reduction. First, because it fails to see the ways in which mantra-like repetition (of the kind that is present in the type of art that Morton values) is already built into traditional form. The repetition of rhyme words has the effect of strategically dulling our rationality in order to let in more oneiric elements. Mutlu Konuk Blasing says it better:

> The lyric works with the material experience of the somatic production and reproduction of words as sounds and sounds as words, whether spoken, written, or read. Formal schemes that abstract and stylize the distinctive sonic and grammatical shape of a language serve to foreground its material reality and put up an organized resistance to meaning, both as sense and as intention.[28]

Second, Peter McDonald, commenting on rhyme, indicates how it can never unambiguously be a sign of mastery:

> [R]hyme is one of the loudest announcements of authorial control, a daring of the reader to join the poet in welcoming the victory over mere accident in the working of poetic form; at the same time, it brings that control into the most profound doubt, by sounding out the impersonality of language's relations.[29]

Pound, Morton, and Antony Easthope, among many others, can only see the phonemes studding the poem's column of text on the page and immediately think that the text, or the author, is trying to control or mitigate the chaos of existence. They cannot see how rhyme is also, on the material level of the language of the poem, an illumination of that very chaos.

Third, in Yeats more particularly, we see especially in the late work an obsession with copies, mirrors, repetitions, family generations, all of which subordinate the ego to larger continuums. After reading Balzac he remarks: "For a long time after closing the last novel one finds it hard to admire deeply any individual strength that has not family strength behind it" (*CW5* 56). And that feeling pervades the late work beyond the Balzacian afterglow.

> [...] all must copy copies, all increase their kind;
> When the conflagration of their passion sinks, damped by the body or the mind,
> That juggling nature mounts, her coil in their embraces twined [...] (*CW1* 154, *ll* 7–9)

The Romantic movement valorized individual originality in art—an aesthetic ideology which is still firmly entrenched in creative-writing pedagogy—yet we may do better to listen to Yeats when he says: "Talk to me of originality and I will turn on you with rage" (CW5 238). Sato's sword may well be a symbol of adversity maintained against encroaching chaos, but such a stance cannot be held by one person, it must have "family strength" behind it. W. J. McCormack details at length Yeats's strategic erasures of the commercial aspects of his family in the nineteenth century in favor of its eighteenth-century aristocratic associations;[30] the great gazebo that he built with other quasi-aristocratic figures turns out to be just "a gimcrack Victorian fabrication."[31] Nevertheless, Yeats's comical maneuverings in his family history do not invalidate the idea of "family strength" that is integral to his intellectual and aesthetic outlook in this period.

But even that "family strength" cannot withstand the release of anarchy upon the world. Neither can it withstand the "charnel house" in Morton's description. For Morton's idea of attunement to the non-human is really just a fiction, as much a complex machine as that of traditional poetic devices. We can never be fully attuned to the non-human without being dead, as Wallace Stevens's snowman will tell you. Morton's chosen artworks merely *figure* that ground zero, just as artworks have always *figured* such states, though in radically different ways. Morton thinks that art should approximate these states—that they should be a kind of spiritual preparation, a kind of lulling of the ego toward its death. Yeats agrees, but would prefer to go "open-eyed" to that charnel house, and he calls upon centuries-old poetry machines in order to do so, or as he says: "I must choose a traditional stanza, even what I alter must seem traditional" (CW5 238). Such complex machines do not seek to *upgrade* the charnel house; they are used to dramatize its awfulness more clearly. And the agency of dramatization, Yeats reminds us, is not the sovereign intelligence of poets, but of larger forces—of the community, local or national; of the natural world—as those forces go *through* the poems.

V

On the one hand, as Shiels shows, Yeats is one of the founding figures of a global anglophone poetic idiom; but on the other, it is as though the English language itself wants to prevent poets from rhyming with "world." Indeed, it is as though Yeats has heard the language's instructions, and his later work does not try to find a rhyme for the word at all (though he still frequently uses the word). But, of course, he does stick with rhyme even as he comes ever nearer an apprehension of the erasure of civilization and its culture. Morton wants art to be a simulation of that disintegration; Yeats wants to face that disintegration riding upon tradition. Perhaps it is because he thinks it will make a bigger explosion on impact; perhaps he has not fully absorbed the idea of the erasure of humanity (who, really, can?); perhaps his ideas are merely an adumbration of the simple biological fact that living beings wish to replicate themselves, whether through children or likenesses of themselves and their lives.

Whatever the explanation, I have tried here to show how Yeats's poetic practice when facing what would later be called a hyperobject is exemplary. I think it's important to register this idea, as it significantly renews the repertoire of ways in which our culture can conceive of its own end—indeed, can conceive of the end of all cultures and possibly planetary death. His rhymes more than their rhyming tell.

Notes

This article was first presented as a lecture at the Yeats International Summer School, Sligo, in 2018.

1.   Barry Shiels, *W .B. Yeats and World Literature: The Subject of Poetry* (Farnham: Ashgate, 2016), 3.
2.   Shiels, *W. B. Yeats and World Literature*, 10.
3.   Shiels, *W. B. Yeats and World Literature*, 10.
4.   Shiels, *W. B. Yeats and World Literature*, 129.
5.   Shiels, *W. B. Yeats and World Literature*, 101.
6.   Shiels, *W. B. Yeats and World Literature*, 129.
7.   Shiels, *W. B. Yeats and World Literature*, 56.
8.   Shiels, *W. B. Yeats and World Literature*, 117.
9.   Shiels, *W. B. Yeats and World Literature*, 117.
10.   Aamir R. Mufti, *Forget English! Orientalisms and World Literature* (Cambridge, Mass.: Harvard University Press, 2016), 11.
11.   Mufti, *Forget English!*, 17.
12.   Emily Apter, *Against World Literature: On the Politics of Untranslatability* (London: Verso, 2013), passim. Gayatri Chakravorty Spivak, "The Politics of Translation," Outside in the Teaching Machine (New York: Routledge, 1993), 179–200. Tim Parks, "The New Dull Global Novel," Where I'm Reading From: The Changing World of Books (New York: New York Review of Books, 2015, e-book).
13.   Alexander Beecroft, *An Ecology of World Literature* (London: Verso, 2015, epub), 216.
14.   Parks, "The New Dull Global Novel."
15.   Frank Kermode, *The Sense of an Ending: Studies in the Theory of Fiction* (Oxford: Oxford University Press, 1968), 95.
16.   Timothy Morton, *Hyperobjects: Philosophy and Ecology after the End of the World* (Minneapolis: University of Minnesota Press, 2013), 36.
17.   Jeffrey VanderMeer, *Annihilation* (New York: Farrar Straus Giroux, 2014, e-book), 105.
18.   Morton, *Hyperobjects*, 70.
19.   Morton, *Hyperobjects*, 164.
20.   Morton, *Hyperobjects*, 160.
21.   Morton, *Hyperobjects*, 126.
22.   Morton, *Hyperobjects*, 171.
23.   Morton, *Hyperobjects*, 181.

24. Morton, *Hyperobjects*, 185.
25. Ezra Pound, *Selected Prose, 1909–1965*, ed. William Cookson (London: Faber and Faber, 1973), 345.
26. T. S. Eliot, "Ulysses, Order, and Myth," *Selected Prose of T. S. Eliot*, ed. Frank Kermode (London: Penguin, 1975), 177.
27. Morton, *Hyperobjects*, 178.
28. Mutlu Konuk Blasing, *Lyric Poetry: The Pain and the Pleasure of Words* (Princeton, NJ: Princeton University Press, 2007), 27.
29. Peter McDonald, *Sound Intentions: The Working of Rhyme in Nineteenth-Century Poetry* (Oxford: Oxford University Press, 2012), 41.
30. W. J. McCormack, *Blood Kindred: W. B. Yeats: The Life, The Death The Politics* (London: Pimlico, 2005), 367.
31. McCormack, *Blood Kindred*, 370.

THINGS, THOUGHTS, AND WALTER PATER IN "NINETEEN HUNDRED AND NINETEEN"

Tom Walker

"Nineteen Hundred and Nineteen" was not always called, nor was it dated, "Nineteen Hundred and Nineteen." The first printed version of the poem, appearing in the pages of *The Dial* in September 1921, was titled "Thoughts upon the Present State of the World" and dated "May 1921" (*VP* 428); before that, an extant manuscript version was alternatively, if somewhat indecisively, headed "The Things ~~Return come~~ that come again."[1] Such shifts have given rise to much commentary. For Rob Doggett, where the first printed title suggests some straightforward reflections on a series of passing events, the final title and dating (reinforced by the added postscript date "1919") resonates with "a sense of objective truth and the weight of history and historiography." Such a resonance, though, is darkly shadowed by irony: "the expected progression evoked by the date is undercut by a chaotic vision of the present, which is in turn further undercut by the poem's refusal to sanction any concrete historical narrative as a means for comprehending (and, in turn, valorizing) that present."[2] Nicholas Grene sees the poem's shifting titles as best understood in terms of the regressive sequence of dates deployed in the preceding three opening poems of *The Tower* (1928). Moving from the 1927 dating of "Sailing to Byzantium" backwards through "The Tower," dated 1926, and "Meditations in Time of Civil War," dated 1923, each poem unravels what the previous poem seemed to fix, constituting a "backward, darkening, spiralling movement one could call a widening gyre."[3] In this vein, the move from the first to the final printed title also ties the poem more closely to Yeats's "theory of the gyres and to the imagination of millennial disaster," as gestured towards too in the abandoned manuscript titles: "'Nineteen Hundred and Nineteen' is written out thus in words rather than given in numerals and, as such, it evokes irrationally an idea of the millennium minus one [...] not apocalypse now, but apocalypse tomorrow."[4] However, beyond the temporal and historical determinacies and indeterminacies that the poem, including its final choice of title, enacts and critiques, the displaced earlier titles also point towards the poem's concern with things and thoughts.

Reading the poem under the moniker "The Things ~~Return come~~ that come again," for instance, immediately foregrounds the "things" now gone in the first part's opening line. Similarly, to approach the poem as titled "Thoughts upon the Present State of the World" is to underline the cluster of thought referred to in the opening section's second stanza: "We thought it would outlive all future days. / O what fine thought we had because we thought / That the worst rogues and rascals had died out" (*VP* 428, *ll* 14–16). Moreover, this is a poem in which things are subject to thought and thoughts are evoked as things. Not only are the opening stanza's things gone, but so too is the collective mindset to which they "seemed" miraculous. In the second section, Loie Fuller's dancers are initially presented as enwinding "a shining web, a floating ribbon of cloth"—so, as a thing. But the dancers then become subject to the processes of mental perception, again evoked through the word "seemed," in appearing to be moved around by "a dragon of air […] fallen among" them. Thinking about thinking makes up much of the third section, as is suggested by the deployment of a range of further cognates for the processes of the mind: "compares," "satisfied," "meditation," "affirms," "imagined," "half-imagined," "dreamed," "seemed," "learn," "crack-pated." Yet such thinking is also partly conducted through equating the soul to a swan, a figure that in turn becomes somewhat concrete in terms of the physical presence of the bird's "wings" and "breast." In the fourth section, past talk of the abstract values of "honour" and "truth" has now been brought down to the display of the "weasel's twist" and "tooth"—parts of an animal that are decidedly un-self-conscious. Those mocked in the fifth section include those who had "burdens on the mind" and so labored to leave to posterity a "monument"—marking another transition of thoughts into things.

Of course, classifying parts of an animal or a troupe of dancers as "things" alongside an animate object such as a monument raises questions of definition, as does the point at which satisfaction or affirmation might lie within or outside of the domain of thought. Such problems of categorization, though, seem to be repeatedly foregrounded within a poem marked, as Michael Wood observes, by a wider disturbance or instability of "apparent oppositions or distinctions:" "the whole poem in one sense is about what happens when we can't tell the difference between a march and a lurch."[5] A phrase such as "the night can sweat with terror" from the first section's fourth stanza reconfigures a process at least partly of mind, being terrified, as a thing produced solely via a bodily process, "sweat with terror." This is itself then displaced in terms of agency and affect from the human mind or body altogether, onto a period of time, "the night." Such estrangements also serve to thoroughly distance this activity in kind from the next line's piecing of "our thoughts into philosophy"—of human thoughts thoughtfully thought into thought, as it were. To be an "ingenious lovely" thing, as in the opening line, is to be at the least the product of thought, of ingenuity. The first printing of the poem in *The Dial* has "ingenuous" for "ingenious" (*VP* 428). But whether a mistake or a later change of mind (and the evidence from the manuscripts and typescripts is not wholly conclusive), this is in either case a thing somehow created via thought—innocent, clever, or perhaps somehow both. Moreover, this thing is also able to be perceived as lovely, and so to be thought of as well. To then seem miraculous both through being ingenuous/ingenious and lovely, and through being uncommonly impervious to time ("Protected from the circle of the moon / The pitches common things about"), further raises questions as to the thought at work within and through the object itself—not least, its possible incarnation or materialization of the divine. An unsettling permeability between things and thoughts is repeatedly in play.

Discussing how Yeats reverses rather than simply adopts "forms of abstraction," Wood points towards Angela Leighton's consideration of the poet's curious literalization of figurative language.[7] In relation to the golden bird at the end of "Sailing to Byzantium," Leighton describes how "Yeats's neoplatonism"—in terms of the flexibility it allows between a soul and the form it might take—"gives him a wild freedom with language, an ability to turn simile into fact."[8] There certainly seems to be a similarly Neoplatonic side to this movement between the figurative and the literal at work in the evocation of the swan in the third section of "Nineteen Hundred and Nineteen."[9] However, in then contrasting this Neoplatonism with Yeats's supposed aestheticism-derived sense of art as a separate realm, Leighton somewhat elides the extent to which Yeats during the 1920s is also starting to implicate art and indeed aestheticism itself within his sense of a destabilizing traffic between thoughts and things. Pointing to Yeats's enduring debt to the writer and critic Walter Pater, she casts this influence as a matter of style rather than substance.[10] Yet the supposedly corroborating passage she points to from *The Trembling of the Veil* (1922) is altogether more equivocal than such a distinction would suggest (*Au* 235). There Yeats reflects on the centrality of Pater's influence as a philosophical "sage" on "The Tragic Generation" of writers he encountered in London in the 1880s and 1890s. Having recently re-read Pater's *Marius the Epicurian* he is also unsure as to whether its style ("the only great prose in modern English") or "the attitude of mind of which it was the noblest expression" brought about the downfall of his friends. Quite where Pater's philosophy and prose style begin and end is, for Yeats, unclear. This combination has an apparently direct effect on these poets in the realm of ideas ("Pater had made us learned") and outward form (they are "ceremonious and polite" in their dealings with each other). However, Yeats also goes on to wonder about the connection between such behavior and the antithetical paradoxes of the corporeal forms that their lives and art actually took, as they lived "lives of such disorder" and sought "to rediscover in verse the syntax of impulsive common life." Any comfort that an aesthete's categorical separation between life and art might offer seems far from view; the instability and permeability of things and thoughts will simply not allow for it.

Turning back to "Nineteen Hundred and Nineteen," its initial appearance in *The Dial* followed consecutively on from a serialization across the three previous issues of "Four Years, 1887–1891," the first part of *The Trembling of the Veil*—when he first meets the generation who will go on to become tragic. Such a publication context casts the poem as suggesting a writer now turning to offer their impressions of the present, having just offered a retrospect on the fin de siècle. Thus the "we" looked back on in the first stanza might be seen to include within what Wood aptly describes as its "movable moral and political community" of "anyone who was wrong about the world," just this "Tragic Generation."[11] They too had their "pretty toys" and "fine thought." And before them again comes Pater—but a Pater decidedly of substance and not just style. As Elizabeth Muller has recently argued, Pater's work was a persistent and important influence on Yeats into the middle and latter stages of his career, particularly in terms of the substance of Pater's ideas about the art of Ancient Greece.[12] Accordingly, Pater's writings on Greek sculpture seem to be one of the possible sources for the things and the ideas about those things present in the poem's first stanza. Richard Finneran suggests that: "The bees, also ascribed to Phidias in early printings of the poem, may derive from a reference in Walter Pater's *Greek Studies* (1895) to 'the golden honeycomb of Daedalus'" (*CW1* 495)—a possibility then also relayed in A. Norman Jeffares's annotations.[13] That particular phrase comes from Pater's essay "The Beginnings of Greek Sculpture," but one might less tentatively add that several other ideas and phrases from across Pater's *Greek Studies* also seem to be in play in this opening stanza.[14]

The "ancient image made of olive wood," for instance, might derive, as Jeffares has it, from Sophocles's *Oedipus at Colonus*, or the accounts of Herodotus or Pausanias he also cites.[15] But Pater's "A Study of Dionysus" likewise evokes "the old miraculous olive-tree still growing" in the Erechtheus, before its destruction during the Persian sack of Athens.[16] A notion of "ingenious lovely things" seeming miraculous also forms a key part of the account of "the sensuous, decorative materiality of Greek sculpture prior to Phidias" through which Pater challenges "the neoclassical notion of sculpture as abstract thought in white marble," as Lene Østermark-Johansen outlines.[17] "The Heroic Age of Greek Sculpture," the first part of "The Beginnings of Greek Sculpture," turns to the writings of Homer to capture a lost (ingenuous even) period when the "miraculous power" of works of art was closely tied to their handcrafted ingenuity:

> If the golden images move like living creatures, and the armour of Achilles, so wonderfully made, lifts him like wings, this again is because the imagination of Homer is really under the stimulus of delightful artistic objects actually seen. Only those to whom such artistic objects manifest themselves through

real and powerful impressions of their wonderful qualities, can invest them with properties magical or miraculous.[18]

From a different angle—the persistence of primitivism (ingenuous again) in classical Greek religious sensibilities—the miraculous nature of the work of Phidias himself is also considered at length in "A Study of Dionysius:"

> If men felt, as Arrian tells us, that it was a calamity to die without having seen the Zeus of Olympia; that was because they experienced the impress there of that which the eye and the whole being of man love to find above him; and the genius of Pheidias had availed to shed, upon the gold and ivory of the physical form, the blandness, the breadth, the smile of the open sky; the mild heat of it still coming and going, in the face of the father of all the children of sunshine and shower; as if one of the great white clouds had composed itself into it, and looked down upon them thus, out of the midsummer noonday; so that those things might be felt as warm, and fresh, and blue, by the young and old, the weak and the strong, who came to sun themselves in the god's presence, as procession and hymn rolled on, in the fragment and tranquil courts of the great Olympian temple; while all the time those people consciously apprehended in the carved image of Zeus none but the personal, and really human characteristics.[19]

This final paradoxical emphasis on the divine somehow embodied and perceived in both the made nature of the literal object, "the carved image," and the graspable mundanity of what it represents, "personal" and "human characteristics," also seems inversely in play in Yeats's notion of a "sheer miracle"—a miracle that might at once be absolute and purely immaterial, in evoking the eternal, and made contingently and materially manifest in a crafted object that is sensually attractive.

Such ideas are mobilized in "Nineteen Hundred and Nineteen" to evoke not a moment when art was distinct from, but rather when it was central to, life. Explicitly this moment is of course located in ancient Greece. Its probable mediation via Pater, though, also allusively suggests that the dream or idea of such an empowered and integrated relationship of art to life might also be seen to operate in relation to the more recent past and the collective "we" then turned in the poem's second stanza. Moreover, this we, in its very vagueness, can somewhat more expansively be linked to Pater's notion of a transhistorical spirit. In the preface of *Studies in the History of the Renaissance* (1873), Pater famously conceives of his subject as an "outbreak of the human spirit" characterized by a "care for physical beauty" and a "worship of the body"—of some kind operation of mind interacting with not just any thing, but with a human thing, the body, that itself seemingly combines matter and thought.[20] Just such an outbreak, even if in an attenuated or incoherent form, has clearly been in play during Yeats's youth. But the "we" perhaps also gestures towards any such Renaissance, of any kind of investment in a humanistic unification between mind and matter, as well as the human and the divine. The reversals enacted upon such an outbreak within the poem certainly seem decidedly corporeal. In the first section human bodies, desensitized in becoming "a drunken soldiery," start to separate a human from a part of its very body, in leaving a murdered mother "to crawl in her own blood." In the second section, the determinism of the Platonic Year renders the body at least partly insentient, in dancing without agency. The operations of mind in the third section are condemned as a product of bodily misfunction, of being "crack-pated." The "wise" in the fifth section have had their very eyes short-circuited, while the mockers will not "lift a hand" for the good. The final section then culminates in a complete, twisted separation of thoughts and things within the site of the body. Robert Artisson, an evil spirit and so an illusory body, is "without thought." Yet the false corporeality of his image provokes irrational desire in a real human body, "the love-lorn Lady Kyteler." In turn this leads her to offer him the token of bodily sacrifices, in the form of the parts of disembodied birds. The dream that looking with care on physical beauty and on worshipping the body will lead to an outbreak of the human spirit is undermined. From Paterian "ingenious lovely things," we arrive at a faintly echoing "bronzed peacock feather" that is decidedly not a thoughtfully sculpted or observed thing, but rather a remnant of a bird that in its beauty is still to be placed alongside the bloody "red combs of her cocks." They are both the product of forces, whether irrationally human or inhumanly deterministic, that will in time challenge the ontological and epistemological stability of all thoughts and things.

Notes

1. W. B. Yeats, *The Tower* (1928): Manuscript Materials, ed. Richard J. Finneran with Jared Curtis and Ann Saddlemyer (Ithaca, NY: Cornell University Press, 2007), 198–99.
2. Rob Doggett, *Deep-Rooted Things: Empire and Nation in the Poetry and Drama of William Butler Yeats* (Notre Dame, IN: Notre Dame University Press, 2006), 74–75.
3. Nicholas Grene, *Yeats's Poetic Codes* (Oxford: Oxford University Press, 2008), 26.
4. Grene, *Yeats's Poetic Codes*, 27–28.
5. Michael Wood, *Yeats and Violence* (Oxford: Oxford University Press, 2010), 4.
6. Yeats, *The Tower* (1928): *Manuscript Materials*, 199–255.
7. Wood, *Yeats and Violence*, 29–30.
8. Angela Leighton, *On Form: Poetry, Aestheticism, and the Legacy of a Word* (Oxford: Oxford University Press, 2007), 149–50.
9. See Tom Walker, "'the lonely flight of mind': W. B. Yeats, Louis MacNeice and the Metaphysical Poetry of Dodds's Scholarship," in eds. Christopher Stray, Christopher Pelling, and

Stephen Harrison, *Rediscovering E. R. Dodds: Scholarship, Education, Poetry, and the Paranormal* (Oxford: Oxford University Press, 2019), 217–19.

10. Leighton, *On Form*, 150.
11. Wood, *Yeats and Violence*, 43.
12. Elizabeth Muller, "Defining Beauty: The Paterian Yeats," *International Yeats Studies 2*, no. 1 (Nov. 2017): 24–44.
13. A. Norman Jeffares, *A New Commentary on the Poems of W. B. Yeats* (London: Macmillan, 1984), 230.
14. Walter Pater, *Greek Studies: A Series of Essays* (London: Macmillan, 1910), 193.
15. Jeffares, *A New Commentary*, 229–30.
16. Pater, *Greek Studies*, 41.
17. Lene Østermark-Johansen, *Walter Pater and the Language of Sculpture* (Farnham: Ashgate, 2011), 238.
18. Pater, *Greek Studies*, 204–05.
19. Pater, *Greek Studies*, 30–31.
20. Walter Pater, *Studies in the History of the Renaissance*, ed. Matthew Beaumont (1873; Oxford: Oxford University Press, 2010), 5.

"Number Weight & Measure:" "Nineteen Hundred and Nineteen" and The Labor Of Imagination

Rosie Lavan

It is of more than passing interest that, of the thirty-four chapters in the two volumes of R. F. Foster's biography of W. B. Yeats, only one bears a direct quotation for its title. Chapter Five, in volume II, *The Arch-Poet*, is called "Weight and Measure in a Time of Dearth," and it covers the period 1920–21 (*Life 2* 193). Foster is quoting a letter Yeats wrote to Lady Gregory on April 10, 1921, in which he quoted William Blake in his account of his work towards the sequence of poems which would become "Nineteen Hundred and Nineteen." The work was not easy and the progress was uncertain, but Yeats's commitment to the labor of the writing was serious, underscored by the maxim he summoned from Blake:

> I am writing a series of poems all making up one poem on the state of things in Ireland & am now in the middle of the third. I do not know what degree of merit they have or whether I have now enough emotion for personal poetry. I begin to find a difficulty in finding themes. I had this about twelve years ago & it passed over. I may have to start another Noh play & get caught up into it, if these poems turn out badly. The first poem is rather in the mood of the Anne poem but the rest are wilder. Newspapers & letters alike await now till my work is finished: "bring out weight and measure in a time of dearth" Blake wrote. (*CL Intelex*, 3900)

Yeats was slightly misremembering the quotation, though the inaccuracy does not suggest anything beyond haste in correspondence. The line he has in mind comes from *The Marriage of Heaven and Hell*, a text he knew intimately, and there it reads: "Bring out number weight & measure in a year of dearth."[1] In retrieving this quotation from memory Yeats is snatching the necessary sentiment for this brief letter, which is implicitly a diversion from the urgent primary labor of the troublesome poems, yet offers no release from the preoccupation that poetry itself might be evading him. The letter is often quoted by critics examining the contexts and composition of "Nineteen Hundred and Nineteen:" Nicholas Grene, Helen Vendler, and Michael Wood have all done so in prominent studies in the past twelve years, and it has proved an essential document in clarifying the actual dating of the poem, as opposed to the date with which Yeats titled it.[2] Foster cites the letter at greater length, notably not only including, but also pursuing, the Blake reference in his gloss on it:

"The weight and measure were undeniable; for all the doubts of this letter, the complex poem-series became one of his masterpieces" (*Life 2* 193). This too is undeniable, but it is the aim of this essay to consider the space between the two halves of Foster's sentence, exerting more pressure on the "weight and mea-sure," and the version of Blake that stands behind this masterpiece.

When Yeats describes the incipient "Nineteen Hundred and Nineteen" to Gregory, he fluctuates between the specific and the general: he is telling her about that poem, but he is also reflecting rather despondently on writing poet-ry. "Personal poetry" is personally exacting and he doubts his present capacity for it; the "themes," which in retrospect bear all the majestic desolation of "The Circus Animals' Desertion," are elusive. There is discernment over possible distractions: a Noh play might prove to be generatively engrossing, a way of working through the block with other work; but newspapers and letters, the demotic and the everyday, need to be left aside. It is not unusual to find Yeats attesting to such creative challenges. Indeed, Vendler begins *Our Secret Disci-pline* (2007) by reminding us that: "Over and over, in the intervals he had set aside for writing poems, he complained of the 'strain'of writing lyrics, of the 'ex-haustion' they caused."[3] In this context, the Blake maxim introduces the virtues of self-discipline and prudence. Weight and measure are the instruments of the dedicated artist, economizing his creative resources as he faces a process he expects will be strenuous and protracted. Read in these terms, the composition of "Nineteen Hundred and Nineteen" as Yeats describes it begins to sound like a marathon, as opposed to what Seamus Heaney called the "sprint mode" of writing, when poems appear gifted by sudden inspiration.[4] And Yeats himself sounds very like Heaney's valorized Yeats, the poet who "offers the practising writer an example of labour, perseverance." In Heaney's self-affirming portrait, Yeats "proves that deliberation can be so intensified that it becomes synony-mous with inspiration. Above all, he reminds you that art is intended."[5] In the letter, Yeats is seeking that truth for himself, trusting in labor, perseverance, and dedication as he invokes a very unmystical Blake.

Heaney's word "synonymous" makes deliberation and inspiration equiv-alent in meaning, and that equivalence glosses the tension between the workmanlike practical application and the unbidden poetic stimulation Yeats is grappling with in the letter. His quotation from Blake, and the condition and process it describes, offer a vantage point on the construction and the mystery of "Nineteen Hundred and Nineteen." Rather than examining Yeats's sustained and sustaining philosophical engagement with Blake, here the questions of in-spiration, imagination, and vision will be considered in more quotidian, but no less illuminating, terms. The constellation of references and influences within "Nineteen Hundred and Nineteen," from Phidias to Loie Fuller, and from El-len Quinn to Lady Kyteler, cohere around an expression of poetic inadequacy which Yeats placed at the center of this sequence, in the third poem. That expression defies, or more properly defines, the achievement of the poem, a monument in its own way to the work of the poet.

When Yeats deployed that phrase from Blake in his letter to Gregory, he neutralized its original paradoxical force. The contortions of Blake's "Proverbs of Hell" are apparently overlooked in a quotation which is immediately and strategically personal. It is also revealing, leading us back to Yeats's earlier consideration of this phrase in relation to Blake's own artistic challenges. In the "Proverbs of Hell," Yeats's maxim is one of a series of elliptical and often perverse statements, in tone and intention far removed from the sincerity of purpose he seems to express, and need, in his letter to Gregory. Presumably, in his state of mind in April 1921, he would have found some of the other proverbs far less comforting: Blake's satire and subversion notwithstanding, "Prudence is a rich ugly old maid courted by Incapacity" might have struck him as especially discouraging, but it is in this tonally intemperate context that number, weight and measure need to be understood.[6] However, this was not the first time that Yeats moved to decontextualize and redirect the implications of this phrase. In the introduction to his 1905 edition of Blake's poems, extracted from the three-volume Quaritch edition of the *Works of William Blake* (1893) on which he worked with Edwin Ellis, he discussed Blake the contrarian, at odds with an age to which he refused to adapt:

> He would not modulate his passion, for he was ever combative against a time which loved moderation, compromise, and measured phrase, because it was a time of "unbelief and fear" and of imaginative dearth. Had he not said, "bring out number, weight, and measure in a time of dearth?" [sic] and with him there was no dearth; and also that "the road of excess leads to the palace of wisdom?" His fault was not that he did not moderate his passion, but that he did not feel the error he so often warns himself against, of being angry with individuals instead of "states" of mind.[7]

The rhetorical question at the heart of this extract takes too much for granted. It just about functions as an impatient gloss on what comes before and after, but it also sounds like a non-sequitur. Sheltered in parentheses it might seem a less conspicuous and more logical corroboration of Yeats's argument in Blake's own words. But as it stands, this question raises questions—around, for example, the coincidence and distinction of those terms "dearth" and "measure"—which persist when Yeats draws on the quotation for his own purposes later.

What is clear, though, in the long paragraph from which this extract is taken, is that in 1905 Yeats was as determined to make the proverb personal to Blake the artist as he would be to claim it for himself in 1921. Doing so means disregarding the provocative pose of the "Proverbs of Hell." He outlines Blake's denunciation of "the art of his day" and its influences, and then proceeds with this characterization of Blake's temperament and predicament:

> He made, in a blind hopeless way, something of the same protest made afterwards by the pre-Raphaelites with more success. They saw nothing but an artistic issue, and were at peace; whereas he saw in every issue the whole contest of light and darkness, and found no peace. To him the universe seemed filled with an intense excitement at once infinitesimal and infinite, for in every grass blade, in every atom of dust, Los, the "eternal mind," warred upon dragon Urizen, "the God of this world."[8]

Again, Yeats's meaning is evasive: the transition from the Pre-Raphaelites ("[t] hey saw nothing but an artistic issue") to Blake ("he saw in every issue") is more convoluted than his euphonic repetition and cadence, which muffle the difference between surface and depth, suggest. When the Pre-Raphaelites see, they simply see: it is a matter of appraisal, and even of unexamined transformation of the world into art. Blake's seeing is complicated by vision, a total and ineluctable apprehension which is carried in that tiny word "in." But this too, as Yeats learnt from Blake, is "an artistic issue."

Taking "Nineteen Hundred and Nineteen" as one of two major examples, Vendler argues that the Yeatsian sequence exemplifies "how, by means of abstraction, large and recalcitrant events can be brought within the precincts of poetry."[9] It is possible to proceed from her very helpful assurance, while at the same time acknowledging the Blakean challenge which precedes the discovery of those "means of abstraction" with which the finished poem presents us. In this poem, Yeats can be seen to confront "the whole contest" in its most basic representational terms: how could that not be the case, when we remember the ambition, the urgency, and the impossible capacity of its earlier title, "Thoughts upon the Present State of the World," and when we consider, in Vendler's summary, the disturbing plurality of its concerns?

> In these various poems, we are sometimes agents of free will, sometimes helpless creatures of Fate. We are makers of beautiful things; we are destroyers of beautiful things. We live on a human scale; we live on a cosmic scale. We are rememberers; we are forgetters. We are believers; we are mockers. We are creative minds; we are creatures of erotic abjection. We are debased animals; we are the creators of abstract notions of honor and truth. All of these assertions are held in tension within the sequence.[10]

Vendler also rightly calls attention to the plurality of grammatical voices Yeats deploys in the poem. Caught between the dominant first-person plural (in I, IV, and V) and the "impersonal voice" of II and VI, the first-person singular emerges only in the third poem. Here, Yeats centralizes the "artistic issue:" in the first stanza expressing a patently unsatisfying satisfaction with the comparison of the "solitary soul to a swan," provided the bird is caught in a "troubled mirror;" and in the second, regretting the man absorbed through "his own secret meditation." The third and final stanza is a vision of the end:

> The swan has leaped into the desolate heaven:
> That image can bring wildness, bring a rage
> To end all things, to end
> What my laborious life imagined, even
> The half-imagined, the half-written page;
> O but we dreamed to mend
> Whatever mischief seemed
> To afflict mankind, but now
> That winds of winter blow
> Learn that we were crack-pated when we dreamed. (*VP* 431, *ll* 79–88)

As in the extract from Yeats's introduction to his Blake selection, the euphonious repetitions mask the syntactical complexities at work in this stanza. The stakes could not be higher: the willful image is accorded its own agency, and the wildness and rage it brings end "all things," but this, somehow, is not everything. Yeats also implicates, within this projected destruction, "all that my laborious life imagined," condensing the work into the life to the point of indivisibility, but reinforcing its lamentably incomplete achievement in "[t] he half-imagined, the half-written page." The destructive accomplishment of the image triumphs over the frustrated efforts of the laborious life, so all that remains to be done in the rest of the stanza is to retreat into the tripping, denigrated sphere of the dreamers and the dream.

Both Vendler and Neil Corcoran hear Shakespeare in this final stanza. Vendler describes this "trimeter lilt [. . .]" embodying a Shakespearean song recalling *King Lear*."[12] Corcoran, writing back to Vendler in his consideration of Yeats in *Shakespeare and the Modern Poet*, brings a welcome empiricism to his discussion of the echoes, assenting to the fact that the lines "do recall *Lear* in their weather, their evocation of universal suffering, and their hinting at madness"—though we might question how universal that dreaming "we" really is.[13] Both critics agree that through these allusions Yeats puts us in the company of the Shakespearean fool, sealing the reference with that compound "crack-pated" which, as Corcoran points out, is "a nonce-word, presumably, for 'crack-brained," but he argues for the surer resonance of the song "Blow, blow, thou winter wind" in *As You Like It*.[14] It is worth dwelling on this reach to Shakespearean comedy. Later, discussing "Lapis Lazuli" and "An Acre of Grass,"

Corcoran considers the word "frenzy" in the frantic penultimate stanza of the latter poem:

> Grant me an old man's frenzy.
> Myself must I remake
> Till I am Timon and Lear
> Or that William Blake
> Who beat upon the wall
> Till Truth obeyed his call (*VP* 575–76, *ll* 13–18)

Here Yeats's Blake steps forward, caught in a particular light, and physically opposing obstruction until his own conviction brings abstracted Truth to heel. Parsing the interesting displacement of Hamlet by Timon to accompany Lear, Corcoran suggests briefly that Theseus's speech at the opening of Act V of *A Midsummer Night's Dream* might be detected "in this poem by a poet reaching the end of his life."[15] In that speech, the Duke of Athens evokes "The poet's eye, in a fine frenzy rolling," as he seeks to dismiss as "more strange than true" the tales which the four young lovers have brought back from the wood to the city.[16] In relation to "Nineteen Hundred and Nineteen," though, and the Blakean challenge of its composition, there are further connections to pursue.

Theseus's much-quoted speech, with its contention that "The lunatic, the lover and the poet / Are of imagination all compact," is often, and understandably, detached from its original referents. Shakespeare is using Theseus's speech to satirical ends, invoking contemporary skepticism towards, in Sukanta Chaudhuri's words, "the quasi-Platonic views of Shakespeare's time about love, poetic inspiration and the divine furor of poets and visionary philosophers."[17] Chaudhuri goes on to note the distortions of Romantic engagements with this speech, and offers a clarifying set of assertions:

> It would be simplistic to see Theseus as taking a merely rationalist stand against the action of the imagination (a term which, in any case, did not mean in Shakespeare's time what it does today [. . .]). For Theseus 'imagination bodies forth / The forms of things unknown', and 'the poet's pen / Turns them to shapes' (5.1.14–16). In other words, the poet validates the imaginary forms *as forms*: they are authentic mental constructs even if they correspond to nothing material.[18]

Chaudhuri glosses "imagination in the old sense" as "the faculty of recalling and reordering visual impressions or images planted in the mind, perhaps to create unreal creatures and objects," as distinct from the intervening Coleridgean definition.[19] "Nineteen Hundred and Nineteen" is not resistant to the earlier understanding of the faculty. Borrowing further illumination from Chaudhuri's analysis, the "forms" throughout that formally varied poem are validated by this Shakespearean measure, and yet the "authentic mental constructs" are more than etymologically enmeshed with an authorial crisis, as Yeats presents in the third poem the perceived—or projected—flight of agency and conviction.

What is enduringly brilliant about this speech and its satire is that Shakespeare ensures Theseus's argument functions equally effectively as a testament to the achievements of the imagination and as a dismissal of them. Harold F. Brooks put this well in his 1979 commentary on the remarks: "Theseus intends them as censure; but his eloquence, summoned like Balaam to curse, blesses altogether."[20] This is poetry making nothing happen, with all the famous ambiguity of that famous statement from Auden's elegy for Yeats.[21] Theseus uses the imagination as a great yet unimpressive leveler: what difference is there to discern between the shapes that emerge from the poet's transforming efforts, and the tricks the imagination can play on the anxious mind in the dark? Hippolyta, in response, is clear in her conviction that these experiences are made credible because all four lovers attest to them, but whatever the facts of the night they have attained "great constancy" and will remain "strange and admirable" to her, surviving, to borrow from Auden again, as a "way of happening."[22] The supreme irony of Theseus's speech lies in our consciousness of Shakespeare's dramatic contrivance: just because we enter a pact with the playwright does not mean we cannot see past the limits of the play. In the words of another of the play's editors, Peter Holland, "The man who mocks 'antique fables' is a character from one."[23] Again, this leads back to Yeats and the third part of "Nineteen Hundred and Nineteen:" the rebellious swan, and the "laborious life," the "half-imagined, the half-written page" are performative expressions of poetic incapacity in a poem of supreme accomplishment.

When the Cambridge critic E. M. W. Tillyard delivered a series of lectures about Shakespeare's last plays at the Sorbonne in 1936, he too turned to this scene in *A Midsummer Night's Dream*, using it to represent one of a writer's strategies for managing what he called "planes of reality." In a discussion which also embraced Virginia Woolf's recently published novel *The Waves* (1931), Tillyard drew in the figure of Blake and imagined him as a poet of exemplary resistance to the possibility of unity Theseus's speech embodies:

> In the eighteenth century a poet liked to pretend that things were simpler than without prejudice he would have found them; with the result that Blake, in revolt against his age, passionately protests his own fourfold vision. Perhaps the normal poetic method is to strive to give some sort of unity to whatever planes of reality are apprehended. Something of this sort may be found in *A Midsummer Night's Dream*. [. . .] There are many different realities and we may make excursions into them; but the light of common day is sweet and healthy, let us view things in it. Such, anyhow, is the tenor of Theseus's famous comment.[24]

Tillyard went on to discuss the alternative to the unifying impulse of this "normal poetic method." In other plays, he said, Shakespeare handles these different planes of reality by "communicating the sense of their existence without arranging them in any pattern of subordination."[25] Again he turns to *The Waves* as the modern exemplar of this method. In its own way, and with its own formal and intellectual strategies, "Nineteen Hundred and Nineteen" offers another such exemplar. That is not to suggest that the sequence's range is straightforwardly harmonized under its title, but rather to acknowledge that here—by Yeats's own private admission, in the letter to Gregory—we see a poem emerging from an imagination under the strain of doubt. That strain survives as an artistic effect which seems to crack the polish of trust in achievement in the third poem, but it is also converted into the will to apprehend and comprehend in the sequence as a whole the strange, true subjects it absorbs—made admirable, and granted constancy, through being represented in poetry. In that sense, we can return to the title under which the poem was first published in *The Dial*, "Thoughts upon the Present State of the World," and recognize that it is as accurate as it is portentous: thoughts traverse our own planes of reality, retaining their variety and discontinuity even as we might try to contain a situation in time (like the "Present State") and a place (like "the World") in inadequate singulars.[26]

Some twenty years before he struggled with the images and events which would be transfigured into "Nineteen Hundred and Nineteen," Yeats visited Stratford-upon-Avon. The essay which recalls this trip is memorable for its sweeping denunciation of Victorian scholarship on Shakespeare, and notably the work of John Butler Yeats's friend, Edward Dowden. Tellingly, Blake—and specifically the Blake of the "Proverbs of Hell"—is summoned against the odious efficiency drive of nineteenth-century readers:

> It did not occur to the critics that you cannot know a man from his actions because you cannot watch him in every kind of circumstance, and that men are made useless to the State as often by abundance as by emptiness, and that a man's business may at times be revelation, and not reformation. [. . .] Blake has said that "the roaring of lions, the howling of wolves, the raging of the stormy sea, and the destructive sword are portions of Eternity, too great for the eye of man," but Blake belonged by right to the ages of Faith, and thought the State of less moment than the Divine Hierarchies. Because reason can only discover completely the use of those obvious actions which everybody admires, and because every character was to be judged by efficiency in action, Shakespearian criticism became a vulgar worshipper of success (*E&I* 103).[27]

This is a more positive invocation of "the whole contest" he elsewhere understood as a challenge for Blake: the proverb about the roaring of lions stands for a higher vision, pitted against the narrow, the utilitarian, and the vulgar. It might also, in this context, be understood as testament both to the impossibility of codifying the full achievement of the artist, particularly if the critic's eyes are clouded by their own interests and, conversely, to the always incomplete achievement of the artist. In other words, it reminds us of the poet's labor as Yeats perceived it. "Nineteen Hundred and Nineteen" permits an unusually full view of this labor; its very real challenges were admitted by Yeats in his letter to Lady Gregory, and then remembered and performed in the third section of finished poem. The "half-imagined," "half-written page" endures alongside and within the masterpiece, haunting the poet who lived that "laborious life."

Notes

1. William Blake, *The Marriage of Heaven and Hell*, in Blake, *The Complete Poems*, ed. Alicia Ostriker (London: Penguin, 1977), 183, line 19.
2. See Nicholas Grene, *Yeats's Poetic Codes* (Oxford: Oxford University Press, 2008), 23–24; Helen Vendler, *Our Secret Discipline: Yeats and Lyric Form* (Oxford: Oxford University Press, 2007), 64; Michael Wood, *Yeats and Violence* (Oxford: Oxford University Press, 2010), 57.
3. Vendler, *Our Secret Discipline*, 1.
4. Dennis O'Driscoll, *Stepping Stones: Interviews with Seamus Heaney* (London: Faber, 2008, pbk. 2009), 261–62.
5. Seamus Heaney, "Yeats as an Example?" in Heaney, *Preoccupations: Selected Prose 1968–1978* (London: Faber, 1980, pbk. 1984), 110.
6. Blake, *Complete Poems*, p. 183, line 9.
7. William Blake, *Collected Poems*, ed. W. B. Yeats (London: Routledge, 2002), xxxix.
8. Blake, *Collected Poems*, xxxix.
9. Vendler, *Our Secret Discipline*, 61.
10. Vendler, *Our Secret Discipline*, 71.
11. Vendler, *Our Secret Discipline*, 63.
12. Vendler, *Our Secret Discipline*, 72.
13. Neil Corcoran, *Shakespeare and the Modern Poet* (Cambridge: Cambridge University Press, 2010), 42.
14. Corcoran, *Shakespeare and the Modern Poet*, 42.
15. Corcoran, *Shakespeare and the Modern Poet*, 58.
16. William Shakespeare, *A Midsummer Night's Dream*, ed. Sukanta Chaudhuri (London: Bloomsbury, 2017). UK eLD e-Books, 5.1.10–12.
17. Shakespeare, *Midsummer Night's Dream*, Introduction, 204.0/832.
18. Shakespeare, *Midsummer Night's Dream*, Introduction, 205.3/832.
19. Shakespeare, *Midsummer Night's Dream*, 5.1.8n.
20. Shakespeare, *Midsummer Night's Dream*, ed. Harold F. Brooks (London: Methuen, 1979, repr. 1984), cxl.
21. W. H. Auden, "In Memory of W. B. Yeats," in Auden, *Collected Poems*, ed. Edward Mendelson (London: Faber, 1976, rev. edn. 1991), 248.
22. Shakespeare, *Midsummer Night's Dream* 5.1.26, 27; Auden, Collected Poems, 248.
23. Shakespeare, *Midsummer Night's Dream*, ed. Peter Holland (Oxford: Clarendon Press, 1994), 55.
24. E. M. W. Tillyard, *Shakespeare's Last Plays* (London: The Athlone Press, 1990), 63–64.
25. Tillyard, *Shakespeare's Last Plays*, 65.

26. W. B. Yeats, "Thoughts upon the Present State of the World," *The Dial* LXXI (July–Dec. 1921), 265–69.
27. See also Blake, *Complete Poems*, 184, lines 5–7.

Presence Of An Absence: Yeats's Solitary Swan

Kelly Sullivan

The cover image to Yeats's 1928 *The Tower*, the volume in which "Nineteen Hundred and Nineteen" appeared, shows the stark upright lines of Thor Ballylee and its inverted reflection in rippling water. Dividing the image and its reflection is a leafy branch; the only mark on the smooth water are lines of slight movement that subtly displace the reflected tower. The composition emphasizes the blocky, linear quality of the once-defensive tower, set against the stylized organicism of the branch. Despite the stillness of the scene, the effect is not entirely peaceful. Part of the aura of unease comes in the significant absence of birds or animal life.

In a 1927 letter to his friend T. Sturge Moore, the artist who created the cover, Yeats makes clear his priorities for the image: "Do what you like with cloud and bird, day and night, but leave the great walls as they are"(*CL InteLex* 5,000). Despite the significance of the natural world, it is the human-made and its destruction—the walls and rubble of civilization—that most concerns Yeats in this book. Yet the reflection of the tower within the water also echoes a significant avian image within: the swan of section III of "Nineteen Hundred and Nineteen." The poet claims he will be "Satisfied if a troubled mirror show" the swan "An image of its state" as it pauses before choice (*VP* 430, *ll* 62–64). Thus the "great walls" of Thor Ballylee reflected in the vaguely troubled waters of the cover in turn recall the great body of a swan half-risen from a lake with its wings thrown wide for flight. It is as if, in showing us the reflective waters, the swan is made present by his absence.

This image of a swan preparing for flight, captured in the moment just before an action, is self-consciously loaded with meaning. The swan represents a soul, and here we see it on the cusp of potential. Yet more radically, after an interrupting stanza, the swan "has leaped into the desolate heaven:" "it took off when the poem wasn't paying attention," jokes Michael Wood, but this quip captures something of the swan's agency.[1] It has wrested control from the poet, made the choice to fly, and moved from a symbolic swan to something more literally avian. This distinction between representing and experiencing—or, to put it another way, between echoing or directly showing—preoccupies aspects of Yeats's poetic oeuvre, particularly in relation to birds and other animal life. That the swan, like the tower itself, represents something seems clear; and that the bird also trammels upon whatever it briefly stands for comes clear in the poet's reaction, his rage at the bird ascending toward "the desolate heaven." The swan's leap is the central preoccupation of "Nineteen Hundred and Nineteen" even as its enclosing stanza "seeks to register this deed and to ignore it."[2] Significant in its absence is the moment of crossing over, an experience of choice and action that, the poem suggests, remains unknowable even as it may be the ultimate understanding to which poetry aspires.

Poems in both *Michael Robartes and the Dancer* (1921) and *The Tower* increasingly engage images of birds and other wildlife, often using them first as symbols only to find they "wing" out of control and cannot be tamed into fixed meaning.[3] These volumes also track Yeats's interest in and frustration with ethical and political themes, and his decreasing sense of confidence in human nature and behavior. Linking this ethical and political interest to the animal allows us to see a poem like "Nineteen Hundred and Nineteen" as preoccupied with the limitations of human experience and understanding. In some parts of this poem such a preoccupation helps reveal a modernist interest in individual isolation, what Fredric Jameson describes as a sense of the inability to communicate experience in any way, that everyone "is equally locked into his or her private language, emprisoned in those serried ranks of monads."[4] Yeats's attitude toward the unknowability of human nature extends to an exploration of and bewilderment with human violence, particularly the ongoing violence of world war followed by revolution and uprising. Helen Vendler argues the "original enigma" of the poem is "the human race's urge to obliterate the very civilizations it has constructed."[5] And Wood calls Yeats "a poet almost everyone associates with violence."[6] In "Nineteen Hundred and Nineteen," Yeats's constant return to debilitating and frustrating human destruction renders the symbolic birds a part of this destruction—the swan may escape the poem, but instead of other poems's joy or at least wonder at the otherness of the animal, in 1919, the defiant swan brings rage. As an uncontainable emblem, it vacillates between being symbolic of and subject to human destruction.

THE SWAN HAS LEAPED

In section I of "Nineteen Hundred and Nineteen," Yeats seeks a way of distancing humanity from the ills of the contemporary moment but finds no "comfort" in assuming this is yet another phase of history. Now that "the nightmare / Rides upon sleep," humans (in the collective "we") are likened to weasels "fighting in a hole" (*VP* 429, *ll* 25–26, 32). This reference conjures up the trench warfare of the First War, but also swiftly indicts man as like a mammal known for its surplus killing of prey even when it has just fed, a distinction it shares with, among a handful of other animals, humans. The second section describes a troupe of dancers conjuring a dragon out of ribbons and cloth, an aestheticized evocation of the "dragon-ridden" days of the War of Independence erupting in the first poem. Thus, it is emblems of war and blood-mired reality that converge in the third section of the poem, despite its seemingly peaceful imagery. In an act of narrating the creation of a symbol, Yeats calls up "some mythological poet" (himself, in this instance, regardless of any other poet he may have in mind) who compares "the solitary soul to a swan" and finds in this image a temporary satisfaction akin to the comfort he sought in the first section in attempting to situate present political violence in a continuum of human history (*VP* 430, *ll* 59–60).

Yeats reinforces the emblematic role the swan plays in describing it half out of the water, "the wings half spread for flight / the breast thrust out in pride," and suggests the bird is cognizant of its role as a symbol—the speaker feels "Satisfied if a troubled mirror show it, / Before the brief gleam of its life be gone, / An image of its state" (*VP* 430, *ll* 65–66, 62, 64). Its "state" is one of choice (as Vendler emphasizes), either "to play, or to ride" the "winds that clamour of approaching night" (*VP* 431, *ll* 67–68).[7] As a symbol, this swan suggests grace, elegance, power, and pride in its stance on the water, qualities coupled with swans' association with fidelity. Yet the image is also significantly static—no actual swan on the waters of Coole demesne, this emblematic swan seems rigidly fixed in an attitude of power and potential—capable of toying with ill-blowing winds or harnessing them. The association of nightmares with "riding," invoked in the first section of the poem, helps inflect both these options with a sense of dread or doom.

If the swan poised for flight represents pure potential in choice, Yeats's account of the labyrinth of "art or politics" suggests that human choices and actions—the pursuit of knowledge, civilization, aesthetics—lead to confusion. Worse, involvement in the labyrinth means missing the moment at which the swan takes flight, suggesting an opacity of knowledge about both the "solitary soul" and the swan itself. The swan's leap, that absent action, preoccupies the poet. The avian ascent into air happens as the poet mires himself in the labyrinth of poetry or politics; the bird "has leaped," an action that takes place off the page. The man lost "in his own secret meditation" misses both the symbol and reality (*VP* 431, *l* 69). The moment of choice and action seemingly cannot be represented in the poem itself, and points to ephemeral experience or to a wholly other consciousness. This unrepresentable action is the heart of this poem, even as it the stanza "seeks to register this deed and to ignore it."[8]

Why does this decision so enervate the poet? Why does it even "end" the very page he hopes to write, signaling the death of poetry, the blend of imaginative dwelling and futuristic dreaming that makes up these political poems? Wood argues the poem most appreciates the potential of the swan "poised to leap but never leaping, because all leaps wreck the pure potentiality of the wings half spread for flight."[9] The image of "pure potentiality" clarifies the swan as a symbol (the potential inherent in a soul, or the potential for an individual to recognize, just for a moment, his or her "state"). Yet the poem's sleight-of-hand in positioning the swan's choice and action of leaping out of the frame (mirroring the avian absence in the cover of *The Tower*) emphasizes what we miss, that for which there is no potential recording. If the heaven that the swan has entered appears desolate, it may be all the more liberating for it. Desolation seems to undo any Christian meaning inherent in "heaven," deliberately calling up and canceling out significance so the swan ascends into nothingness. Yeats's swan defies what the poet elsewhere referred to as the limiting, anthropocentric way Wordsworth (and by implication the Romantic poets) "has to burden the skylark with his cares before he can celebrate it."[10] If Yeats tries to burden the swan with the responsibility of representing a soul, the creature defies him and points to the inevitable failure of lyric poetry (another emblem of civilization). Yet the swan-as-symbol allows Yeats to have it both ways: in implying the failure of art to convey meaning or representation, the bird represents failure and conveys its depths. The swan echoes through the presence of its absence.

This emphasis on presence through absence, a sleight of hand that suggests what we cannot see or know and therefore emphasizes evocation over representation, connects to other absences of knowledge in poems from this period in Yeats's writing. This swan, like gulls and hawks elsewhere, may come close to representing a human soul, but ultimately its consciousness—its decision, instinct, and the meanings that inhere in playing or riding—are opaque to us. They are not meaningless, but we can at best only understand that the bird experiences life as a bird and cannot know what this life may be like. This preoccupation with the swan's leap gestures to a frustration with the human need for trappings of civilization: art and politics. If we are capable of destroying what we have created ("break in bits the famous ivories"), section III comes close to suggesting we would to better to ignore the labyrinth of aesthetics and instead observe the swan at the moment of flight (*VP* 430, *l* 47).

The association of the image of the departing swan with "rage" links to the implied failure of communication or transmission of knowledge (*VP* 431, *l* 80). This opacity or incommunicableness finds parallels in the labyrinth and in the shifts from first person plural ("if our works could/ But vanish") to singular possessive ("my laborious life") to a castigation of a collectively-deluded past ("we were crack-pated when we dreamed"). In increasingly angry statements, Yeats muses on the possibility that it would be better if all our works vanished with our death, wishes away the very endeavor he engages in—the poem we are reading—and finally denies any empathy with his and civilization's ambitions for a better future. Neither collective ambition nor aesthetic or political work brings knowledge, and in losing the moment at which the swan leaps, the poet finally misses out on the potential empathy he might share with another consciousness.

John Shoptaw frames questions of non-human empathy in relation to risk: poets risk feeling their way into an empathic relationship with the non-human, trusting that this process will show forth truth in its representation.[11] But "Nineteen Hundred and Nineteen" explores and fixates not on empathy, animal or otherwise, but on the seemingly perpetual dissolution of relationships, civilities, even civilizations. That the avian has a place in this—beyond symbol, through its tense shift between figurative and literal—connects to the centuries-long place of animals in human culture. Onno Oerlemans suggests that although humans have been "curious" about animal behavior, culturally we have marginalized them as unknown. This in turn leads to a vacillation in the animal's place within or beyond human culture: "Our awareness of animals is simultaneously bound by human history and culture and outside of that history and culture, which is true too of animals themselves."[12] Central to the concept of "civilization" that troubles "Nineteen Hundred and Nineteen" is a distinction between the human and the animal (with the weasels symbolically linked to the human capacity to shoot a woman in her doorway), yet the breakdown of civilization endemic in this poem has the effect not of drawing the human down to an animal level, but of drawing our attention to the arbitrary and easily violated boundaries we use in such definitions.[13]

The etymological weaving in this stanza helps clarify the thinness of such boundaries. "Solitary" and "solitude," both linked to "soul," derive from *solitudinem*, "loneliness, a being alone; lonely place, desert, wilderness."[14] In most of his other poems, Yeats's swans are paired, yet this swan is itself solitary, tying in with the theme of "ghostly solitude" broken by "triumph" in section I and marred by it in section III; solitude is abandoned for "a holiday" in section V. Wood stops just short of suggesting that what Yeats might want in section III is the solitude that comes from not attempting to understand others and, more significantly, leaving no archive by which others might attempt to understand oneself. One etymological connection links this to a desire for "wilderness," that antithesis to civilization. If this is a poem concerned about ongoing violence and the irrational damage humans do to the very civilization they have conceived (a poem for our times as much as it was Yeats's), it is also a poem about the "uncommunicableness" (to use Louis MacNeice's word) of one's own experience of the world.[15]

Put another way, the poem might offer a reflection of "some poet's" tired symbols and "half imagined, half written page," but it can never enable us to experience the swan's leap or the sense of utter confusion in the midst of a labyrinth of one's own making (*VP* 431, *l* 83). These things—the animal other and the terrifying richness of intellectual or imaginative creating—have no fully successful equivalent in poetry or prose. If "triumph can but mar our solitude," it is because it tames it, brings it in from the wilderness (*VP* 431, *l* 78). Thus the swan, in escaping its role as symbol, asserts the value of what is wild, beyond human civilization. In doing so, it thematically links to lines from Yeats's *The Resurrection* (begun between 1925 or 1926).[16] At a moment of climax, one character asks, "What if there is always something that lies outside knowledge, outside order? What if, at the moment when knowledge and order seem complete, that something appears?"[17] The poem suggests the limits of the lyric, forcing us to experience the disconcerting effects of confusion, chaos, violence, and the limits of knowledge. But it is in this experience of limitations that we find "that something that lies outside knowledge." For this reason, "Nineteen Hundred and Nineteen" is a deeply ambitious poem at the moment it is most pessimistic.

COMBS OF HER COCKS

The labyrinth that prevents the speaker, in section III, from watching the swan take flight offers little consolation or shared aesthetic vision. Instead, cultural constraints (the desire to figure out art or politics) fit with a pattern in the rest of the poem in which human endeavor has been driven to chaos in abstraction, or destroyed by irrepressible human violence. Avian images in other poems, particularly those of *Michael Robartes and the Dancer*, often show a generous interest in the non-human. "The Wild Swans at Coole" imagines fifty-nine swans suddenly lifting off from the water, but they scatter, wheel, and return. Yeats made a significant revision to this poem, moving the third stanza to the end so the poem concludes with a final note of uncertainty—the poet recognizes he will, someday, find the swans gone.[18] Yet by projecting this event into the future, the stanza suggests mysterious, transient beauty rather than dissolution. These swans also break free of symbolism, resisting his attempts to count them, even slyly resisting their association with love and fidelity in their odd numbering. But they allow him to empathize with a future viewer whom they will delight. By contrast, the solitary swan in section III obliterates a future-oriented view. The swan undoes its own symbolism to leap into nothingness, suggesting that whatever meanings and values we believe adhere in language or culture will be undone, that just because something "sheer miracle to the multitude" does not mean it will last (*VP* 428, *l* 2). In this poem, Yeats both historicizes and prophesizes that even accomplishments and cultures collectively made and celebrated will be destroyed.

The final section of "Nineteen Hundred and Nineteen" returns to the avian theme in relation to violence. Yeats describes "That insolent fiend Robert Artisson," a demon who "lurches past" much like the "rough beast" "slouching toward Bethlehem" in the earlier but related "The Second Coming" (*VP* 433, *ll* 126–28). Lady Kyteler, a fourteenth-century noblewoman accused of witch-craft and of having a sexual relationship with the demon, brings him sexual offerings that include "bronzed" peacock feathers, echoing the golden bees of the opening section, and the "red combs of her cocks" (*VP* 433, *l* 130). The combs may have erotic significance linked to their role in distinguishing roosters from hens, or in their cultural associations with decadence and dandies.[19] Yet the sacrificial image suggests nothing of beauty—unlike the peacock feathers, coxcombs are grotesque when detached from the bird itself, and call up the violent action of animal sacrifice. This folk cultural reference brings the poem full circle, suggesting violent debasement in 1919 as much as in medieval or mythological Ireland, with the striking central image of the murdered woman encased in a series of mythologizing instances of violence and destruction of civilization. The coxcomb offering undoes any remaining thought of avian beauty or human veneration for the unknowable animal consciousness, or for the aesthetic accomplishments of high culture. Vendler concludes that in "Nineteen Hundred and Nineteen" we appreciate most the "powerful attempt by the poet to ingest his country's tragic contemporary moment whole [...] and to project his exploration of the abstract enigma of violence into a set of chosen symbolic forms."[20] The unobserved flight of the swan at the center of the poem suggests endemic human violence links to unknowability, and ultimately to the failure of aesthetic form to contain or describe this solitary state.

NOTES

1.   Michael Wood, *Yeats and Violence* (Oxford: Oxford University Press, 2010), 71.
2.   Wood, *Yeats and Violence*, 70.
3.   For more and other interpretations of avian and animal imagery in Yeats's work, see Nicholas Grene, "Beasts and Birds," in *Yeats's Poetic Codes* (Oxford: Oxford University Press, 2008); Rachel Billigheimer, "'Passion and Conquest': Yeats's Swans," *College Literature* 13, no. 1 (1986): 55–70; Lucy McDiarmid, "The Avian Rising: Yeats, Muldoon, and Others," *International Yeats Studies* 1, no. 1 (2016): 74–85; Jacob Bender, "'The Waters of the Wild': W. B. Yeats, Julia De Burgos, and Romantic Wilderness," *Journal of the Midwest Modern Language Association* 50, no. 2 (Fall 2017): 31–55; Anita Feldman, "The Invisible Hypnotist: Myth and Spectre in Some Post-1916 Poems and Plays by W. B. Yeats," YA 21 (2018): 63–121; Herbert J. Levine, "'Freeing the Swans': Yeats's Exorcism of Maude Gonne," ELH 48, no. 2 (Summer 1981): 411–26; and John Rowlett, "Ornithological Knowledge and Literary Understanding," *New Literary History* 30, no. 3 (Summer 1999): 625–47. Patrick Smiddy establishes that the swans at Coole Park in 1917 were almost certainly Mute Swans (*Cygnus olor*) in Smiddy, "The Wild Swans at Coole," *The Irish Naturalist's Journal* 34 no. 2 (Oct. 9, 2015): 149–50, and J. Lyndon Shanley shows the direct influence of Thoreau's *Walden* on the composition of "The Wild Swans at Coole" in Shanley, "Thoreau's Geese and Yeats's Swans," *American Literature* 30 no. 3 (Nov. 1958): 361–64.

4.   Fredric Jameson, "Beyond the Cave: Demystifying the Ideology of Modernism," *The Bulletin of the Midwest Modern Language Association* 8, no. 1 (Spring 1975): 19.
5.   Helen Vendler, Our Secret Discipline: Yeats and Lyric Form (Cambridge, MA: Belknap Press, Harvard), 65.
6.   Wood, *Yeats and Violence*, 7.
7.   Vendler, *Secret*, 71.
8.   Wood, *Yeats and Violence*, 70.
9.   Wood, *Yeats and Violence*, 71.
10. Quoted in Bender, "Waters of the Wild," 34.
11. John Shoptaw, 'Why Ecopoetry?' in *Poetry* (Jan. 2016): 395–408.
12. Onno Oerlemans, *Poetry and Animals: Blurring the Boundaries with the Human* (New York: Columbia University Press, 2018), 2.
13. See Oerlemans, Poetry and Animals, 5 and passim; and Carey Wolfe, *Animal Rites: American Culture, the Discourse of Species, and Posthumanist Theory* (Chicago: University of Chicago Press, 2003).
14. *Online Etymological Dictionary*, s. v. "solitude," accessed July 15, 2019, https://www.etymonline.com/search?q=solitude.
15. MacNeice, "Postscript to Iceland," in *Collected Poems* (London: Faber and Faber, 2007), 98.
16. According to Feldman, "The Invisible Hypnotist," 79.
17. Quoted in Feldman, "The Invisible Hypnotist," 84.
18. See Feldman, "The Invisible Hypnotist," 102–03, 112. Feldman also remarks that the swans in this earlier poem appear as "truly 'wild' because […] their meaning as totems or symbols or emblems is still latent, still potential" (112).
19. In his *The Historie of Ireland* (1577), Raphael Holinshed explains that Kyteler "sacrificed in the high way ix red cockes, & ix peacocks eies;" quoted in Richard J. Finneran, "Notes to the Poems," in W. B. Yeats, *The Tower: A Facsimile Edition*, ed. Finneran (New York: Scribner, 2004), 115. Yeats's change of peacocks's eyes for bronzed feathers recalls the golden birds of "Sailing to Byzantium" and also points to a further aestheticization verging on decadence, with the organ of sight transmuted into the bronzed eyespots of the peacock feather. Yeats likely understood the peacock's use of tail fathers in courtship, thus further linking violent human ritual to observable animal behavior. My thanks to Lauren Arrington for pointing this out.
20. Vendler, *Secret Discipline*, 79.

Vanishing Presences: Women And Violence In "Nineteen Hundred And Nineteen"

Claire Bracken

The initial sense of the female subject in Yeats's poem "Nineteen Hundred and Nineteen" is marked by vanishing appearance—her presence is there, but barely. The fleeting quality is surprising given that many of the women to which the poem refers are drawn from real life or historical record; one of the things I aim to do in this essay is to restore their presence. In Elizabeth Butler Cullingford's essay on "Yeats and Gender," she notes Yeats's contradictory representation of women, providing a comprehensive and detailed overview of the feminine in his work as celebrated yet demonized, idealized yet critiqued. She charts his shifting representations of women from early valorization to a more reactionary, anti-suffrage critique, to his later resistance to the Catholic Church and his "sexually bold female speakers."[1] I argue here that "Nineteen Hundred and Nineteen," written in 1921, ultimately presents a conservative vision; its representations of the feminine move from fleeting and disappearing imaginings in the early sections of the poem to a more visible, but demonized, presence by its end. The shift underscores the poem's subtext: Yeats attempts to shore up the privilege of a white masculinity that—for most of the early sections—he ostensibly critiques. I trace this dynamic via analysis of the gendered politics embedded in different configurations of disappearance in the poem, exploring how women's disappearance becomes replaced at the poem's end, as the Western male subject-artist vanishes in a protectionist gesture that maintains its future possibilities of selfhood. The poem's final apocalyptic vision of modernist horror is borne by women and a racialized male figure, who are made to appear in the poem's final section.

The first section of "Nineteen Hundred and Nineteen" announces a great loss: of decency, civilization and culture, all "lovely things" that "are gone" (*l* 1)[2]. Helen Vendler notes how the "sequence begins in the voice of one who values such icons and images," the loss of which, Michael Ragussis argues, is marked by Yeats as a complete illusion.[3] As Michael Wood sums it up: "In fact, the whole of the first part of 'Nineteen Hundred and Nineteen' invites us to a double reading, or tells two stories, the first about loss, the second about the folly of our believing we ever had what we think we have lost."[4] In its temporal structure, the past becomes a repository of (illusionary) loss, and the present reveals the stuff of "nightmare." This current time of "Now" is revealed in the fourth stanza of this six-stanza section, and at its center is the figure of a murdered woman, Eileen Quinn, who was shot by the Black and Tans on November 1, 1920, as she sat with her baby in her arms.[5]

Eileen Quinn begins to vanish even before Yeats's nameless reference to her. There has been some confusion over her name in written sources, with some critics and commentators calling her Ellen and others Eileen. Yeats heard the story from Augusta Gregory, as the murdered woman was the wife of Malachi Quinn, a well-known neighbor of Gregory's. In her journal, Gregory recounts, "it was Malachi Quinn's young wife who had been shot dead – with her child in her arms [...] I was so angry at the official report of Eileen Quinn's shooting."[6] Here, Gregory calls her Eileen; however, in his biography of Yeats (which also uses Gregory as the source), Roy Foster calls her Ellen. Analyzing the confusion, Michael Wood states:

> Fergus Campbell, as we have seen, calls the dead woman Ellen Quinn, as do Roy Foster and many other scholars. Lady Gregory calls her Eileen, and so do more recent commentators, including Helen Vendler. Lucy McDiarmid thinks the first appellation is an error, a confusion of identities springing from the fact that Lady Gregory's maid and informant is called Ellen. This makes sense, but then the *Galway Observer* for 6 November 1920 opens up the whole question again, since it calls the murdered woman both Ellen and Eileen.[8]

The *Galway Observer*'s article opened by naming her as Ellen but later in the article refers to her as Eileen:

> Mrs. *Ellen* Quinn (24), who was shot on Monday evening, while sitting on the lawn in front of her farmhouse in Kiltartan, near Gort, bled to death the same night [...] The court has considered the evidence and the medical evidence [sic] are of the opinion that Mrs *Eileen* Quinn, of Corker, Gort in the county of Galway, met her death due to shock and hemmorrhage [sic] by a bullet wound in the groin fired by some occupant of a police car proceeding along to Gort-Ardrahan road on the 1st of November, 1920. They are of the opinion that the shot was one of the shots fired as a precautionary measure, and in view of the facts record a verdict of death by misadventure.[9]

A review of newspaper reports clears up the question of Eileen Quinn's name; Eileen emerges as the much more likely option, as the majority of sources name her. The first report of the attack, on November 2 in the *Irish Independent*, lists her as Eileen, as do subsequent reports in the *Freeman's Journal, Connacht Tribune, Evening Echo, Skibbereen Eagle, Freeman's Journal, Sligo Champion*, and the *Connacht Telegraph*. There is one newspaper report from the Freeman's Journal on November 3 that names her as Ellen—this same text is reproduced in the aforementioned *Galway Observer, The Leitrim Observer* and *Sligo Champion*—as well as mentions of her as Ellen in two other reports in *The Irish*

Examiner and the *Skibbereen Eagle* respectively.[11] Thus, it would seem that the initial *Freeman's Journal* report produced the confusion with their incorrect naming. Moreover, given that Lady Gregory was on personal terms with the family, it is unlikely she would have gotten the name wrong. As McDiarmid has pointed out, Foster's naming of her as Ellen is likely a confusion with a woman who worked with Gregory, given that the journal is Foster's primary source for the incident and is in fact mentioned as giving the initial news of Eileen's shooting to Gregory. Moreover, *The Skibereen Journal* report on her death gives the details of her father's name, Gilligan, and townland, Raheen. The 1911 census lists an Eileen Gilligan, age fifteen, living in Raheen. This would concur with her age of death in 1920, which was widely reported as twenty-four.[12]

Eileen Quinn's name is important, especially given her namelessness in the poem (unlike the two other named historical female figures, Loie Fuller and Lady Kyteler). Her murder is, as Vendler notes, an "atrocity that lies at the heart of Yeats' sequence," and it motivates the meditations and reflections of the poem itself.[13]

> Now days are dragon-ridden, the nightmare
> Rides upon sleep: a drunken soldiery
> Can leave the mother, murdered at her door,
> To crawl in her own blood, and go scot-free;
> The night can sweat with terror as before
> We pieced our thoughts into philosophy,
> And planned to bring the world under a rule,
> Who are but weasels fighting in a hole. (*ll* 25–32)

Violence is at stake here for Yeats: the violence of the modern world, both in terms of the post-World War era and the current time of war in Ireland; as Wood notes, "the drunken soldiery were his emblem."[14] More specifically, it is violence against women that is constructed as a horrific effect of the contemporary moment. Gendered violence is inferred in the Athena reference, where her "ancient image made of olive wood"—one of those "lovely things" —could easily be destroyed ("To burn that stump on the Acropolis"): this aggression towards the feminine is at its most saturated in the image of Eileen Quinn's murder (*ll* 6, 1, 46).

However, the intensity of the imagery does not necessarily render subjectivity to "the mother." She is nameless, her specificity trapped within the collective inference of "the," representing all mothers of a dying nation, a dying culture. Her description as "mother" is linked to the fact that she was holding a baby in her arms when she was shot. Additionally, some newspaper reports stated that Quinn was seven months pregnant at her death.[15] In Yeats's poem, she is simply a symbol of the approaching apocalypse. While Wood argues that the use of the word "her" twice in these lines ("her door;" "her blood") provides the woman with specificity, going on to say that "it isn't possible to lose her," I suggest the opposite. Quinn is very much lost, both in Yeats's poem and—as we have seen—the subsequent reporting of her own proper name.

The structure of Yeats's lines about Quinn highlight this, opening with "the nightmare" of "a drunken soldiery" and ending with them going "scot-free" (*ll* 25–28). In between these, in a relative clause that contains and minimizes her, we have "the mother" who is acted upon ("can leave," "murdered"). Her only activity is the horrifying image "to crawl in her own blood," and it is this abject excretion of blood—the double symbol of her life and death—into which she merges, becoming the matter and stuff of "nightmare" itself. The image of "sweat" in the subsequent line connects with "blood" as excreted bodily fluid, and this "sweat" is the very stuff of the night that sweats with terror. There is a repetition of "the" as "the mother" is retranslated from human subject to space itself: "The night" of line 29. Eileen Quinn disappears into matter, as her death for Yeats becomes not just a symbol of contemporary horror, but the affective environment of that horror too.

A disappearance is also effected on Loie Fuller in the second section of "Nineteen Hundred and Nineteen." One of the most arresting images of the poem is that of Fuller and her dancers, who also reform as matter, "A shining web, a floating ribbon of cloth" (*l* 50). Loie Fuller was an American dancer, described by Sally Sommer as "An overnight sensation in Paris in 1892 [...] Her ideas about modernism in dance, stagecraft, music, and scenic design influenced her contemporaries and shaped visions of the future."[16] Fuller is most renowned for her Serpentine Dance, recorded in an 1896 film by the Lumière Brothers. Fuller's costume of multiple and extended pieces of cloth was integral to the dance, as was a complex lighting scheme which brought an intense array of color: "Surrounded by a funnel of swirling fabric spiraling upward in the space around her and bathed in colored lights of her own invention, Fuller's body seems to evaporate in the midst of her spectacle."[17] Foster notes that "WB may have seen her in a private performance [...] he remembers 'a dance I once saw in a great house, where beautifully dressed children wound long ribbons of cloth in and out as they danced.'"[18]

Fuller's figure appears in the first line of the poem's second section which, coming after the first section's despair over the disintegration of culture, stability, and order, attempts to capture some of the chaotic spirit that swirls in and out of this changeable time:

When Loie Fuller's Chinese dancers enwound
A shining web, a floating ribbon of cloth,
It seemed that a dragon of air

Had fallen among dancers, had whirled them round
Or hurried them off on its own furious path; (*ll* 49–58)

The stanza asserts Fuller's primacy, leading with her name and establishing the dancers as objects of her possession. Critics regularly make the point that Fuller's dancers were in fact Japanese, not Chinese, referring to her engagement of two separate troupes of Japanese dancers during the period 1900 and 1908.[19] In a brief account of this collaboration in her memoir *Fifteen Years of a Dancer's Life*, Fuller frequently refers to these dancers as "my Japanese,"[20] at one point remembering her championing of one female dancer in proprietary terms:

> When the rehearsal was over I gathered the actors together and said to them:
> "If you are going to remain with me, you will have to obey me. And if you don't take this little woman as your star, you will have no success."
> And as she had a name that could not be translated, and which was longer than the moral law, I christened her on the spot Hanoko.[21]

Yeats's establishment of Fuller as a poetic subject echoes these assumptions of white, Western privilege, as the putative owner of the "Chinese dancers," the orchestrator of chaotic principles that modernism invariably marks in racially othered terms.

The swirling movement of the "Chinese dancers" also refers to the material cloth—Chinese silk—used in Fuller's performance, which intensifies the racial commodification (signaled also in the Orientalized image of the "dragon"), encompassing one of the effects of the stanza, the dissipation of the subject more generally in the whirlings of the Yeatsian gyre.[22] Wood notes that "What we are shown are the great billowing sheets of silk Loie Fuller spun wildly around herself at great speed, as if she were simultaneously engineering a great storm and dangerously caught up in it."[23] As the cloth swirls, Fuller's own prominence—so powerfully announced—dissipates into the stanza; the opening word suggests this, as the "When" pushes us away from the immediacy of Fuller's being and towards the temporality of the dance. According to the aesthetics of the dance, Fuller disappears, merging with the "Chinese dancers" that create a winding, billowing, circling "ribbon of cloth." In the poem, she dissipates into the dancers, who are then dissipated into the dance, "whirled around" "by a dragon of air."

Reading the structure of the stanza closely, we can see that the "dragon of air" is generative of aggressive practices of masculinity and—following on from the poem's first section—contains an effect of violence towards women. Ragussis notes "a furious movement that resists the order the artist attempts to impose on it."[25] Fuller's "dragon of air" clearly echoes the "dragon-ridden" days that bring in "a drunken soldiery" of aggressive masculinity in the poem's representation of Quinn's death. As the speaker of section two states, "All men are dancers and their tread / Goes to the barbarous tread of a gong" (*ll* 57–58). Thus, barbarous masculinity is encouraged by the swirling wind of change, with "tread" especially taking on an ominous quality of threat. The poem's horror towards this violence oscillates between representations of women as victims, with Quinn's murder functioning in the poem as a symbol of the current state of Ireland, and complicit, as Loie Fuller and her dancers bring on the very wind of destruction that is a symbolic marker for the contemporary moment. Possession matters again here, as the use of the possessive apostrophe in line one of the second section makes Fuller somewhat responsible for the ensuing chaos.

In the poem's third section, violence has an undertone of sexual threat. Women disappear entirely here, in a section entirely focused on male action, moving from the collective image of "all men" to the "solitary soul," perhaps the artist facing the chaotic winds. This "soul" is compared to a swan:

> The wings half spread for flight,
> The breast thrust out in pride
> Whether to play or to ride
> Those winds that clamour of approaching night. (*ll* 65–67)

Ragussis persuasively reads "to play or to ride" as differing alternatives that are then explored in stanzas two and three respectively, arguing that stanza two is "the poem's most explicit criticism of the artist and the politician" constructing an elaborate (and futile) "labyrinth" to navigate the winds.[26] He sees the third stanza, where the swan leaps "into the desolate heaven" (*l* 79), as "the active acceptance of the destructive winds, and the solitude that necessarily follows upon that acceptance."[27] The swan's domineering and phallic assertion in stanza one, with "The wings half spread for flight, / The breast thrust out in pride" is channeled into a "wildness," "a rage" "to end all things" in the third stanza, which connects to representations of violent masculinity in the first two sections of the poem. Moreover, considered alongside "Leda and the Swan" (1923), also published in *The Tower* and composed two years after "Nineteen Hundred and Nineteen," the swan carries tentative suggestions that its violence is sexual. The later poem—with its inclusion of Leda as a subject—could be said to write in a femininity that is absented and invisible in this section of "Nineteen Hundred and Nineteen."

This intimation of sexual violence reaches its peak in the final section of the poem. Having blown through the winds of mockery and despair in section five, the opening of section six opens in these ominous terms: "Violence upon the roads: violence of horses" (*l* 113). The final section replaces the earlier disappearances of the female subjects with a much more visible feminine charged force in the form of "Herodias' daughters:"

> Herodias' daughters have returned again,
> A sudden blast of dusty wind and after
> Thunder of feet, tumult of images,
> Their purpose in the labyrinth of the wind
> And should some crazy hand dare touch a daughter
> All turn with amorous cries, or angry cries,
> According to the wind, for all are blind. (*ll* 118–24)

These daughters are associated (and indeed merge) with the air and wind, but they are not lost in it; they retain their presence. They have voice ("cries") and "purpose." They do not dissipate into the stanza, as both Fuller and Quinn do, but rather stay visible amidst and within the wind. Here Yeats makes clearest the gendered context of the destructive winds of the poem: a wild feminine force, something that has been prefigured in the representations of both Quinn and Fuller as their bodies are shown to merge with the apocalyptic night and wind. Foster notes that Yeats's source for this image is "Arthur Symons's 'Dance of the Daughters of Herodias', harbingers of vengeance and anarchy," representing the destructive dance of the daughters, Salome's especially, which reaps death and beheading.[28]

In Yeats's poem, that sexual violence is a potential outcome of the wind is conditionally implied in the lines: "And should some crazy hand dare touch a daughter / All turn with amorous cries, or angry cries" (*ll* 122–23). The "handsome riders" "vanish" with their horses, becoming instead the impersonal "hand" of assault (*l* 17, *l* 123). As Vendler points out, "Behind these screen images of supernatural incursions into the natural world, Yeats at last reveals the origin of human violence: the sexual satisfaction attending on it, a powerful satisfaction that is always irrational."[29] The dance of Herodias's daughters connects them to Fuller, who is figured as orchestrating the chaos of section two.[30] Here too the "daughters" are figured as generating the very wind that inflicts sexual violence on them. Thus, Yeats uses an undercurrent of sexual violence to symbolize the destructive chaos of contemporary modern life, configuring a deeply disturbing subtext of victim-blaming, as the fault is laid at the dancing feet of the destructive daughters.

The poem's gendered unconscious is made evident in a tracing of the sexual politics of vanishing. The "drunken soldiery" of section one, the "barbarous" "tread" of section two, the "swan" of section three and the "handsome riders" of section six all "vanish" (*l* 17) and that vanishing is a protectionist gesture that ultimately shores up the subject of the poem: the white, Western male subject/

artist. Until the final section, it is this subject, alternating between the pro-
nouns "he," "we," and "I" who sits at the center of the poem. This is a "he" "who
can read the signs nor sink unmanned / Into the half-deceit of some intoxicant
[…] who knows no work can stand […] Has but one comfort left: all triumph
would / But break upon his ghostly solitude" (ll 33–40). Phallic manhood and
knowledge are connected here, the knowledge of the futility of art in a redemp-
tive and redeeming sense. This theme is reactivated in section three, with its
"man in his own secret meditation:"

> Some Platonist affirms that in the station
> Where we should cast off body and trade
> The ancient habit sticks,
> And that if our works could
> but vanish with our breath
> that were a lucky death,
> for triumph can but mar our solitude. (ll 69–78)

The word "vanish" here connects with the "lovely things" that have been lost
("Man is in love and loves what vanishes") (ll 1, 42); what is being suggested
is that these objects of the artist's creation—art, culture, beauty—are illusory
parts of a "labyrinth" "made in art or politics" to shield the self from the inevitable crumbling of all stability, order, and decency.[31] A "lucky death" would be to
vanish, along with the "work," into the oblivion of "solitude," which the speaker
imagines as a form of escape. This is a very different type of disappearance and
vanishing to Eileen Quinn, Loie Fuller, and the "Chinese dancers" who lack access to escape; rather they are the very stuff, the matter, of "nightmare" itself, as
their subjectivities dissipate into blood and wind, sweat and tears. Gender and
race intersect here. Despite her figuration as proprietary Western modernist
artist (presented in control of racialized others), as a woman in the poem Fuller's disappearance is not fully allowed and she returns in the dancing daughters
of the final section. Thus, Fuller's representation operates on two deeply problematic levels: on the one hand she functions as an example of the assumed
superiorities of the white, Western modernist artist and, on the other, she is
part of the poem's feminine stratum of disappearing appearance used to prop
up and support the vanishings of a white, Western artist that is invariably male.

In section six, the riders "vanish" and fade out, while the witchy images
of women fade in. The women's visible presence allows for the disappearance
of the poem's white male subject, as they instead embody apocalyptic representation and the burden of modernist fear, anxiety, and terror. The poem's
final historical reference is to a woman: Lady Kyteler, a Kilkenny Anglo-Nor-
man accused of witchcraft in the fourteenth century. Vendler notes that Yeats

"borrows his final symbol for that demonic sexual undoing of culture from the chronicles of witchcraft, invoking the tale of the empty-eyed 'insolent fiend Robert Artisson,' insusceptible in his insolence to all the conventions of romance, who has exercised his sexual power over 'the love-lorn Lady Kyteler,'" while Ragussis interprets "the fiend and his sexual victim" within the poem's more general theme of "the rape of innocence."[32] We see in this haunting final section, when the "wind drops" and a figure comes into view (the "fiend" who "lurches"), an othering that is racialized. The modernist "nightmare" that the entire poem addresses becomes embodied in the demon figure of Artisson, to whom Lady Alice Kyteler was supposedly in thrall.

Maeve Brigid Callan identifies Kyteler's case as "Ireland's only medieval witchcraft trial."[33] The trial proceedings were recorded by its delusional prosecutor, who claimed that "Alice herself had admitted that, in exchange for her submission and sexual services, she received the entirety of her considerable estate from her incubus, Robert or Robin son of Art, who might come to her as a cat, a hairy black dog, or a black man with two big friends holding an iron rod."[34] Yeats's source was St. John Seymour's *Irish Witchcraft and Demonology*, which describes Artisson's apparent shifting of shapes in racial and animalistic terms.[35] This is also implied in the description of "insolent" Artisson as he "lurches past" "great eyes without thought," recalling the racialized "rough beast"—"somewhere in the sands of the desert"—"with a gaze blank and pitiless" in "The Second Coming."[36] Such representations betray a problematic modernist tendency, the projection of the chaotic forces seen to be indicative to modernity onto racialized bodies.[37]

Anxiety about whiteness is built into this process, as suggested in the configuration of Artisson's "stupid straw-pale locks," an example of Nietzsche's blonde anti-Christ, which Anthony Bradley argues is a symbolic source for "The Second Coming" and "Nineteen Hundred and Nineteen."[38] Racial liminality is thus used as an example of what Ragussis categorizes as "A Vision of Evil" in the poem, an anti-artist and a figure of sexual aggression that serves as a warning to the white, male *thinking* subject-artist.[39] It is this subject-artist who is allowed to vanish off the page, via a "lucky death" that brings about an escape from the "nightmare," as well as protecting that subject-self from annihilation in what, as Ragussis argues, is the "impersonal" final section. In this way the vanishing male self is (problematically) preserved.

Women and a racialized, dehumanized male figure in "Nineteen Hundred and Nineteen" are made to carry the horrifying burden of modernist apocalyptic disintegration. Artisson is the poem's final figure of sexual assault, activating deeply troubling stereotypes of black men and sexual aggression. Herodias's daughters' "amorous cries" indicate a worrying subtext of rape as somewhat desirable and enjoyable for women.[41] Similarly, by drawing from the annals of witchcraft, Yeats implies that Lady Kyteler summons the aggressor (like Fuller with her dancers), the final image of sacrificial offering compounding her subservience to demonic power. In the context of sexual violence towards women, this series engenders a disturbing connotation of victim blaming. In gendering the winds in feminine terms—as orchestrators of the wind that generates the violence—the poem makes this deeply troubling implication that it is women's own fault. The riders that "vanish" in the poem's last section—the male subjects of the poem's "we"—are protected by disappearances that safeguard their potential future. What remains, the "coupling"[42] of "fiend" and woman, is an "apocalyptic" present with no future, an abject vision where the poem's final image—of male dismemberment at the hands of woman, "those red combs of her cocks"—compounds the poem's demonization of the feminine, and signals an all-pervasive fear of women's power.

Notes

I would like to thank a number of people for their insights on this piece: Lucy McDiarmid for excellent scholarly recommendations, and Susan Cahill, Kara Doyle, and Mary McGlynn for their reading of drafts and sharp critical insights. I would also like to thank Lauren Arrington for her careful editing and excellent recommendations and Geraldine Curtin at NUI Galway Special Collections for providing me with a scan of an article from *The Galway Observer*.

1. Elizabeth Butler Cullingford, "Yeats and Gender," in *The Cambridge Companion to W. B. Yeats*, ed. Marjorie Howes (Cambridge, UK: Cambridge University Press, 2006), 167–84.
2. Unless otherwise noted, citations from "Nineteen Hundred and Nineteen" refer to Variorum edition.
3. Helen Vendler, *Our Secret Discipline: Yeats and Lyric Form* (Cambridge, Mass.: Belknap Press of Harvard University Press, 2007), 65; Michael Ragussis, *The Subterfuge of Art: Language and the Romantic Tradition* (Baltimore, Md. & London: Johns Hopkins University Press, 1978).
4. Michael Wood, *Yeats and Violence* (Oxford: Oxford University Press, 2010), 36.
5. There are some inconsistencies in dating Quinn's death in both Augusta Gregory's journals and Roy Foster's biography of W. B. Yeats. In a journal entry of Nov 5, 1920, Gregory initially hears of the murder as taking place the day before. Isabella Augusta Gregory, *Lady Gregory's Journals, Vol. 1, Books One to Twenty-Nine, 10 October 1916–24 February 1925*, ed. Daniel J. Murphy (Gerrards Cross, Buckinghamshire: Colin Smythe, 1978), 197. So by that account, Eileen Quinn's murder is listed as Nov. 4. Likewise, Foster, for whom Gregory's journal is a source, states that: "On 26th of October the news of MacSwiney's death came to Gort. Ten days later Ellen Quinn was shot outside her front door in Kiltartan." Foster, *W. B. Yeats: A Life. The Arch-Poet, 1915–1939* (Oxford: Oxford University Press, 2003), 181. However, the military inquiry into the circumstances of her death took place on Thursday, Nov. 5, with her death officially recorded as Nov. 1. For example, see "The Chief Secretary's Explanation: Anticipating Ambush," *Irish Independent* (Dublin), Nov. 5, 1920, 5.
6. Gregory, *Lady Gregory's Journals*, Vol. 1, 197, 200.
7. Foster, *The Arch-Poet*, 181.
8. Wood, *Yeats and Violence*, 28. Lucy McDiarmid also made the same observation to me in a private conversation; I appreciate the insight.

9. "Horrible Outrage near Gort: A Woman Killed with Child in Her Arms," *The Galway Observer*, Nov. 6, 1920; emphases added.

10. "Shots from a Lorry: Young Woman Seriously Wounded," *Irish Independent*, Nov. 2, 1920, 5; "Her Dying Words: Father Considine Tells What Mrs Quinn Said," *Freeman's Journal* (Dublin), Nov. 5, 1920, 5; "Death of Mrs Quinn: Verdict in the Court of Military Inquiry," *Freeman's Journal*, Nov. 6, 1920, 5; "Touching Funeral Scenes," *Connacht Tribune*, Nov. 13, 1920, 2; "Military Inquiry Held: Story of the Tragedy," *Evening Echo* (Cork), Nov. 5, 1920, 2; "Woman Shot Dead," *Skibereen Eagle*, Nov. 6, 1920, 3; "Gort Lady's Death: Castle Report of 'Most Regrettable Case,'" *Sligo Champion*, Nov. 20, 1920, 5; "Deaths and Reprisals," *Connaught Telegraph*, Nov. 6, 1920, 3.

11. "Houses Burned in Co Clare," *Freeman's Journal*, Nov. 3, 1920, 5; "A Young Woman Shot in Galway," *Leitrim Observer*, Nov. 6, 1920, 3; "Gort Lady's Death: Castle Report of 'Most Regrettable Case;'" "Shooting of Mrs Quinn: Statement by Rev. John Considine," *Irish Examiner*, Nov. 15, 1920, 6; "Shooting of Mrs Quinn: Court Finds a Verdict of Misadventure," *Irish Examiner* (Cork), Nov. 6, 1920, 5; "Young Mother Shot Dead," *Skibereen Eagle*, Nov. 6, 1920, 1.

12. See "Census of Ireland," The National Archives of Ireland, accessed Aug. 16, 2019, www.census.nationalarchives.ie/. Eileen Quinn's name is further confirmed by the release of a a radio documentary released after the writing of this essay. This documentary, produced by Eileen Quinn's grand-niece Orla Higgins, about the murder of Eileen Quinn. See "Reprisals", Documentary on One, RTE, https://www.rte.ie/culture/2019/0823/1070497-documentary-on-one-shining-a-light-on-irelands-troubled-past/. The documentary's name "Reprisals" references another Yeats' poem "Reprisals" that refers to Quinn's murder.

13. Vendler, *Our Secret Discipline*, 64.

14. Wood, *Yeats and Violence*, 46.

15. See for example, "Young Mother Shot Dead."

16. Sally R. Sommer, "Loie Fuller's Art of Music and Light," *Dance Chronicle* 4, no. 4 (1981): 389.

17. Ann Cooper Albright, Traces of Light: Absence and Presence in the Work of Loïe Fuller (Middletown, Conn.: Wesleyan University Press, 2007), 5.

18. Foster, *The Arch-Poet*, 704.

19. Stanca Scholz-Cionca, "Japanesque Shows for Western Markets: Loïe Fuller and Japanese Theatre Tours Through Europe (1900–08)," *Journal of Global Theatre History* 1, no. 1 (2016): 46–61. Also, see Wood, *Yeats and Violence*, 50 on this point about critics and the characterization of the Japanese dancers as "Chinese."

20. Loie Fuller, *Fifteen Years of a Dancer's Life, With Some Account of Her Distinguished Friends* (London: Herbert Jenkins, 1913), 208; 213; see http://hdl.handle.net/2027/uc1.$b40785.

21. Fuller, *Fifteen Years of a Dancer's Life*, 208–09, 213.

22. Thus, I suggest a further reading of the "Chinese dancers." Chinese silk is the type of cloth that Fuller dressed in for the performance, thus this material meaning needs to be read in a concurrent and simultaneous reference to the Japanese troupes. In the essay, "Loie Fuller's Art of Music and Light," Sally Sommer describes her as such: "Wearing costumes made from hundreds of yards of China silk, she danced beneath a dazzling array of multi-hued electric lights, which set the material aflame" Sommer, "Loie Fuller's Art of Music and Light," 392.

23. Wood, *Yeats and Violence*, 49.

24. Discussing her presentation in the Lumière Brothers's film *The Serpentine Dance*, he remarks on "how often she disappears from view into the material of her own practice. It's as if she keeps getting eaten by a dragon of air, or at least of millinery." Wood, *Yeats and Violence*, 51.

25. Ragussis, *The Subterfuge of Art*, 95.
26. Ragussis, *The Subterfuge of Art*, 96.
27. Ragussis, *The Subterfuge of Art*, 97.
28. Foster, The Arch-Poet, 197. See Arthur Symons, *Poems by Arthur Symons: Volume II* (New York: John Lane, 1902), 105.
29. Vendler, *Our Secret Discipline*, 75.
30. Yeats also connects the daughters of Herodias with the Irish Sidhe: "Sidhe is [...] Gaelic for wind, and certainly the Sidhe [the pagan gods of ancient Ireland] have much to do with the wind. They journey in whirling winds, the winds that were called the dance of the daughters of Herodias in the Middle Ages. When the country people see the leaves whirling on the road they bless themselves, because they believe the Sidhe to be passing by." Quoted in W. B Yeats, *W. B. Yeats: The Poems*, ed. Daniel Albright (London: Everyman, 1992), 657–58.
31. See Ragussis, *The Subterfuge of Art*, 96 for a powerful reading of this section.
32. Vendler, *Our Secret Discipline*, 75.
33. Maeve Brigid Callan, *Templars, The Witch, and the Wild Irish: Vengeance and Heresy in Medieval Ireland*. (Ithaca, NY: Cornell University Press, 2017), 81.
34. Callan, *Templars, The Witch, and the Wild Irish*, 86.
35. St John D. Seymour, *Irish Witchcraft and Demonology*, (Baltimore, Md.: Norman, Remington 1913), 29.
36. See Yeats, W. B. Yeats, 235. I would like to thank Mary McGlynn for this insight on the beast's blank gaze and Artisson's eyes. Vendler is one of many critics that connects the beast of "The Second Coming" and Artisson; Vendler, Our Secret Discipline, 76. Fleissner argues that the beast of "The Second Coming" "very likely stood for something characteristically African, indeed even the 'dark continent' itself." Robert F. Fleissner, "On Straightening out Yeats's 'Rough Beast,'" *CLA Journal* 32, no. 2 (1988): 205.
37. I think this is one of the (critical) implications of Achebe's intertextual use of the poem for *Things Fall Apart*.
38. Anthony Bradley, *Imagining Ireland in the Poems and Plays of W. B. Yeats: Nation, Class, and State* (Basingstoke, Hampshire: Palgrave, 2011), 82, 116.
39. Ragussis, *The Subterfuge of Art*, 99. However Ragussis interprets Artisson differently (105): "while Artisson is an embodiment of evil. His thoughtlessness becomes for Yeats a refreshing escape from a maze of complicated and contrived thoughts [...] even his name's curious suggestion of the artist."
40. Ragussis, *The Subterfuge of Art*, 99.
41. See Cullingford, "Yeats and Gender" for an excellent analysis of this same dynamic in "Leda and the Swan."
42. Vendler, *Our Secret Discipline*, 76.

"Dragon-Ridden" Days:
Yeats, Apocalypse, And The Anthropocene

Malcolm Sen

"You don't have to agree with trump [sic] but the
mob can't make me not love him.
We are both dragon energy."
Kanye West, Twitter, 2018[1]

"Having emerged from previous mass extinctions, humans are at once
part of the ebb and flow of life and non-life on earth, but are nevertheless
the first being to witness, mourn and articulate
extinction as an explicit event."
Claire Colebrook, "Extinction," 2018[2]

Dragon Energy

Dragons, being imaginary creatures, escape the umbra of extinction shadowing multiple species on earth today. We can trace their lineage from Homer (at least in the European tradition) to the personal mount of Daenerys Targaryen, Drogon, in *Game of Thrones*; or, from *Beowulf* to J. R. R. Tolkien's *The Hobbit*. Because they are textual creatures, dragons display a resilience and capacity to mutate that makes them eloquent ontological signifiers in mythic narratives, as motifs of epistemological uncertainty in folklore and cultural memory, and as embodiments of extra-human/pre-modern intrusions in the workings of history. Whereas Chinese dragons are often beneficial to the human species, European variants (including those found in Celtic folklore) are not. Dragons spell death and destruction; they demand human sacrifices, as in the legend of St. George. Their appearance suggests power and menace of extraordinary dimensions, as in Lewis Carroll's Jabberwock. (The Jabberwock was first illustrated by John Tenniel in 1871 as a dragon, and the tradition continues well into the present day, in Tim Burton's *Alice in Wonderland*, for example.) Dragons collude with destructive forces; their power to annihilate everything that stands for "human" is unwittingly referred to in Kanye West's words above.[3] I suggest in this essay that the image of the dragon offers us a portal into the highly ornate symbolic structures of W. B. Yeats's historiography and his vision of the apocalyptic.

Two reasons prompt the focus of this study. The intellectual trajectory of literary criticism has long established the importance of symbolism in analyzing Yeats's poetry and drama, but it has not sufficiently paid attention to the symbol of the dragon. I concentrate on the phrase "now days are dragon-ridden" to read Yeats's "Nineteen Hundred and Nineteen" in ways that help elucidate the dragon's crucial function in the poem. This also leads me to point out the contemporary "relevance" of the poem and the iconicity of the dragon that addresses the environmental tropes of the poem. Like many other Irish literary narratives, Yeats's prodigious output needs to be reevaluated using the tools supplied by the environmental humanities and postcolonial ecocriticism.[4] Isolating the symbol of the dragon, I contend, reveals our contemporary vulnerability to ecological processes already set in motion by the time Yeats wrote and under whose shadow our futurity unconvincingly unfolds. Re-visiting this mythic creature from the precarious perspective of anthropogenic climate chaos is presentist, but unabashedly so. After all, our modern fetish with the medieval is a testament of a beastly modernity. The dragon, I argue in this essay, leads us into the ontological and epistemological realms that haunt the merging of history and geology at this present time, a conflation that ultimately gives rise to the concept of the Anthropocene. This essay conceptualizes how we might view the intrusion of the dragon in Yeats's poetic rendition of history at a time when humans are not only historical subjects but also geological agents.[5] To view the dragon in this manner is to realize that Yeats's apocalypse proleptically comments on our Anthropocene.

For a poet as fascinated with the idea of apocalypse as Yeats was, the awe-inspiring atavism embodied by the dragon seemed especially alluring. In his early career the creature is ironically anthropomorphized, a symbolic stand-in for the empiricists who challenge the romantic sensibility of poets, as in "The Realists," a poem that appears in the collection *Responsibilities*.

> What can books of men that wive
> In a dragon-guarded land,
> Paintings of the dolphin-drawn
> Sea-nymphs in their pearly wagons
> Do, but awake a hope to live
> That had gone
> With the dragons? (*VP* 309, *ll* 2–8)

Here, the dragon is a monstrous metaphor for the realists who enervate artistic vision; they are antithetical to the fairyland romanticism suggested by dolphins and "Sea-nymphs." Later in life and after a prestigious public career, Yeats's introspective poems in *The Winding Stair and Other Poems* of the 1930s see the dragon animated as a symbol of self-limiting delusions—an erector of unnecessary boundaries in the section "Her Triumph," in "A Woman Young and Old:"

> I did the dragon's will until you came
> Because I had fancied love a casual
> Improvisation, or a settled game [...]
> And then you stood among the dragon-rings.
> I mocked, being crazy, but you mastered it
> And broke the chain and set my ankles free. (*VP* 533, *ll* 1–9)

In this poem the dragon is susceptible to human agency, vanquished by an ingenuity of Odyssean dimensions. The poem is a reversal of Yeats's earlier stance in "Michael Robartes and the Dancer," where he chastises "dragonish women like Con Markiewiwicz" (the phrase is Daniel Albright's) who ruin themselves through education:[6]

> Opinion is not worth a rush;
> In this altar-piece the knight,
> Who grips his long spear so to push
> That dragon through the fading light,
> Loved the lady; and it's plain
> The half-dead dragon was her thought,
> That every morning rose again
> And dug its claws and shrieked and fought. (*VP* 385, *ll* 1–8)

If dragons are mutable creatures, then Yeats's poetry supplies ample examples of this genetic propensity. However, whereas the dragon can only annihilate symbolically, our period of multi-species extinctions is not textual but increasingly biopolitical.

Perhaps the most apocalyptic image of the dragon in Yeats's poetry occurs in "Nineteen Hundred and Nineteen." In the lines quoted below the annihilating force of dragons is not only more acute than previous iterations of this image but is also presented as antithetical to an orderly world.

> Now days are dragon-ridden, the nightmare
> Rides upon sleep: a drunken soldiery
> Can leave the mother, murdered at her door,
> To crawl in her own blood, and go scott-free;
> The night can sweat with terror as before
> We pieced our thoughts into philosophy,
> And planned to bring the world under rule,
> Who are but weasels fighting in a hole. (*VP* 429, *ll* 25–32)

The dragon is a cataclysmic force in "Nineteen Hundred and Nineteen"—a pathological infection of existential proportions, seeking the death of "the mother," as if to erase the possibility of generational propagation. Its toxicity, implied by "Now days are dragon-ridden," infects at an individual level too and produces a delirious vocabulary of the subconscious: "the nightmare / Rides upon sleep." The dragon is this nightmare and its contagious intrusion affects Time itself: the night sweats with terror. As is clear, the deployment of this image operates at a number of levels in this poem that demands that we further unpack the traditional suggestion that the dragon is representative of Yeats's conceptualization of apocalypse. I concentrate here on the pathology of the dragon in "Nineteen Hundred and Nineteen" and the ecology of the poem to demonstrate how the conceptualization of the socio-political and temporal aspects of this apocalypse and the understanding of the "world" posited by Yeats can be viewed from a twenty-first century perspective. Concentrating on Yeats's image of the dragon allows us to understand the poem's ecology, that is the web-work through which violence and apocalypse, art and politics, is constructed. My main contention here is that the dragon proleptically antic- ipates dominant questions of human culpability and vulnerability associated with the Anthropocene. It makes sense to ask what the apocalypse, depicted in "Nineteen Hundred and Nineteen" through "dragon-ridden" days, might mean in 2019. The original title of the poem, "Thoughts upon the Present State of the World," uncannily appeals to future generations to ask exactly such a question. As Michael Woods proclaims in his book-length study of the poem, the "Now" preceding "days are dragon-ridden" is interminably contemporaneous: "What's interesting about now is how it shifts in time; and how it is never without a then."[7] Yeats, who once declared that "I took satisfaction in certain public di- sasters, felt sort of ecstasy at the contemplation of ruin," made apocalyptic ends a recurrent feature of his poetry.[8] "Nineteen Hundred and Nineteen," in this re- gard, is clearly a progenitor of "The Second Coming," a poem that was actually written in 1919. The Sphinx-like "rough beast" of "The Second Coming" gains wings in the later poem—the contagion is air-borne and all-encompassing—as if what was forecast has come to pass. What arrives after the apocalypse is the subject of this essay.

HISTORICAL ENDINGS

In Yeats's philosophy of history the cyclic movement of epochs held extinc- tion at bay, so that "death was both contemplated and overcome." The historical structure alluded to in the line "We pieced our thoughts into philosophy" is a contracted version that *A Vision* expands in greater detail: "What if every two thousand and odd years something happens in the world to make one sacred, the other secular; one wise, the other foolish; one fair, the other foul; one divine, the other devilish?" (*CW14* 22). In such a historical method the apocalypse is a temporal inconvenience, which offers a future potential for renewal of the species. If apocalypses reveal some hitherto hidden knowledge, as the Greek root of the word clarifies, Yeats's conceptualizations of such destruction reveal the birth of a new geopolitical order. As Seamus Deane notes:

> But Yeats's world and that of the Romantic movement in general is not really quite so different from its bourgeois counterpart as it would have liked to be. Neither world will yield to the fact of extinction; each preserves, in different ways, belief in the eternity of the world and in the eternity of consciousness. Both are rooted in the fear of death.[9]

However, it is the very reincarnation of history, "the most fervently held of all Yeats's private beliefs," that is under scrutiny today.[10] The Anthropocene is not a period of visually stimulating, instantaneous disaster; rather, its stratigraphic and atmospheric layers are etched over time, through a slow accretion of ecological violence affecting both human and non-human nature.[11] The naming of our geological epoch also signals the slow death of the human, the extinction of the *anthropos*, since all geological timescales mark both a beginning and an end. How to narrate that which annihilates the human subject altogether? When Yeats contemplates the apocalypse he imagines the end of a social order, especially the death of the Anglo-Irish aristocracy—not necessarily of the world. In our time there is no re-birth foretold at the end of the Anthropocene. The Anthropocene marks the end of the world (itself a human cultural construct) but, to be clear, not the end of the planet (the spatial body which remains caught in a gravitational ellipsis around the sun, at least for the next five billion years). It is little wonder that the Anthropocene has been called an "an intellectual behemoth;" for these reasons it is significantly more complex and thus more resistant to textual representation than the apocalypse.

"Nineteen Hundred and Nineteen" is often read in conjunction with overtly political poems such as "September 1913" or "Easter 1916" for good reason. The stanza quoted above directly refers to the death of Eileen Quinn, a pregnant mother of three, who was "shot dead [...] with her child in her arms," by Black and Tan soldiers. The story, as is well known, was recorded by Lady Augusta Gregory in her journal. But the publication history and the thematic progression of "Nineteen Hundred Nineteen" suggests that, although Yeats may have been responding to the Anglo-Irish War, he was also interested in a universalist, historiographical commentary on modernity.[12] The fact that Lady Gregory's notes on the murder of Eileen Quinn by the ex-military soldiers do not occur until 1920 bears further testimony to this. The title of the poem therefore becomes a synecdochal shorthand; the Anglo-Irish War that it points to in turn becomes a concentrated example of a universal pattern of colonial and nationalist violence.

Helen Vendler contends in her reading of "The Second Coming" that "Unlike the canonical Apocalypse, the Modernist apocalyptic utterance is not certain of its visions."[13] This is borne out by the last lines of "The Second Coming," which begin with certitude but end with bewilderment: "I know / That twenty centuries of stony sleep / Were vexed to nightmare by a rocking cradle" that ends with a question, "And what rough beast, its hour come round at last / Slouches towards Bethlehem to be born?" (*VP* 402, *ll* 21–22). Vendler notes that "The non-parallel syntax shows that the poet's knowledge is limited. He is convinced that a new force is imminent, for which the cosmic cradle has been set rocking; yet what sort of beast it will be is as yet undetermined."[14] "Nineteen Hundred and Nineteen" is radically different in this regard: it not only identifies the beast that is born but also catalogues the wave of destruction in its wake.

When Yeats casts his "dragon-ridden" days in "Nineteen Hundred and Nineteen" he also demonstrates language's capacity to outlast the apocalypse, to bear witness and record the present. The first section of the poem provides such a litany, chronicling the "ingenious lovely things" that are now no more. In an overtly bourgeois rendition of loss, Yeats catalogues "Amid the ornamental bronze and stone / An ancient image made of olive wood — / And gone are Phidias' famous ivories / And all the golden grasshoppers and bees" (*VP* 428, *ll* 5–8). These symbols of human creativity stand in opposition to the destructive forces of political violence that Yeats was witnessing first-hand in the second decade of the twentieth-century in Ireland. The death of Irish soldiers in the First World War, among whom was Lady Gregory's son Robert, the violence of the Easter Rebellion in 1916, and the political strife following the Government of Ireland Act in 1920, all indicated to Yeats the ending of an era. Although "Nineteen Hundred and Nineteen" is not simply a political poem, it is from politics that the violence emanates: "Public opinion ripening for so long / We thought it would outlive all future days. / O what fine thought we had because we thought / That the worst rogues and rascals had died out" (*VP* 428, *ll* 13–16). In this sense Yeats's futurology in "The Second Coming" transmutes to a historian's record-keeping skill in "Nineteen Hundred and Nineteen." History becomes akin to a ransacked museum, Art is commoditized:

> But is there any comfort to be found?
> Man is in love and loves what vanishes,
> What more is there to say? that country round
> None dared admit, if such a thought were his,

Incendiary or bigot could be found
To burn that stump on the Acropolis,
Or break in bits the famous ivories
Or traffic in the grasshoppers or bees. (*VP* 429, *ll* 41–48)

It is important to notice that Yeats's Modernist aesthetics reveals a post-apocalyptic worldview that does not foretell the end of the world per se but the end
of a specific worldview and a way of life. The end of the classical age and the
arrival of violent modernity as apocalypse proleptically anticipates a common
trope of contemporary post-apocalyptic narratives. In our time the apocalypse
is not the end of the world but the end of the First World way of life; that is, the
return of industrialized nations to a medieval condition where the infrastructure of modernity has crumbled. Yeats's timescale is more dense in this regard:
he speaks of the death of the classical age and the arrival of modernity as a
return of the so-called dark ages. The medievalism first suggested in the long
first section of the poem through the image of the dragon mirrors "a dragon of
air" in section two:

When Loie Fuller's Chinese dancers enwound
A shining web, a floating ribbon of cloth,
It seemed that a dragon of air
Had fallen among dancers, had whirled them round
Or hurried them off on its own furious path;
So the Platonic Year
Whirls out new right and wrong,
Whirls in the old instead;
All men are dancers and their tread
Goes to the barbarous clangour of a gong. (*VP* 430, *ll* 49–58)

Yeats changes Fuller's "danse serpentine" to a "dragon of air;" the beautiful sym-
metry of his historical design is enmeshed in an arachnid web, "enwound" and
"whirled," to return us to the old ways.[15] As Woods remarks, "It's telling that the
new should go and the old come back, rather than the old finally giving place to
the new, so the magical circuits are at least good for an angry paradox."[16] That
paradox is embodied not by the scales of justice, "right and wrong," but by the
scales of the dragon, the intrusive and destructive return of the medieval in the
modern. Yeats's litany of loss, his depiction of the transmutation of aesthetics
into commodity fetishism, of humanity being engulfed by a dragon, tells of the
death of philosophy that had attempted to "bring the world under a rule." In the
third movement of the poem, the utopian vision is nostalgically remembered:
"O but we dreamed to mend / Whatever mischief seemed / To afflict mankind,
but now / That winds of winter blow / Learn that we were crack-pated when

we dreamed" (*VP* 431, *ll* 84–88). Here, the corporeal violence is acute, but "crack-pated" also uncannily suggests that the dream originates from a catatonic or a posthumous condition.

Critical focus on Yeats's representation of violence and apocalypse, much like its approach to Yeats's draconic symbolism, rarely unpacks the multilayered aspects of these dense terms. At a time of climate chaos those terms do not appear as simple rhetorical tools but rather resonate with contemporaneity. How might we approach Yeats's apocalypse anew? One way to do this is to identify what distinguishes the apocalypse from the Anthropocene. Here, we will recognize that while language survives the apocalyptic event, it does not outlast the Anthropocene. Claire Colebrook writes that "The twenty-first century is at once and the same time marked by a sense of impending human extinction (both literally, with the biological species coming to an end, and figuratively, with all that passes itself off as human facing annihilation by way of technological, ecological and political catastrophe)..."[17] Among the signifiers of the "human" facing extinction, language especially stands out because it is through language that the "world" is created. There is no post-apocalyptic ability to record the demise of the Anthropocene and narrate the progression of the next geological epoch. Here, "Nineteen Hundred and Nineteen," and the species narratives that form its vocabulary, is informative because it anticipates the temporal incertitude and linguistic challenges of narrating and comprehending the scale of contemporary extinction. Yeats imagines the return of the medieval as the normative condition of the modern, thus bearing testimony to the fact that, if this is the apocalypse, it is impossible to speak of it without being post-apocalyptic. The apocalypse and the Anthropocene are thus radically different in their conceptual import: the former promotes a paradoxical condition of naming that which has already passed, and the latter is a process of passing whose end-point is the death of the human, of language, and the world. The Anthropocene names our geological epoch as the "Age of Human" but at the same time spells the death of that apex species and its world. "Nineteen Hundred and Nineteen" thus helps us visualize the tense relationship between that which has already passed and that which has yet to occur.

Michael Wood cites Frank Kermode's assessment of Yeats's poem "In Memory of Major Robert Gregory" to describe the pleasures of reading "Nineteen Hundred and Nineteen:" "It is a poem worthy of much painful reading."[18] The latter poem is, as I am contending here, especially worthy of being analyzed in a contemporary frame. In 2017, at a talk delivered at the Yeats International Summer School, Fintan O'Toole noted that:

There are many ways to measure the world and economists, ecologists and anthropologists labour mightily over them. I suggested another one: the Yeats

Test. The proposition is simple: the more quotable Yeats seems to commentators and politicians, the worse things are. As a counter-example we might try the Heaney Test: if hope and history rhyme, let the good times roll. But these days, it is the older Irish poet who prevails in political discourse—and that is not good news.[19]

While Yeats's phantasmagoric vocabulary has resurfaced in the public sphere since 2016—from *The Wall Street Journal* to Twitter and everywhere else in between—the resurrection has been read as a result of the geopolitical uncertainties in a post-Trumpian and post-Brexit world. Political discourse is a cornerstone of Yeats's poetry and at times, art is synonymous with politics, as in the poem under consideration here: "A man in his own meditation / Is lost in the labyrinth that he has made / In art *or* politics" (*VP* 431, *ll* 69–71, emphasis mine). But Yeats's political themes are also the reason why ecological and environmental motifs in his poetry matter a great deal. As Bruno Latour's recent exhortation reminds us, bringing us down to earth is the contemporary task of politics.[20] The separation of nature from culture—or of ecology from economy, of history from geology — is a product of a modernity whose end-point has been extractive capitalism, alarming levels of resource depletion, unprecedented species extinctions, and financialized capital's novel methods of selling servitude. The metabolism of modernity parasitically digests its host, and the vulnerability of ecosystems mirrors the fragile territorial politics of 2019. It is now increasingly clear that ecological degradation and resultant geopolitical transformations lead to the "crisis ordinariness"—to use Lauren Berlant's phrase—of contemporary politics. This is a period when honor and truth, the two moral signifiers in section four of "Nineteen Hundred and Nineteen," can truly be considered politically obsolete, "for we / Traffic in mockery" (*VP* 432, *ll* 111–12).

Rather than focusing on Yeats's relevance to contemporary geopolitics I am proposing that Yeats provides us with conceptual tools to understand the enormous scale of our geological present. Yeats's planetary scope, cosmological timeframes, and his interest in non-human, naturalistic imagery, allow us to unearth some crucial epistemological questions about non-human nature, artistic representations of the nonhuman world, and history's co-evolution with ecology. As Christophe Bonneuil writes, "To see the Anthropocene as an event rather than a thing means taking history seriously and learning to work with the natural sciences, without becoming mere chroniclers of a natural history of interactions between the human species and the Earth system." Yeats, especially in his later poetry, demands such a felicity with what is often considered to be outside the purview of the literary critic or the historian. A central component of the interdisciplinary work in our field is to recognize the rhetorical imbrication of human nature with non-human nature within our representative systems that might help us forge what is of utmost importance: "new narratives for the Anthropocene and thus new imaginaries."[21] The present state of climate chaos, apart from being the product of industrialization and late modernity, also reveals a conceptual problem of harnessing the multi-scalar, multi-generational nature of ecological degradation causally linked to human history. The naming of the Anthropocene serves to bring the planetary and existential scope of such degradation and the imbrication of the human within "nature."

EARTHLY EXTINCTIONS

The only rule that outlasts the machinations of history in Yeats's poem is the geometry of planetary paths, suggested by the "Platonic year."[22] Indeed, the orbital trajectories of planetary bodies is a key component of his philosophy of history. This planetary vision recurs in Yeats's later poetry. Marjorie Howes has pointed out that Yeats opens "The Second Coming" with the impersonal stance of an epic viewer-from-above of the entire earth: "Things fall apart; the centre cannot hold." She further argues that, "One Yeatsian map would show the whole earth from space. It would cast Ireland, or certain elements of Irish culture, as just one point of access among many to the eternal truths, beauties, or conflicts whose essences were constant throughout the world."[23] A similar logic is at play in "Nineteen Hundred and Nineteen." Yeats's conflation of a planetary framework with history certainly demands the rectifying lenses of postcolonial and race studies, but his grand, wide-angled, and simultaneously microscopic scrutiny is also instructive of the kind of scalar thinking required in the Anthropocene. The epic scope of the visual economy of "Nineteen Hundred and Nineteen" depends on the image of the dragon.

We might approach this by engaging the ecology of this poem. The entanglement of history with planetary ecology suggests that history evolves within and through the assemblages of accelerated biodiversity loss and multispecies extinctions that directly affect the continuity of our species. Elizabeth DeLoughrey contends that "Due to their enormous scales and their discursive histories, the figures of nonhuman nature, the human, Earth, and now the Anthropocene share a universalizing geologic."[24] Here, Yeats's suggestion that history can be apprehended through nature demands some elaboration. The naturalistic symbolism of early poems, such as the "bee-loud glade" in the pastoral "Lake Isle of Innisfree," turns into artifice in this poem. The animal imagery of "Nineteen Hundred and Nineteen" further conflates the human and the animal; for example, the appearance of a solitary soul cast as a swan in section three. Yeats's menagerie affords a special place to avian symbolism, from the Orientalized peacocks and peahens in the early poems to the swan and other birds in his later works. They help us understand, for example, key political poems such as "Easter 1916."[25] "Nineteen Hundred and Nineteen" also ends with avian imagery: "Bronzed peacock feathers, red combs of her cocks," which stand in opposition to the opening stanza's "golden grasshoppers and bees." Nonetheless, the winged creature that allows a truly hemispheric perspective from which to view the planetary chaos unfolding in "Nineteen Hundred and Nineteen" is the mythical dragon; the "violence of horses" at the end of the poem is instigated by the pathological fear instilled by "dragon-ridden" days in the opening. The structure of the poem also suggests a growing perspectival resolution; from space to place, from the heady depths of philosophical rumination, subconscious nightmares, and the airborne dragon, Yeats brings us down to earth in the final stanza: "Violence upon the roads."

Dragons, however, can be airborne or reside in oceanic and subterranean depths, as contemporaries of Yeats's pointed out. Standish O'Grady, in his translation of *Acallam na Senórach* (Colloquy with the Ancients), supplies us with the reason why the Fianna, despite having banished all monsters out of Ireland, did not kill "the reptile" in the glen of Ros Enaigh.[26] In O'Grady's re-telling, Cáilte replies, "Their reason was that the creature is the fourth part of Mesgedhra's brain, which the earth swallowed there and converted into a monstrous worm."[27] Apart from many other strange and wonderful things the *Acallam na Senórach*, one of the most important tales of the Fenian cycle, also narrates the figure of the serpent, or the monstrous worm, whose refuge is deep underground and who is an offshoot of the fossilized/preserved brain of an ancient king of Leinster. The magic realism of this text allows Oisín and Caílte to speak to Saint Patrick, who finally banishes serpents from Ireland. In Celtic mythology, as in many other cultural traditions, reptiles, serpents, and dragons share a fluid relationship, appearing sometimes from the bowels of the earth, at others arising from oceanic depths, or plunging from the sky, earthbound. Dragons encompass the stratigraphic, aqueous, and atmospheric realms of this planet; the world of the Celtic Revival could not escape their rhetorical power.[28]

These oceanic and topographical signifiers focus our attention on Yeats's draconic symbolism in a way that might *naturalize* the dragon from myth into history. If the dragon can help us approach key epistemological and ontological questions related to the Anthropocene, as I suggest in my opening remarks, it does so through an intellectual lineage in which extinction features prominently. The dragon defies death itself but simultaneously speaks to our contemporary time of escalating extinctions. A recent study by the anthropologist David Jones argues that tales surrounding dragons, which span cultures and nations, originates from a primal fear of snakes, eagles, and panthers. This fear, as Jones argues, is a genetically in-built response encoded in our evolutionary history. It is understandable why the dragon thus becomes an archetypal signifier of humanity's destruction in numerous texts. A corollary argument explains the predominance of draconic imagery in world cultures by proposing that these myths were narrative attempts by our ancestors to rationalize the sighting of fossilized remains of large predators, such as dinosaurs. What both these theoretical strands share in common is the theme of extinction, whether imagined (as in the first instance) or real (as in the second example). In the eighteenth and nineteenth centuries, the discourse surrounding the ecological concept of extinction troubled the species narratives that a Christian worldview had promulgated. If God had created the world, how could he allow something as self-negating as biological extinction? As Ursula Heise writes:

> Most life forms that have ever existed—over 99 percent, according to some scientists—are extinct. Extinction is, therefore, one of the most basic characteristics of the planet's ecology. Species disappear because they change through gradual adaptation to such a degree that they can no longer be considered the same species, or because all individuals die off before they can reproduce.[29]

When Richard Owens "discovered" and named dinosaur fossils in 1842, he helped gain traction for both evolutionary theory and extinction as a biological fallout of evolutional history. Extinction finally seemed not an anomaly but a process which reflected the natural order of things. The so-called background rate of extinction—a rate of normal extinctions of species—reflected processes of natural selection, adaptation, or inability thereof, towards changing ecological scenarios such as habitat loss. However, this normality appears to be in a distant past in the Anthropocene, which among other catastrophes narrates a hundred-fold increase in extinction levels among vertebrate and plant species. The situation is dire enough that the otherwise staid tone of the *Proceedings of the Natural Academy of Sciences of the United States of America* was recently undercut by renowned scientists who titled their groundbreaking paper on contemporary extinction levels with these opening words: "Biological Annihilation." In the article the authors go on to prove how "Dwindling population sizes and range shrinkages [of vertebrates] amount to a massive anthropogenic erosion of biodiversity and of the ecosystem services essential to civilization."[30] There are numerous other such reports; for example, "Humans have driven nearly 600 plant species to extinction since 1750s," runs the title of a recent article in the *New Scientist*.[31]

If, as has been proposed, one of the markers of the Anthropocene is an irradiated planet after the first nuclear tests were carried out in the 1940s, then mass extinctions have become an ontological signifier of this geological epoch in the twenty-first century. Dragons, in this scheme of things, are avatars of dinosaurs, the iconic species of the extinction narrative (although subversively, they do not die out themselves). Dragons emerge in the contemporary moment from the abyssal depths of modernity not through biological adaptation or re-silience, but because of their archetypal alterity; they are an iconic reminder of existential ends and the slow violence of species extinction. Thus, their wrath-ful presence in twentieth-century literature needs to be historicized through an environmental lens so that dragons are not simply signifiers of evil and myth, cordoned off into the realms of fantasy, but reincarnated as synecdochal signifi-ers of the Anthropocene. They remind us of fossilized pasts and chthonic ends, the lithic layers that humanity compacts itself into in the geological scheme of modern times.

Thus, in 2019, we might read Yeats's incantation of the dragon as an un-witting but timely reminder of the adjacency of our future end as a species. It is fitting that "Nineteen Hundred and Nineteen," written as a bitter cry against the fall of an aristocratic past and as a response to unfolding crises of state-for-mation, demands to be a commentary on the present state of the world. At this time when biology and politics, philosophy and ecology, history and ge-ology merge, the dragon emerges as a figure of clarifying alterity. The phrase "dragon-ridden" needs no further elaboration for poetic import: it is already malevolent. As an amalgamation of mythic rationalizations of mega fauna fos-sils, religious cosmology, and a shorthand for the genetically-induced human fear of large predators, perhaps the dragon can never go extinct. Its plastic pop-ularity in modernity, along with its ability to transgress the magical possibilities of fable and enter the historical mode, makes it, as Donna Haraway writes in a not dissimilar context, "outside the security checkpoint of bright reason." The dragon is an ideal figure of otherness with "a remarkable capacity to induce panic in the centers of power and self certainty."[32]

The question that remains unresolved is this: if the dragon is the figure of the other, and if it is an uncanny image of the Anthropocene, the past resur-rected to hurtle us into a precarious future, then is it human or beast? Yeats circumnavigates the planetary and the particulate in the final section of this poem; as "evil gathers head," "dusty wind" engulfs the tableau of destruction. Like his former exercises of draconic imagery Yeats anthropomorphizes the dragon in the figure of "Robert Artisson"—apart from the dragon, the only other actively evil subject in the poem—whom he calls an "insolent fiend." Even Lady Kyteler, the medieval "witch," is cast as "love-lorn," and not really malevolent at all. Following the same uncanny logic, we recognize that Artis-son is no human either. He "lurches past, his great eyes without thought," much like the slouching beast of "The Second Coming." If *our* days are "dragon-rid-den," it is because we live "Under the shadow" of Artisson's "stupid straw-pale locks." The totemic items of the "Bronzed peacock feathers" and the "red combs of cocks," ritualistically given to Artisson, feed the *anthropos* who destroys the human and the world.

NOTES

1. Kanye West (@KanyeWest), "You don't have to agree with trump […]," Twitter, April 25, 2018, https://twitter.com/kanyewest/status/989179757651574784?ref_src=twsrc%5Etfw% 7Ctwcamp%5Etweetembed%7Ctwterm%5E989225812166696960&ref_url=https%3A%2F%2Fwww.theguardian.com%2Fmusic%2F2018%2Fapr%2F25% 2Fkanye-west-donald-trump-dragon-energy

2. Claire Colebrook, "Extinction," in *Posthuman Glossary*, eds. Rosi Braidotti and Maria Hlavajova (London: Bloomsbury, 2018), 151.

3. Thanks are due to Jason Moralee for reminding me of Kanye West's tweet.

4. My forthcoming studies chart such a critical trajectory in detail. In the meantime, see Sharae Deckard, ed., "Food, Energy, Climate: Irish Culture and World-Ecology," *Irish University Review* 49, no.1 (May 2019) and Derek Gladwin, *Contentious Terrains: Boglands, Ireland, Postcolonial Gothic* (Cork: Cork University Press, 2016).

5. See Dipesh Chakrabarty, "The Climate of History: Four Theses," *Critical Inquiry* 35, no. 2 (Winter 2009): 197–222.

6. W B Yeats, *The Poems*, ed. Daniel Albright (London: Everyman, [1990] 1999), 604.

7. Michael Woods, *Yeats and Violence* (New York: Oxford University Press, 2010), 6.

8. Cited in Marjorie Garber, *Loaded Words* (New York: Fordham University Press, 2003), 185.

9. Seamus Deane, "Yeats and the Idea of Revolution," in *Celtic Revivals* (London: Faber & Faber 1985), rep. in ed. Jonathan Allison, *Yeats's Political Identities* (Ann Arbor: Michigan University Press, 1996), 136.

10. Deane, "Yeats and the Idea of Revolution," 136.

11. See Robert Nixon, *Slow Violence: The Environmentalism of the Poor* (Cambridge, MA: Harvard University Press, 2013).

12. See Toby Foshay, "Yeats's 'Nineteen Hundred and Nineteen': Chronology, Chronography and Chronic Misreading," *The Journal of Narrative Technique* 13, no. 2 (Spring 1983): 100–08.

13. Helen Vendler, "The Later Poetry," in eds. Marjorie Howes and John Kelly, The Cambridge Companion to W. B. Yeats (Cambridge: Cambridge University Press, 2006), 80.

14. Helen Vendler, "The Late Poetry," 80.

15. To see the Lumière Brothers's 1896 cinematic rendition of Loie Fuller's Danse Serpentine, visit https://youtu.be/YNZ4WCFJGPc

16. Michael Woods, *Yeats and Violence*, 52.

17. Colebrook, "Extinction," 151.

18. Michael Woods, *Yeats and Violence*, 6.

19   Fintan O'Toole, "'Yeats Test' Criteria Reveal We Are Doomed," *Irish Times* (Dublin) July 28, 2018, https://www.irishtimes.com/opinion/fintan-o-toole-yeats-test-criteria-reveal-we-are-doomed-1.3576078.

20. Bruno Latour, *Down to Earth: Politics in the New Climactic Regime* (Cambridge, UK: Polity Press, 2018).

21. Christophe Bonneuil, *The Shock of the Anthropocene: The Earth, History and Us*, trans. David Fernbach (London: Verso, 2017), xiii.

22. For a comprehensive explanation of "The Platonic Year," also known as "The Great Year," see Michael Woods, *Yeats and Violence*, 53–54.

23. Marjorie Howes, "Yeats and the Postcolonial," in Majorie Howes and John Kelly, eds., *The Cambridge Companion to W. B. Yeats* (New York: Cambridge University Press, 2006), 210.

24. Elizabeth DeLoughrey, *Allegories of the Anthropocene* (Durham: Duke University Pres, 2019), 2.

25. See Lucy McDiarmid's "The Avian Rising: Yeats, Muldoon, and Others," *International Yeats Studies* 1, no. 1 (2016), https://tigerprints.clemson.edu/iys/vol1/iss1/10. See also Nicholas Grene, Yeats's Poetic Codes (Oxford: Oxford University Press, 2008), 104–129.

26. The Colloquy with the Ancients, trans. Standish Hayes O'Grady, Medieval Irish series (Cambridge, Ont.: In parentheses, 1999), 67; see http://www.yorku.ca/inpar/colloquy_ogrady.pdf.

27. *The Colloquy with the Ancients*, 67.

28. For example, another contemporary of Yeats, John Millington Synge, ethnographically narrates stories of ominous sightings of sea monsters by Aran Island villagers. John Francis Campbell suggests a link between Synge's sea monsters and dragons in Campbell, *The Celtic Dragon Myth*, trans. George Henderson, reprint edn. (Felinfach Lampeter: Llanerch, 1995).

29. Ursula Heise, "Extinction," in *Keywords for Environmental Studies*, eds. Joni Adamson, William A. Gleason, and David N. Pellow (New York: New York University Press, 2016), 118.

30. Gerardo Ceballos, Paul R. Ehrlich, and Rodolfo Dirzo, "Biological Annihilation via the Ongoing Sixth Mass Extinction Signaled by Vertebrate Population Losses and Declines,"in *Proceedings of the Natural Academy of Sciences of the United States of America* 114, no. 30 (July 25, 2017), E6089.

31. Adam Vaughn, "Humans Have Driven Nearly 600 Plant Species to Extinction since 1750s," *NewScientist* (June 10, 2019), https://www.newscientist.com/article/2205949-humans-have-driven-nearly-600-plant-species-to-extinction-since-1750s/.

32. Donna Haraway, *When Species Meet* (Minneapolis: University of Minnesota Press, 2008), 10.

A Review Of Yeats's Legacies: Yeats Annual No. 21

Warwick Gould, ed., *Yeats's Legacies: Yeats Annual No. 21, A Special Issue* (Cambridge, UK: OpenBook, 2018), lxviii + 609 pp., ISBN 978-1-78374-455-8.

Reviewed by Alexander Bubb

The theme of this year's edition of the redoubtable Annual was "Yeats's Legacies," with a marked focus on the final twenty years of the poet's life, and the first decade of his (textual) afterlife—including a close look at some of his very last works, such as *On the Boiler*. The book's title echoes the call for historical reflection that has been sounded during Ireland's ongoing round of centenaries (the Easter Rising, the War of Independence, and now two years that will require the most sensitive retrospection). It was in part prompted also by the two auctions that took place in Autumn 2017 of Yeats family documents, drawings, furnishings, and mementoes. Warwick Gould's editorial introduction helpfully enumerates the lots, their selling prices and—when known—their buyers based on his own first-hand observations; it also features a number of those high-quality color reproductions that have become such an admirable feature of the *Annual*. These aid us not only to visualize the *writing space* of W. B. Yeats, as Gould comments, but also the *reading space*—see for example the young poet, painted by his father, lounging in the overgrown garden at 3 Blenheim Road, thinking a green thought in a green shade, or the reference card index he used much later at Broad Street in Oxford (est. £100–150, hammer price £2,400). Also reproduced is a delightful sketch that Jack B. Yeats inserted into a letter to Lady Gregory, showing a sign-painter at work on the slogan:

MAKE PROVISION FOR
YOUR OLD AGE!!!!
BUY JACK B YEATS' PICTURES
WHY INSURE LIFE
WHAT IS LIFE WITHOUT HIS PICTURES
WHY TAKE SHARES IN A COMPANY
EVERY PICTURE
A SHARE OF THE WORLD

It will be some years yet before publications begin to appear bearing directly upon these sale items, but as tokens of a writer embedded in his place, time, and family (significant considering the conclusion Yeats came to during composition of *On the Boiler*, as William H. O'Donnell's essay relates, that man stands "between two eternities, that of his family, that of his soul"), the trove offers a suggestive textured backdrop to the subsequent essays (*CL InteLex* 7259). The editor's own extended piece, "Satan, Smut & Co," is fundamentally concerned with what Gould calls "the quotidian realities of Irish public life" (180), and the need to restore Yeats to that complex, animated, and productively confusing "actuality" that some of his interpreters, preoccupied with critical narratives of Modernism and other overarching concepts, have been tempted, perhaps, to wish away. The revisions Yeats made in late 1924 to his dedicatory vers- es to *Representative Irish Tales* (1891), for example, were executed specifically for publication in *To-Morrow*, the periodical which the newly-crowned Nobel Laureate was mischievously promoting as part of a campaign of provocation against the Free State's new laws on the regulation of blasphemous and inde- cent publications. That of course was tied intimately to Yeats's stand against censorship in the Seanad, but also to the little-known campaign of vigilantism that took place in this period, orchestrated originally by Canice Craven of *Our Boys* and cheered on lustily by his editorial colleague at the *Catholic Bulletin*, Timothy Corcoran.

Gould tells the story with verve, drawing on a number of overlooked or un- derused sources such as Louis M. Cullen's 1989 history of the Dublin bookseller and stationer Eason & Son. Easons were the somewhat uneasy distributors of *Our Boys*, a monthly periodical modelled on the *Boy's Own Paper* but intend- ed as an Irish substitute for it, carrying wholesome sentiments into the hearts of the nation's youth and expelling the impious and degrading influences put there by imported, "unclean" literature. Seeking to win notoriety—and a great- er market share—for his own beleaguered publication, in 1925 Craven publicly burned piles of *Pears' Annual* outside the *Our Boys* offices because it contained Cecil Sharp's version of "The Cherry Tree Carol." This, then, is without doubt the second of two lurid episodes Yeats refers to in his article for the *Spectator* of September 1928:

> Ecclesiastics, who shy at the modern world as horses in my youth shied at mo- tor-cars, have founded a "Society of Angelic Welfare". Young men stop trains, armed with automatics and take from the guard's van bundles of English newspapers [...] A Christian Brother publicly burnt an English magazine because it contained the Cherry Tree Carol, the lovely celebration of Mary's sanctity and her Child's divinity, a glory of the mediaeval church as popular in Gaelic as in English, because, scandalized by its naïveté, he believed it the work of some irreligious modern poet [...] (*CW10* 214–18)[1]

I confess that when I originally read these words ten years ago, I half-fancied the first episode to be some exaggerated version owing its imagery to Yeats's well-known fondness for westerns and adventure stories. It thus came as quite a surprise to discover that this great train robbery actually happened—at Dundalk in 1927—along with various less-romantic incidents involving threats and boycotts imposed on unfortunate newsagents who dared to stock *The News of the World*. Such manifestations of the "bitter fissiparity" (124), as Gould calls it, exhibited in the daily life of the early Free State, along with the neighboring color reproduction of an *Our Boys* front cover with its wholesome jumble of sculls, footballs, cricket bats, and hurleys, calls to mind a contemporary cartoon shown in a recent lecture by Roy Foster. In this sketch the clutter is made up of instruments of modern entertainment, among them a saxophone and its presumed owner, a black musician, who is being swept away head-over-heels by the giant broom of a muscular young patriot. However terrifying, frankly, such images are, I cannot help but regret Gould's implied analogy with Islamic moral policing, through the throwaway use of such words as "madrassa" (148) and "jihad" (145) that, taken by themselves, should not be thought of as necessarily carrying any extremist connotations. This, to my mind, slightly muddies the otherwise clear expostulation of this fascinating material. And by alienating us from the context it has the potential to interrupt further, branching routes of thought into such countervailing issues as Yeats's own history of objection to the spread of urban mass culture in Ireland—notably his dislike for the bawdy music hall, which he deprecates in *Autobiographies* (*CW3* 87).

Gould's introduction explains that his original theme for this volume was intended to be the "vain battles" (lxv) that Yeats participated in throughout his career, making both rhetoric and poetry out of quarrels with others. That volume is still envisaged (and keenly anticipated by this reviewer) but in the meantime several of the essays do address themselves either to Yeats's zest for controversy, or to the contentious politics that subsequently came to surround individual works. O'Donnell has meticulously researched the publication history of On *The Boiler*, a tortuous process set in motion by F. R. Higgins's inexplicable decision to entrust printing of Yeats's self-styled "Fors Clavigera" to a firm so inexperienced that they were not even equipped with italic type! With her focus instead on the late 1920s, Lauren Arrington offers insights from her upcoming book on Yeats's circle at Rapallo, detailing how the poet's thought was transformed under the combined impressions of Mussolini's Italy and the Japanese books passed on to him by his American friend. As she puts it, "if *A Vision* gave Yeats metaphors for his poetry, then Pound and the Noh gave him metaphors for his politics" (283), referring to the complex analogy between contemporary Ireland and medieval Japan that Anita Feldman, an expert on the Noh, also discusses in her essay. Feldman's contribution is one of two to focus explicitly on the 1916 Rising and its aftershocks. The first, by Denis Donoghue, uses personal family memories to illustrate the "anthem"-like status (59) that "Easter 1916" obtained among nationalists born in the interwar years. The essay raises several problems that remain unresolved at the close. Donoghue lays great stress on the difference between "change," the word that recurs throughout the poem, and "transformed," which is applied only to the figure of John MacBride. "Transformation is what culture does" (58), writes Donoghue—but what is this culture? The demotic "book of the people" that Yeats spent much of his youth trying to read, or the high culture of which he became a staunch defender? The essay ends by expressing the hope that Ireland's politicians will come finally to celebrate "without embarrassment" (61)—though not without circumspection, surely?—the anniversary of the Rising, and celebrate too the fact that Ireland has retained its democratic values and never subsided into the Blueshirt "cruelty" (61) that offered such a dangerous temptation to the poet. But isn't it Yeats's very preoccupations with the persistence of culture, and with that decisive intervention "the sublime act" (58), that predisposed him to authoritarian forms of governance? Donoghue's essay is anchored in the controversies of three years ago, but it will speak no doubt also to the Civil War commemorations, and it complements its neighboring essays by touching again on the matter of Yeats's "actuality" and daily existence. He begins his essay by citing a remarkable letter of 1915 in which Yeats welcomes Lennox Robinson's proposal to bring his play about Robert Emmet to the Abbey stage. How extraordinary it seems that Yeats would risk bringing a rebel scenario before the public at a time of such acute tension. But then, history looks very different to those who are living it in their present.

It is right that the *Yeats Annual* should be a forum not only for the latest research on Yeats, but also on his family and his wider circle. That side of its mission is supported here by John Kelly, who with his usual eye for precise chronology has used a short story published by Maud Gonne in 1889 to help plot her transition from Colonel's daughter to physical-force nationalist—a timely supplement to the somewhat broader brushstrokes used by Adrian Frazier in his new book on Gonne and her lover Lucien Millevoye, *The Adulterous Muse*.[2] Another recent biographer, Grevel Lindop, has shared material in a neighboring essay from his close investigation of Charles Williams, the poet, occultist, and admirer of Yeats, whom circumstances brought into dialogue with his idol when Yeats commissioned him on behalf of Oxford University Press to produce the *Book of Modern Verse*. Yeats's famous assessment of his 1890s contemporaries in the preface, and Lindop's discussion of the editorial decisions that baffled Williams only just a little less than everybody else, throw an interesting sidelight on the first essay in the volume by Hannah Sullivan. She seeks to explain that counterintuitive progress whereby Yeats's "metrically uneasy" (8) early lyrics were consciously hardened into more constrained and traditional forms, even while "vers libre," as Yeats had known it in his youth, was growing ever more prevalent and viable. It seems churlish to point out lacunae in such a thoroughgoing analytic account, though it seems to me that a missing piece of the puzzle here—and one that would have more closely connected Sullivan's essay with Lindop's—may be retrieved in the shape of W. E. Henley. His collection *In Hospital* (written in the early 1870s) is an early landmark of English free verse and, according to *Autobiographies*, Yeats made a conscious decision not to emulate his mentor's prosody. "I associated [it] with Tyndall and Huxley, and Bastien-Lepage's clownish peasant staring with vacant eyes at her great boots" (*CW3* 121). When he came to assemble the *Modern Verse*, Yeats included four of Henley's poems. But none of them are drawn from *In*

Hospital, and none are in free verse. Incidentally, another of Henley's protégés claims to have made the same rejection at the same time, teasing the avid angler over dinner by remarking that vers libre was "like fishing with barbless hooks." Here I must desist from indulging my own interests, though Sullivan's final point that it is Yeats's confidence with finite verbs (in phrases like "That is no country for old men"), that makes him "so quotable" and "so memorable" (37) in an era when poets avoided direct propositions, may call to mind for other readers too the easily-forgotten figure of Kipling.

As mentioned earlier, none of the essays in this year's *Annual* draws directly on those materials exposed to the public eye by the 2017 auctions, but nonetheless one essay is based entirely on newly-uncovered archival sources, and forms another layer in James Pethica's longstanding contribution to the study of Augusta Gregory. As he constructed an imagined lineage of predecessors who trod with iron heel the winding stair at Thoor Ballylee, Yeats seems to have paid little mind to the people who were living there immediately prior to his purchase of the tower in 1917. The story, told through a series of letters that until recently were held by the Naval & Military Club in London before being deposited in the Bodleian, unfolds thirty years earlier, when Sir William Gregory reluctantly opened legal proceedings against his recalcitrant tenant Patrick Spelman. Spelman was ultimately deprived of his lease, though he was allowed to remain in the tower on the sufferance of his son-in-law, and it is this uneasy family that Yeats would have encountered when Lady Gregory first took him folklore-hunting in the neighborhood. The article is accompanied by transcripts of the letters, one of the most remarkable of which is a petition written to Sir William by Spelman's daughter Elizabeth, in which the old farmer would have it known that he "inherits gentlemanly principles beyond the common herd, and should not be illtreated in his decline of life by you" (253). So Yeats's occupancy, as it turns out, did add its chapter to a history of proud tower-dwellers, and in search of a prototype for his own lordly, masterful utterance he needn't have looked back even so far as the Land War.

That brings us back to battles—some vain, some not—and we may look forward with interest to the upcoming *Annual* on that theme, and to similarly exacting and close-grained studies of Yeats's career in conflict.

NOTES

1. "Angelic Welfare" is an error for "Angelic Warfare."
2. Adrian Frazier, *The Adulterous Muse: Maud Gonne, Lucien Millevoye and W.B. Yeats* (Dublin: Lilliput Press, 2016).
3. Rudyard Kipling, *Something of Myself* (London: Macmillan, 1937), 82.

A Review Of *Classical Presences In Irish Poetry After 1960: The Answering Voice*

Florence Impens, *Classical Presences in Irish Poetry after 1960: The Answering Voice* (London: Palgrave Macmillan, 2018). ix + 210 pp. ISBN 978-3-31-319-68230-3.

Reviewed by Matthew Campbell

In her 1990 volume *Outside History*, Eavan Boland initially declares her garden "free of any need / for nymphs, goddesses, wounded presences." These would-be green-fingered deities like Daphne, who found herself turned into a laurel; but also Ceres, goddess of the harvest who loses her daughter for half of every year. The mythical entities haunt suburban spaces—a garden with a conservatory and roses or the edge of the city at evening. But for all that, Boland says that these spaces have no need for such wounded presences; they continue to lurk ominously at the edges of the domestic, as at the end of "Daphne Heard with Horror the Addresses of the God":

> A suggestion,
> behind it all, of darkness: in the shadow,
> beside the laurel hedge, its gesture.[2]

The poems have presences which gesture at both history and mythology, structures of feeling with which the poet feels familiar but which nevertheless transgress the familial.

The speaker of Boland's poem "The Making of an Irish Goddess" ends as Ceres, worrying about a daughter who might be a latter-day Proserpina—though the daughter is merely out playing on a summer evening. The poem had traversed difficult material to get to its worry, in which the historical becomes mythological, and myths from history retain their power to unsettle. It presents a vision of famine, "the failed harvests, / the fields rotting to the horizon, / the children devoured by their mothers." That image is historically contentious: were there any instances of starving mothers eating their own children during the Great Famine? And it is also aware of what is historiographically contentious, as in the subsequent statement, "myth is the wound we leave / in the time we have." This I take to be an updating of both myth and history—myth as history and vice versa—into a present lived moment, where the latter-day Ceres or Daphne or Proserpina admonish the contemporary self. In the case of *Outside History*, in 1990, the presence of these figures from Roman mythology in Irish poems had been used to make complaint against the perpetuation of political violence and the continued mythologization of the wounded female form.

Florence Impens's *Classical Presences in Irish Poetry after 1960: The Answering Voice* draws our attention throughout to such moments as these in contemporary Irish poetry. In these poems classical myth not only found a home, but also allowed poets to address issues of myth and history which are slanted differently from other anglophone poetry, for all its centuries-long borrowing from the literatures of Greece and Rome. Impens works across a broad canvas, from Yeats and Patrick Kavanagh and Louis MacNeice through to Peter McDonald and Paula Meehan. In three central chapters she gives an overview of classical presences in Seamus Heaney, Michael Longley, Derek Mahon and Boland. If the figures of Virgil and Homer loom largest, then Ovid (as with Boland) plays a strong supporting role. And various fugitive and fragmentary lyric verses also find their way in here, from the expected—Sappho—to the less so, culled from the obscurer reaches of the Loeb classical library. Longley's "Praxilla" is a case in point, a short lyric which takes issue with the criticism of Zenobius (retold by the editor/translator of the Loeb edition of her work) that the Greek poet was "feeble minded" (113). The only reason we have one fragment from Praxilla is where Zenobius demonstrates her bathos, retelling how that along with the sun and moon Adonis in the underworld missed cucumbers. This is the cue for Longley's poem, where he celebrates unpacking the day's shopping with direct quotation from his Greek foremother: "ripe cucumbers and apples and pears." "I subsist on fragments and improvisations" Longley tells us in the poem, one of a number of *ars poeticae* for a late style re-immersing itself in the quotidian of the Greek and Latin that has been a presence in his poetry for decades.[4]

Given the breadth of her project, the value of Impens's work is in the amount of material it brings into play and conscientiously amasses in solid, more or less chronological, detail. Impens has a new story to tell about the oldest things which have been cropping up in Irish poetry since 1960. If the emphasis is on Northern poets (Boland aside), then that is hard to avoid given the particulars of their grammar-school education and the ways that they choose to adapt classical material, not just for contemporary political concerns but also to answer a number of poetical questions that could be better solved with a look backwards beyond the peculiarities of an Irish poetic tradition. The version Impens gives of classical rewriting lands at one point in various versions of *Antigone*, a model for a particular type of Ulster political drama arising out of the late 1960s and early 1970s. The example of Conor Cruise O'Brien and his antagonist Tom Paulin is strong here, as in the account of Tom Paulin's *Riot Act* (170–72).

Impens's canvas is large enough to show that, as historical events moved on, so too did the preoccupation with other versions of the classical, the drama giving way to epic. This is manifest in rewritings of Homer or Virgil, or poetic investigations of lyric, seeking international cross-linguistic connections through translation, adaptation and creative and often synthetic rewriting. A number of texts and styles and languages coalesce. Her account of Heaney's *Midnight Verdict*, a folding of the story of Orpheus and Eurydice into Brian Merriman's *Midnight Court* in the early 1990s context of the controversy surrounding the *Field Day* anthology, is an intriguing example of this, matching canonical classical and Gaelic texts with late-twentieth-century culture wars. Heaney brought contentious materials to this match. Though Impens is censorious of a distortion of tone by the melding of the satiric and the tragic, she does let Heaney off the hook for what she implies is anti-feminist allegory, by calling the treatment "tongue-in-cheek" (68). *Midnight Verdict* retains the ending of Orpheus where the lyrist is torn apart by the Maenads, whereas Merriman's hero had merely woken up in an empty Clare countryside like a true *aisling* poet, his male virginity and his own attitudes to women intact.

It is to Impens's credit that she remains circumspect in the proximity of such controversy. There is much to contend with, not the least of which is the use of poetry, and particularly epic, which tells of myths of imperial foundations and adventures. This is written by poets who are themselves anti-imperial or decolonizing, nevertheless writing in the midst of situations in which the post-colonial paradigm is treated at times by the poets with suspicion, and in the main with hostility. Of course, this is not the case with much Irish criticism, drawn as it continues to be to the sureties of materialist critique. And on the other side, as Impens shows, in the hands of writers such as Yeats, there has been more-than-a-little desire to sit on imperial golden boughs and sing to lords and ladies of Greco-Roman glories. If Heaney or Mahon were beneficiaries of the classical education afforded to the lower middle classes by the UK welfare state, Yeats viewed such a thing with horror: "A Helen of social welfare dream / Climb on a wagonette to scream" ("Why Should Old Men not be Mad," quoted, 17).

It is in her account of education and the ways in which the Irish poetry of the last fifty or so years engages with the classics that Impens is most persuasive. Hers is a deliberately non-linguistic, even non-artistic, analysis. She has little to say about Greek meter, say, or Latinate etymology. The engagement with other languages is by those who mainly have school (and even Church) Latin and—with Longley the exception—little Greek. The majority of Irish versions of almost all of these classical poets and playwrights were by means of English cribs. Ciaran Carson is the exception, as he is a rare example of a polyglot bi-lingual writer. Yet his classical, like his French or Irish, poems have the habit of turning into the Carsonian cento, a tissue of quotation and translation and slanted allusion, even if they usually seem to end up in the accent of one location of Hiberno-English, Belfast. The more clearly internationalist writers—Boland, Mahon, and Heaney—engage with differing cultures and places in different languages and registers. Mahon's long sequences of international displacement, *The Yellow Book* or *The Hudson Letter*, parse Oscar Wilde and Walter Pater and fin de siècle ennui with Homeric journeying and urban dissolution (135–40). When even Longley seems to be reading the poets through their Loeb translators, the poets are seen by Impens as the beneficiaries of Penguin Books as much as the Stormont version of R. A. Butler's Education Act. Oxford World's Classics has picked up Peter Fallon's *Georgics*.

The picture that emerges from Impens's fascinating study, a compilation of much richness which proceeds by empirical accretion as much as by direct

argument, effects a recalibration or re-steering of Irish poetry away from familiar preoccupations and complaints. The contribution of writing by women has
not quite emerged into this account, despite the prominence given to Boland in
the main story of the book. Impens suggest this is because the classical model
has receded in the education of subsequent generations (although a discussion
of Leontia Flynn's recent scabrous versions of Catullus and her reanimation of a
broadly "augustan" satire might have made for a useful coda).[5] There is no place
for Eiléan Ní Chuilleanáin's "The Second Voyage," nor is there space for that
poem's broad conception of a classicism of the sea that goes back to Tennyson's
"Ulysses" and the Irish *Immram*.[6] But to make classicism a presence rather
than the classical would be a different, narrower book. As it is, Impens doesn't
attempt a definition of "classicism," or even "Irish classicism," such concepts
being by turns impossibly precise and diffuse.

Impens reads Derek Mahon's late masterpiece "Calypso" biographically,
as "an allegory of Mahon's hesitations as to his imaginative return to Ireland"
(143), and there is an unmistakeably Atlantic rather than Mediterranean sea-
board scene in the poem. Like "The Second Voyage," Mahon's poem feels the
tug of the sea in its prosodic rigging, a poem of harbor breezes, creaking tackle,
pier-side mutterings, and a half-sensed late-night Oceanic swell. It is set in the
home place but also tells of being haunted by wandering and return. "Calypso" begins with the error of the poet: "Homer was wrong, she never ceased to
please." But the error, the choice of withdrawal from the epic, is eventually,
grudgingly, corrected:

> Homer was wrong, he never made it back; or,
> if he did, spent many a curious night hour
> still questioning that strange, oracular face.[7]

Mahon's ending is of a kind of unknowing, a road taken rather than not taken
but with uncertain results, a classicism which is by turns oracular and strange.
It is, to use Impens's subtitle, a request for an answering voice, except the sheer
size of the classical engagement means that we cannot quite pin it down in
forms other than oracles.

NOTES

1.   Eavan Boland, *Outside History* (Manchester: Carcanet, 1990), 35.
2.   Boland, *Outside History*, 35.
3.   Boland, *Outside History*, 32.
4.   Michael Longley, *Snow Water* (London: Cape, 2004), 57.
5.   Leontia Flynn, *The Radio* (London: Cape, 2018), pp. 41–43.
6.   Eiléan Ní Chuilleanáin, *The Second Voyage* (Meath: Gallery, 1986), 26.
7.   Derek Mahon, *Harbour Lights* (Meath: Gallery, 2005), 60.

A Review Of W. B. Yeats's Robartes-Aherne Writings, Featuring The Making Of His "Stories Of Michael Robartes And His Friends"

Wayne K. Chapman, *W. B. Yeats's Robartes-Aherne Writings, Featuring the Making of his "Stories of Michael Robartes and His Friends,"* Modernist Archives (London: Bloomsbury Academic, 2018), pp. xlix + 373, ISBN 9781472595157.

Reviewed by Neil Mann

It is an excellent idea to bring together in one volume all of the writings that W. B. Yeats devoted to the figures of Michael Robartes and Owen Aherne, recalling A. Norman Jeffares's rather different project of bringing together all the published material related to *A Vision*.[1] Robartes and Aherne are protean compound ghosts in Yeats's personal phantasmagoria, familiar enough to be recalled at a distance of twenty years and be picked up more or less where they had left off, despite a minor confusion of names.[2] In the stories of the 1890s, "Rosa Alchemica" and "The Tables of the Law,"[3] the characters do not meet but share contacts, including the narrator—but on their reappearance they become a form of double act. Robartes is the more consistent over time, the magian voice of *The Wind Among the Reeds* and hierophant of the Order of the Alchemical Rose who becomes a wanderer in the Austro-Hungarian and Ottoman empires. He is the compiler and guardian of the documents that form the basis *A Vision*, finally presiding over a clutch of acolytes at a house in Regent's Park. Owen Aherne is the shadowier figure, defined by inner conflict, "half monk, half soldier of fortune" (*RAW* 18),[4] a modern Templar and orthodox heretic who, in finding himself, loses his sense of sin and God. Recast twenty years later as Robartes's straight man and prompter, he encourages the exposition of the lunar system, his greater conventionality making him a foil for Robartes's accounts of the strange doctrines of the Judwalis and their European parallel, Giraldus. In the world of *A Vision A* (1925), Aherne is Robartes's walking companion in Galway and Connemara, the stay-at-home counterpart to Robartes's rover, but in in the *Stories of Michael Robartes and His Friends* (1932), and therefore *A Vision B* (1937), he becomes more of an assistant, even a dogsbody, as Robartes takes center stage. The G. R. S. Mead to Robartes's Madame Blavatsky or the William Wynn Westcott to Robartes's MacGregor Mathers, Aherne's surname connects him to another fiction, the unpublished, semi-autobiographical *The Speckled Bird*, where Yeats's alter ego is named Michael Hearne (Robartes takes the Christian name). Though Richard Ellmann is simplistic in viewing the pair as "two sides of a penny"[5] and two sides of Yeats's own character, there is certainly something in the sense that they are among the masks that project aspects of personality.

Despite this continuity in Yeats's creative work and the rich seam of material, the problems emerge as soon as one starts to consider the practicalities. As a glance at the table of contents (given on the Bloomsbury webpage) shows, the volume risks being a chimeric hybrid, with awkward gaps between parts that come from very different beasts, starting with the jeweled stories of the 1890s at the head, the dialogues and elaborate fictions of 1917 to 1925 in the body, and the absurdist narratives of 1929 to 1937 at the tail. Furthermore, some of the material involved exists in several distinct published versions, and some passages are extracted from the notes to other published works; other parts are the manuscripts of published works, and yet others are manuscripts unpublished by Yeats, some published before and others published here for the first time. Some of the material has been discussed by many critics and presented in a variety of ways, other research is entirely original, and some of the manuscripts are presented for the first time.

So, the question becomes how to bring together this material into a satisfactory and satisfying volume, and Wayne K. Chapman probably comes as close to achieving this as is possible. He takes the problems and turns them to the volume's advantage. Coherent it cannot be, but the jumble itself becomes the point. And it works.

The three magical stories "Rosa Alchemica," "The Tables of the Law," and "The Adoration of the Magi" had a complicated publishing history, published in magazine and book versions in the 1890s, revised versions in 1908 and again in 1925, and the final form that Yeats gave them in the 1932 *Mythologies*, which is how they are usually presented today.[6] Chapman uses the 1908 version from the Shakespeare Head *Collected Works*—the first time all three were published together—as his text (*CWVP* 1–8), including substantial variants of earlier and later versions in endnotes. Yeats's work for this edition, published by A. H. Bullen, shows him reworking the stories a decade after their first appearance, possibly keeping his memories of Robartes and Aherne alive enough to enable their reappearance in his imaginary circle less than a decade later.[8]

The characters make their full return in a group of manuscripts that surround W. B. Yeats's early attempts to provide a context for what was emerging in the automatic script that he and George Yeats were engaged in from the end of 1917.[9] Chapman has unearthed a manuscript that indicates that Aherne may initially have been revived in a dialogue with "WB Yeats" from late November 1917, looking at the legacy of "Anglo Ireland" and pitting his Catholic sensibility against Mr. Yeats's defense of the ascendancy tradition (*RAW* 37). Based at Thoor Ballyleee, this shifts into being a dialogue between Aherne and Robartes in what would become "The Phases of the Moon." Chapman also gives some of the earliest prose dialogues that were drafted between late 1917 and the first months of 1918.

The end of October 1917 saw the start of the "incredible experience" of the automatic script (*AVB* 8). Almost immediately, Yeats was confecting fictional frameworks, from the first with the European exponent and the Arabian one, and he visited the Orientalist Edward Denison Ross in December 1917 for some plausible Arabic names, writing to Augusta Gregory in January 1918, "I am writing it all out in a series of dialogues about a supposed medieval book the 'Speculum Angelorum et Hominum' by Gyraldous & a sect of Arabs called the Judwalis (diagrametists). Ross helped me with the Arabic" (*CL InteLex* 3384; cf. L 644).[10] And Robartes and Aherne were on hand to bring these figures and their ideas into modern Ireland and London—in "The Phases of the Moon" they mock Yeats in his tower at Ballylee, while in the fictions of *A Vision A*, they do something of the same at his apartments in Bloomsbury.

Even in the very early material, the fictions center on a Renaissance Latin book by Giraldus and an Arabian tribe (to be named), who have separately arrived at the doctrines that are connected by Michael Robartes. He goes to live with the tribe to learn their secrets and tells the fruits of his research to Aherne. The first manuscripts in "Unpublished 'Discoveries', 1917–1920" are mainly concerned with setting up the encounter of Aherne and Robartes, Robartes's surprise that Yeats's Per Amica Silentia Lunae contains glimpses of his doctrine, and Robartes giving his account of how he discovered the esoteric system in a book in "Crackow" and an Arabian oral tradition (*RAW* 76–79). These precede and therefore complement the drafts that were published in Yeats's 'Vision' Papers, volume 4 (*YVP*4), edited by George Mills Harper and Margaret Mills Harper (with Richard W. Stoops Jr.).[11] For clarity, I shall use here Chapman's very helpful stemma (*RAW* 88)—which draws on Catherine Paul's and Margaret Mill Harper's chronology as editors of *A Vision (1925) (CW13)*—to indicate in table form (Table 1) where the various transcriptions are to be found.

The "Appendix by Michael Robartes," which falls outside the process of redrafting, is a terser and more direct account of the doctrines, presumably intended to follow and support what was being shown more allusively in the dialogues. Based on an exposition of "The Great Diagram from the Speculum Angelorum et hominis," the fictional book by Giraldus, it also uses "Arabic names" from "the 'Camel's Back,'" giving diagrams such as "'The holy women and the two Kalendars'" and "'The dance of the Eunuch with the favourite wife'" (*RAW* 95), part of the pastiche of *The One Thousand and One Nights* that Yeats uses as his color. While Walter Kelly Hood, who published the transcript in *Yeats and the Occult* in 1975, gave a dating of 1918 to 1920 (*YO* 206), it is clear from this use of language (and the absence of certain terms) that it falls right at the beginning of Hood's timespan; the caution of someone as expert as Hood reminds us how the publication over the last forty-five years of material associated with *A Vision*—which he was pioneering—has made dating a little easier.

Chapman leaves the rest of the manuscripts to Yeats's 'Vision' Papers and moves on, in his third section, to the published material related to Robartes and Aherne, most of it exposition of *A Vision's* system couched in Arabian fictions. The first poem is "Ego Dominus Tuus," which contains a reference to a "book / That Michael Robartes left" (*VP* 367); it is dated to late 1915 and was published in magazine form in October 1917 (*RAW* 103, n1), before his marriage and thus also before the preceding manuscript material. It is included here, however, as part of the contents of *The Wild Swans at Coole* (Macmillan, 1919).

Table 1

Title	Version	Dates	Manuscript Number	Notes	Transcription Location
"Aherne & Robartes Dialogue Etc – imperfect"	Drafts 1 and 2	Nov. 29–Dec. 16, 1917	NLI 36,263/7/1–2	Exercise Books 1 and 2	RAW 64–87
"Untitled Manuscript"	Draft 3	c. Jan. 1–Mar. 1918	NLI 36,263/9		YVP4 119–135
"Appendix by Michael Robartes"		Jan./Feb. 1918	NLI 36,263/7/3		YO 210–15 RAW 95–100
"'Discoveries' Manuscript"	Draft 4	c. Mar.– Oct. 3, 1918 (finished for typing). WBY reached p. 30 mid-July	NLI 36,263/4		YVP4 62–118
"'Discoveries' Typescript"	Draft 5	c. Oct. 3, 1918–late 1918	NLI 36,263/3		YVP4 11–61
"Version B"		c. late 1918–1920	NLI 30,525 and 36,263/10/1–2	MS of brief headnote of "June 1920," short Robartes-John	YVP4 139–260
				Aherne dialogue, and Extracts ["The Great Wheel" and "The Twenty-Eight Embodiments"]	

Indeed dates here can become slightly slippery as Chapman is also forced by coherence to put a note from the Later Poems (Macmillan, 1922)—connected with poems from *The Wild Swans at Coole* (Macmillan, 1919)—before the material from *Michael Robartes and the Dancer* (Cuala, 1921).

The first published expositions of the system—as opposed to the poems, which came out earlier but are, perhaps, "a text for exposition" (note to the *Later Poems* [1922], RAW 114)—are distributed in fragmentary form in notes to *Michael Robartes and the Dancer* (Cuala, 1921) and the *Four Plays for Dancers* (Macmillan, 1921), as Michael Robartes gives Owen Aherne documents and sends him letters, drawing on what he has found "in the *Speculum* of Gyraldus and in Arabia Deserta among the Judwalis" ("Note on 'The Only Jealousy of Emer,'" *RAW* 127). In many cases, although the fictions obscure ideas slightly, these notes give a clear and direct account of the ideas that would be expressed more fully and technically in *A Vision*. The "Note on 'The Only Jealousy of Emer'" gives a succinct summary of the Great Wheel, for example, while the account of the afterlife in the "Note on 'The Dreaming of the Bones'" is lucid and relatively simple, expressed in terms of "Shade" and "Spiritual Being," but provides a concise version of the more detailed picture that Yeats drew of the *Principles* in *A Vision B*. At the same time, Yeats was also elaborating further the story of the originator of the Judwali doctrines, Kusta ben Luka, within the world of *The One Thousand and One Nights*, creating an epistolary monologue "The Gift of Harun-al-Rashid," to fictionalize his relationship with George and the origin of the automatic script. Chapman includes the poem in its entirety for the mentions of Robartes and Aherne in the notes, and there is a quibble here, as his choice of copytext is not signaled entirely clearly—it is in the page header, but no printing history is given—nor are the idiosyncrasies that it brings explained. Using Cuala's printing from *The Cat and the Moon* (1924) brings in some extraneous apostrophes—"the Caliphs' hang," "Caliphs' to world's end," for example—which it would be helpful to indicate are included for fidelity to a particular printing rather than any reason of substance; this also happens with misprints in Bullen's *Collected Works*.[12]

The formulations of these notes are closer to the myth that Yeats originally thought to create, using a hybrid of pseudo-Arabic and Latin terms with modern reformulations attributed to Robartes, Aherne, and Mr. Yeats, rather than the eventual exposition of *A Vision*. At successive stages the mythical clothing is stripped away a little further, so that by the time of *A Vision A*, Robartes's researches on Giraldus and studies with the Judwalis provide documents that are the source for two versions: the main one by "Mr. Yeats," with extra material penned by "Owen Aherne." Chapman collects all of Aherne's material into this volume, bringing together Aherne's "Introduction," "The Dance of the Four Royal Persons," and the extended comments included in fourth book of *A Vision A*, "The Gates of Pluto," fabricated either to include a Christian perspective or to fictionalize the Yeatses' personal experiences.[13] Chapman includes references to a 1922 draft of the introduction,[14] and relates "The Dance of the Four Royal Persons" to its typescript drafts.[15] He gives full notes and commentary on this material, which is extremely helpful both textually and in terms of references, though one cavil is that calling Watkins Books in Cecil Court a "famous Mecca for pilgrim readers of the hermetic, esoteric, and Theosophical arts" (*RAW* 158) risks being quaint or confusing in the context of Robartes's travels in Arabia.[16]

Making up half of the book proper (i.e. without the general introduction), the last two sections are the most significant, and they cover the drafting and publication of *Stories of Michael Robartes and His Friends* (Cuala, 1931), and some subsequent additions. Chapman's Part Four opens with an introductory essay on "The Making of 'Stories of Michael Robartes and His Friends'"

(*RAW* 166–87), followed by a facsimile of the single main manuscript draft (NLI 13,577) facing a transcription (*RAW* 188–271),[17] then transcriptions of "Related Material in the While Vellum Notebook (mainly the poem "Huddon, Duddon and Daniel O'Leary") (*RAW* 272–78), and finally a lineated variorum text of the published stories based on the Cuala version with variants from *A Vision B* and the Cuala proofs (*RAW* 279–310).[18] His Part Five is centered on two texts: the corrected typescript of "Michael Robartes Foretells," which remained unpublished until transcribed by Hood in *Yeats and the Occult*, and the story given to Denise de l'Isle Adam, an addition to the Stories, interpolated into the version in *A Vision B* (the final form given as a variant in the variorum text mentioned earlier). An essay on "'Michael Robartes Foretells': A Rejected Ending" (*RAW* 312–21) is followed by photographs of NLI 36,272/33 facing a transcription of the typed text and handwritten corrections (*RAW* 322–39); "Denise's Story: W. B. Yeats, Dorothy Wellesley, and the Re-making of 'Stories of Michael Robartes and His Friends: An Extract from a Record Made by His Pupils'" (*RAW* 340–51) is followed by photographs of NLI 30,390 facing transcription of the manuscript (*RAW* 351–59). That the texts are given as appendices to essays, rather than as texts with introductions, goes slightly against the previous practice, as does the relatively full head material describing the manuscript. The slight difference of approach in part indicates that Chapman regards these facsimiles/texts as supporting more discursive essays that go beyond just the manuscript, though there is also evidence of different parts of the book being written at different times, with slight variations of conventions and style, as well as in approach.[19]

Chapman is largely in agreement with George Mills Harper's doubts about "the artistic merit of the 'Stories of Michael Robartes and His Friends' as an organic part of the whole" of *A Vision B*, viewing the stories as "more or less extraneous" to *A Vision* (*YAACTS6* [1988], 293, cit. *RAW* 166). While asserting "the organic integrity of 'Stories' in its own right," he concludes that the fictions were "attached to *A Vision* to assuage fear that the latter might not stand alone" (*RAW* 166). In fact, it would seem the other way round—the stories hardly seem to stand alone without their connection to *A Vision*, though what precisely that connection is has puzzled many. Chapman certainly does not go as far as William O'Donnell who found the text "incontestably uncraftsmanlike,"[20] but there is no clear argument for the value of the stories or for a reading that gives them a coherence and point that they seem to lack. They seem too leaden for comedy and too trivial to bear the weight that Yeats suggests, of presenting "a group of strange disorderly people on whom Michael Robartes confers the wisdom of the east" (to Dorothy Wellesley, July 26 [1936], *CL InteLex* 6622; cit. *RAW* 344). Strange the people may be, but there is little character to any of them, and O'Donnell is only slightly unfair when he notes that even the "love-war-art schema fails clumsily when he lists Huddon as the warrior instead of Daniel O'Leary, who is the only character to mention ever having been in a war."[21]

The stories were certainly born out of the environment of the material surrounding *A Vision* and its system. When Yeats wrote to Olivia Shakespear in

September 1929, he had finished *A Packet for Ezra Pound* and was immersed in clearing "up endless errors in my understanding of the script. My conviction of the truth of it all has grown also & that makes one clear" (*CL InteLex* 5285). Looking forward to *A Vision*'s going to press in spring 1930, he wrote:

> I shall begin also I hope the new version of the Robartes stories. Having proved, by undescribed process, the imortality of the soul to a little group of typical followers, he will discuss the deductions with an energy & a dogmatism & a cruelty I am not capable of in my own person. I have a very amusing setting thought out. (*CL InteLex* 5285; cit. *RAW* 167)

In the following month he would send Frank Pearce Sturm "Six Propositions" (Oct. 9, 1929, *CL InteLex* 5291),[22] formulating his ideas in the form of sutras or Indian "aphorisms," and these broad, generalized Propositions are hardly recognizable as the same system of thought as the technical and detailed descriptions of *A Vision*. In the *Stories*, the few fragments of Michael Robartes's teaching included at the end are far more recognizable and indeed energetic, dogmatic, and cruel, cast in the form of Nietzschean aphorisms, a mixture of shock tactics, paradox, grandiloquence, and classical balance (*AVB* 51–53; *RAW* 304–5).

It is the preceding stories that are less amenable to clear understanding. Narrated by John Duddon, the stories open with him waiting for Owen Aherne with another man and a woman in London. They meet Daniel O'Leary, who gives an account of the moment when he threw his boots at actors speaking verse badly, some aspect of which Robartes has seen in vision, but O'Leary thinks that the other young people "can understand even better than Robartes why that protest must always seem the great event of my life" (*AVB* 35, *RAW* 283). Duddon then moves on to tell of his relationship as a struggling artist with the rich "tall fair young man," Peter Huddon, and a young woman who "insists on calling herself Denise de L'Isle Adam" (*AVB* 35, *RAW* 284). As with O'Leary's failed boot-throwing, Duddon's attempted jealous assault on Huddon is a failure, with Owen Aherne being mistaken for Huddon and falling victim to his heavy stick, circumstances which have now brought the three of them to meet Michael Robartes and "drink a little wine" (*AVB* 36, *RAW* 284). Robartes and Aherne arrive, and Robartes proceeds to tell the story contained in the introduction of *A Vision A*, with some minor changes. The third section takes place "Some six weeks later [...] round the same fire" and involves the introduction of two further characters, disguised by Robartes under the names John Bond and Mary Bell. Bell is vaguely reminiscent of the young Isabella Augusta Persse, having married an older man who worked for the Foreign Office and is the owner of "a large house on the more peaceable side of the Shannon" (*AVB* 44, *RAW* 294).[23] She has an affair with Bond, which produces a child, but she severs connection for five years and only re-enters Bond's life when she comes to ask his advice as an expert on migratory birds to find out how to construct the nest that a cuckoo might build, as her husband's project is to reform cuckoos from laying their eggs in other birds' nests. This quixotic goal is an ironic commentary on the old man's position as a cuckold, but he dies happy when Bell brings him "a beautiful nest, finished to the last layer of down" (*AVB* 49, *RAW* 300). They are summoned to Robartes and London from the husband's funeral by Aherne,[24] but they have specific roles and are not to be his students.

The scene then takes on a ceremonial quality,[25] as Robartes cathechizes Duddon and his companions on whether he has "proved by practical demonstration that the soul survives the body" (*AVB* 50, *RAW* 301–2)—as Yeats had promised Olivia Shakespear, the process is "undescribed." He proceeds to make sure that they also accept his proof of the cyclical nature of civilizations, before he declares "we are here to consider the terror that is to come" (*AVB* 50, *RAW* 302). He then shows them Leda's third egg, "its miraculous life still unquenched," which Bell will bear to the desert "to be hatched by the sun's heat" (*AVB* 51, *RAW* 303), recalling perhaps the earlier vision of the "shape with lion body and the head of a man" arising in "sands of the desert" ("The Second Coming" [1919], *VP* 402).

The account closes with recollected snatches of Robartes's aphorisms, gnomic in their brevity and largely baffling apart from the system's exposition, but actually succinct aphoristic encapsulations of the material in *A Vision*. A letter from John Aherne is appended, further tangling the fiction and metafiction. Along with references to Yeats's actual poems and *A Vision A*, Owen Aherne's brother John mentions the work of Yeats's brother Jack. He also comments that some people find the woodcut of Giraldus resembles Yeats[26] and appears to suggest three separate revelations of the material: to Yeats, Giraldus, and the Judwalis, writing, "That you should have found what was lost in the *Speculum* or the inaccessible encampments of the Judwalis, interests me but does not astonish" (*AVB* 54, *RAW* 307).

The same young people—Huddon, Duddon, O'Leary, and de L'Isle Adam—gather in "Michael Robartes Foretells" and, in the other fragment that Chapman includes, de L'Isle Adam is able to deliver the story that was cut short in the original version, telling how Duddon is incapable of making love to her until she has slept with Huddon.[27] This last element recalls something of the *Spirit*'s relation with the *Celestial Body*, its true affinity, and the *Passionate Body*, its necessary affinity for experience, and there are definite hints of allegory or at least parable in the relations described.[28] We are told that Art is Duddon's profession, War Huddon's, and Love de L'Isle Adam's (*AVB* 37, *RAW* 286), while we are told at the outset that O'Leary works as chauffeur to Robartes and Aherne (*AVB* 33, *RAW* 281).[29] Taking the driver as the *Will of A Vision*, Matthew DeForrest discerns a dance of the four non-royal persons in the interactions of O'Leary (*Will*), Denise (*Mask*), Duddon (*Creative Mind*), and Huddon (*Body of Fate*); this allegory would be attractive if it made greater sense in terms of the system, yet the only man that de L'Isle Adam is not desired by is O'Leary, and the Mask must represent the *Will*'s object of desire.[30] De L'Isle Adam's name, borrowed from the author of *Axël*, may imply that she, like the play's hero, thinks that "as for living, our servants can do that," in some complex of surrogacy and "living each other's death, dying each other's life." Each possible attribution is both provocative and ultimately frustrating and, though it certainly feels as if these ciphers must have more behind them, the attempt to identify correspondences of characters and elements of *A Vision* ends up being rather reductive. Indeed, any "solution," however brilliant it may be, points to the failure of the art to embody the myth in any way that readers have found illuminating or helpful. And fascinating though the manuscript evidence is, there is little to clarify these conundrums. Even Robartes and Aherne do not appear to any great advantage in these stories, yet the final vignette of them setting off for the Middle East with Leda's egg and preparing for "the terror that is to come" seems a fitting close.

As indicated, the transcriptions of "Anglo Ireland," "The Stories of Michael Robartes," "Michael Robartes Foretells," and "Denise's Story" are accompanied by facsimiles of the manuscripts. These are crucial to a real appreciation of the drafts and a huge help to understanding the difficulties that the transcriber faces; they also offer the possibility for dissent or reappraisal. In most cases the quality of reproduction is high, though the draft of *The Stories of Michael Robartes* is evidently on paper of a fairly large format,[31] so that the reduction to the book page renders them less easily legible (this combines with curvature of the image, although they seem to be loose pages, and shearing of edges in a couple of places, e.g. *RAW* 224, 256). In theory the e-book versions—which I have not seen—may enable readers to look more clearly at the manuscripts and zoom in on details, though Bloomsbury's site mentions that both the E-Pub version and the PDF are watermarked, which raises the dispiriting possibility of shadows in inconvenient places.

In general, the care and detail of Wayne Chapman's transcriptions, including the attempts to deal with cancelled text and substitutions in Yeats's notorious hand, are admirable, giving the reader confidence in the transcriptions which are not accompanied by facsimile. It is honest to transcribe the word as it appears without wishing it into something plausible that fits (as was sometimes the case with earlier transcribers), but few choices seem improbable. A good transcription usually indicates some plausible combination of words and syntax—given time, place, and personal idiolect—though there is often no obvious right answer amid all the false starts and changed paths. Very occasionally a transcription does not read naturally, such as when Chapman gives "in the same little wandering ~~tri~~ tribe one will find, ~~the more they~~ the extreme living to tolerable amounts" (*RAW* 79), where the latter part makes little sense and there is no convincing phrasing with "amounts." There is no facsimile to compare, but I would hazard that it should probably be something closer to "the extremes living in tolerable amity" (cf. *YVP4* 122, cit. *RAW* 99, n1). Similarly when Robartes is made to comment that "Mr Yeats so far although at the being of the kin of St John of Patmos has but a few dreams broken dreams twenty years ago and may be half forgotten" (RAW 72–73), it seems clear that, with some or other wording, Robartes is denying Yeats the true vision that was granted to St. John as the basis of his Book of Revelations, and it may be that part of the cancelled text includes a "from" to give "far from being" or that the word has been forgotten. But in Chapman's confusing account, Robartes is "likening him to St. John of Patmos, said-author of the apocalyptic Book of Revelation, final chapter of the New Testament. With 'but a few broken dreams' to go on, Yeats's revelations are being derided as a come-lately form of false prophecy" (*RAW* 73). Contrasting is a form of likening, but it is misleading to imply likeness; and, as the final book of the New Testament, Revelations certainly includes the "final chapter," but it seems a poor choice of word in this context. Furthermore, Apocalypse is simply the Greek version of the name Revelation, so "the apocalyptic Book of Revelation" is something of a redundant doubling, and one that occurs again in "St John's description of the beast of Apocalypse in Revelations" (*RAW* 123, n1).

Elsewhere second thoughts do not seem to have been applied to revise earlier readings, so that a note gives "You protestants have no quibbles" (*RAW* 160), while the transcription facing the facsimile has "You protestants have your quotations but | but I do not see much Platonics about you" (*RAW* 59) (the repetition of "but" is perfectly natural, but here "Platonic" would make better sense that "Platonics" and the manuscript warrants either reading). On a slight tangent here, one thing that strikes me as a reader is the use of vertical lines for line breaks of poems and plays. It has been a useful convention to use vertical lines for describing title pages and manuscripts where the line breaks may or may not be fully significant, while using a slanted line or slash to separate poetic or dramatic writing where the line breaks are important elements of the form.[32] The vertical line may appear more aesthetically elegant, but using it indiscriminately for all line breaks—a shift also seen in the *Collected Letters* and often in the *Yeats Annual*—risks losing a useful distinction, especially in a work such as this, where manuscript transcriptions are found alongside quotations of poetry.

In *Yeats's Robartes-Aherne Writings*, Wayne Chapman succeeds in giving a full sense of Michael Robartes's and Owen Aherne's place in "the phantasmagoria through which alone I can express my convictions about the world" (*VP* 852, *RAW* 102),[33] with all the continuities and disjunctures involved, spanning published texts that were heavily reworked and unpublished drafts that never even reached typescript stage. Robartes and Aherne do achieve a form of independence separate from any single presentation, and this collection of all the relevant material strengthens the reader's sense of their coherence. It would be difficult to see them amid the pantheon of "'all that have ever been in your reverie, all that you have met with in books,'" such as Lear or Beatrice (*RAW* 7), but they are more than conveniences or simple mouthpieces. Robartes in particular comes to embody the system that the Yeatses created in A Vision, his energy and dogmatism giving him a form of committed belief that Yeats felt himself unable to express. Assigned to the Phase 18 with Giraldus and George Yeats herself,[34] the phase of "emotional philosophy," which comes after the *Daimonic* phase of Yeats and the poets, Robartes has the possibility of attaining the "Wisdom of the Heart" and he certainly has emotional intelligence, his passion matched by learning. Owen Aherne is a more ascetic and more circumspect character, whose phase is never given but would probably be later in the cycle, where *primary* orthodoxy affects the temperament, possibly at Phase 25 along with figures such as George Russell and George Herbert, as well as the turbulent clerics Luther, Calvin, and Cardinal Newman. The version of the system drawn from Robartes's papers that Aherne half achieved, according to the Introduction to *A Vision A*, in which he "interpreted the system as a form of Christianity" (*AVA* xxi, *RAW* 149) and favored its objective aspects, is intrinsically just as valid as the more subjective version created by Mr. Yeats and is arguably a more logical reading, seeing the final phases of the Wheel as a form of goal. Aherne's role is that of the questioner, Robartes's that of affirmer. In this volume, Chapman brings together the many pieces through which we see them in a fine patchwork. Including both crafted wholes and unpolished fragments, part of the charm lies in the disparateness of the elements, and it gives a more complete picture of this aspect of the phantasmagoria than has been possible before.

NOTES

1. W. B. Yeats, "*A Vision*" *and Related Writings*, sel. and ed. A. Norman Jeffares (London: Arena, 1990). Chapman indeed fills one of the major oversights in Jeffares's collection, which is the notes to volumes of poetry and plays, where Yeats uses the fictions of Robartes and Aherne to give expositions of *A Vision*'s system in different terms.
2. Aherne's name shifts between John and Owen, until the two are separated as brothers.
3. "The Adoration of the Magi" is the last of the stories told by the same narrator, where both Aherne and Robartes are mentioned but do not appear.
4. Throughout the text, *RAW* is used to refer to the book under review, *W. B. Yeats's Robartes-Aherne Writings*, in order to avoid confusion in the in-text citations.
5. Richard Ellmann, *Yeats: The Man and His Masks* 2nd edn. (Harmondsworth: Penguin, 1979; 1987), especially Chapter 6, "Robartes and Aherne: Two Sides of a Penny," 73–88.
6. The primary texts available are in W. B. Yeats, *Mythologies* (London: Macmillan, 1959); Yeats, *The Secret Rose: A Variorum Edition*, eds. Warwick Gould, Phillip L. Marcus, and Michael J. Sidnell, 1st edn. (Ithaca, NY: Cornell, 1981), 2nd rev. edn. (New York: Macmillan, 1992); and Yeats, *Mythologies*, eds. Warwick Gould and DeirdreToomey (New York: Palgrave Macmillan, 2005).
7. Robartes's appearance in the titles of poems in *The Wind Among the Reeds*, alongside Mongan, Hanrahan, and Aedh, the latter two with associated qualities that contrast with Robartes as "the pride of the imagination brooding upon the greatness of its possessions, or the adoration of the Magi," are examined in the general introduction (RAW xxii–xxvi) rather than included as one of the texts.
8. Yeats had already republished *The Tables of the Law / The Adoration of the Magi* in 1904 with Elkin Mathews, noting that "I do not think I should have reprinted them had I not met a young man the other day who liked them very much and nothing else at all that I have written" (*RAW* xxxv), the young man in question being James Joyce.
9. Robartes is mentioned in the poem "Ego Dominus Tuus," dated 1915 (see below); the poem is given in full, *RAW* 103–05.

10. The spelling of the Latin author is variously Giraldus, Geraldus, and Gyraldus in print, and mainly Gyraldus in the letters, as well as Gyraldous, as here.

11. George Mills Harper, Margaret Mills Harper, and Richard W. Stoops, Jr., eds., *Yeats's 'Vision' Papers*, vol. 4 (New York: Palgrave, 2001).

12. It would save possible puzzlement on the part of the reader to explain why misprints such as "hither and hither" (*RAW* 12, line 397) for *hither and thither* or "and bad it flutter" (*RAW* 12, line 407) for *and bade it flutter* are retained.

13. One further passage from "The Cones—Higher Dimensions" that refers to "the sentence quoted by Aherne about the great eggs which turn themselves inside out without breaking the shell" is included as a footnote to the Introduction, mainly because it is written in the voice of Yeats/Mr. Yeats—itself a dichotomy worth teasing out.

14. Given the completeness of Chapman's project, it is perhaps surprising not to see the variants from the Prospectus for *A Vision*; see "T. Werner Laurie's Prospectus for Subscribers," *The System of Yeats's "A Vision,"* http://www.yeatsvision.com/Prospectus.html.

15. A line or two describing the typescripts would give the reader a little context, though a description of the typescripts can be easily enough checked by those who know to look in Peter Kenny, "Collection List No. 60: The Occult Papers of W. B. Yeats," National Library of Ireland, accessed September 20, 2019, http://www.nli.ie/pdfs/mss%20lists/yeatsoccult.pdf.

16. Islamic distinctions cause problems in the controversial comment that: "Most Sunni and Shia Muslims today disapprove of Wahhabism, nowadays associated with global terrorism" (*RAW* 132), which raises so many issues in such a short sentence that it is best left.

17. William H. O'Donnell's rather cursory treatment in *A Guide to the Prose Fiction of W. B. Yeats* (Ann Arbor, Mich.: UMI Research Press, 1983) notes that the drafts were not polished in the way that Yeats had reworked his earlier prose fiction, "and almost no significant changes were made between the first draft and the published text" (139).

18. The different approach from the stories of *The Secret Rose* (where only major variants are given as endnotes) is partly justified by the far simpler variants, though Chapman chooses to include proofs alongside the other printing, and partly because there was little point in creating a different variorum of the earlier stories alongside *The Secret Rose: A Variorum Edition* (see n6).

19. In the section "Unpublished Fragment, November 1917," the essay "Imaginary Conversations, 'The Phases of the Moon,' and the Robartes Monologue in *The Wild Swans at Coole*" includes references to the *Variorum Poems, Plays,* or other editions from Macmillan and, in the second part, also Scribner's *Collected Works*, where the two references are separated by a semi-colon. It is generally written in high academic style, with phrases such as "as a prolusion" (*RAW* 34, 42) and "the insipient modern age" (*RAW* 48), without contractions. In the following section, "Unpublished 'Discoveries,' 1917–1920," the essay "Creating Story in 'The Discoveries of Michael Robartes,' 1917–1920" separates references to *Variorum Poems* and *Mythologies* by a slash where both are used. The essay is written in a looser style: "It seems pretty clear from this that it is too soon for Robartes and Aherne to confront Yeats, except behind his back" (a paradoxical situation), and "Right away, he plunges into the objections. [...] We hear them; but, supposedly, he doesn't" (*RAW* 83). In both essays, letters are sometimes cited from Wade's Letters and elsewhere from *CL InteLex* (even when also in Wade, without cross-referencing to Wade). We once get Yeats's letter of Jan. 4, 1918 to Lady Gregory in John Kelly's version from *CL InteLex* (*RAW* 89) and once in Wade's tidier version (*RAW* 126, n6). Slightly mystifying too are references to Edward O'Shea's *Yeats's Library* without cross-reference to Chapman's own newer and more accurate *The W. B. and George Yeats Library: A Short Title Catalog* (Clemson, SC: Clemson University Press, 2006). The essay on the White Vellum Notebook switches halfway through from the declared convention of putting "Overwritings are formalized within large curly braces { }" (*RAW* xii),

when the page numbers written into the notebook by Curtis Bradford shift from curly into square brackets on p. 276.

20. O'Donnell, *A Guide to the Prose Fiction*, 140.

21. O'Donnell, *A Guide to the Prose Fiction*, 140.

22. A version of the "Seven Propositions"; see Mann, "Seven Propositions," (rev. Sep. 2008, corr. Apr. 2009), *The System of Yeats's "A Vision,"* consulted September 2019, www.yeatsvision.com/7Propositions.html.

23. Whether or not Yeats knew of Augusta Gregory's affairs with Wilfred Scawen Blunt as a young married woman or John Quinn when a widow, he must have been aware of her more passionate side.

24. Recalling the importance of Hermes in "The Adoration of the Magi," Aherne has an almost psychopompic role, as Robartes says, "'I want the right sort of young men and women for pupils. Aherne acts as my messenger'" (*AVB* 37, *RAW* 286).

25. There is a change of section in AVB but the change comes slightly later in the Cuala text.

26. Edmund Dulac had based the woodcut on Yeats, of course, and Yeats said that he doubted "if Laurie would have taken the book but for the amusing deceit that your designs make possible. It saves it from seeming a book for specialists only & gives it a new imaginative existence" (Oct. 14, [1923], *CL InteLex* 4381).

27. Chapman explains the connection with "an exact transcript from fact" of the goings-on in the Yeatses' sub-let house in Oxford (W. B. Yeats to Dorothy Wellesley, July 26, [1936], *CL InteLex* 6622), though it also recalls an earlier anecdote about George Moore: "I hear also that Moore lately made love to a young woman, who belonged to Sickert & that when she would not have anything to do with him Moore remonstrated with the words 'but Sickert & I always share'" (W. B. Yeats to Florence Farr, [Apr. 14, 1908], *CL5* 173).

28. Compare this with "The Passionate & Celestial Body," where a male *Spirit* moves between two brides; Rapallo Notebook C (NLI 13,580), [59r]; see also Neil Mann, *A Reader's Guide to "A Vision"* (Clemson, SC: Clemson University Press, 2019), 138.

29. His declaration that "I am the chauffeur: I always am on these occasions, it prevents gossip" (*AVB* 33, *RAW* 281) indicates that he is just the chauffeur for collecting possible students, though there is no indication of any previous occasion or other students.

30. Matthew DeForrest is the only writer I am aware of who has seriously tried to work out the possible allegory in these terms. As he notes, "John Bond" and "Mary Bell," together with Robartes and Aherne—make up another group of four, whom he identifies with the *Principles*, and he also traces the course of the stories through the twenty-eight phases that are "every completed movement of thought or life" (AVB 81); DeForrest, "Stories of Michael Robartes and His Friends," *The Canadian Journal of Irish Studies* 18, no. 2 (Dec. 1992): 48–57.

31. The dimensions of the manuscript pages are not given in any of the cases.

32. This is the advice given in the MLA guidelines and *Chicago Manual of Style* 17th edn., 6.111, 13.29, 13.34. A double slash may indicate a stanza break and a double vertical line may be used for a caesura, where relevant.

33. Yeats repeats the formulation in *Later Poems* (1922), where Robartes and Aherne "take their place in a phantasmagoria in which I endeavour to explain my philosophy of life and death" (*VP* 821, *RAW* 114). "Phantasmagoria" was an early-nineteenth-century term for light shows with projected spectral images. Describing a séance in "Swedenborg, Mediums, and the Desolate Places," Yeats notes "All may seem histrionic or a hollow show. We are the spectators of a phantasmagoria that affects the photographic plate [...] Yet we never long escape the phantasmagoria nor can long forget that we are among the shape-changers" (*Ex* 54–55, *CW5* 62–63). Yeats's usage implies a construct that is both voluntary and unconscious, writing of "those strange sights that only show themselves for an instant, when the

attention has been withdrawn; that phantasmagoria of which I had learnt something in London," presumably in the Golden Dawn (*Au* 243, *CW3* 198).

34. Robartes is assigned to Phase 18 (*YVP1* 149; *YVP4* 150), but also to Phase 19 "where expression is almost too facile" (*YVP4* 31; cf. 86).

Notes On Contributors

Zsuzsanna Balázs is an Irish Research Council Postgraduate Scholar in the O'Donoghue Centre for Drama, Theatre and Performance at the National University of Ireland, Galway. She completed her BA in Italian Studies and her MA in Postcolonial Studies at Pázmány Péter Catholic University in Budapest. Her PhD research considers the anti-normative and anti-authoritarian temperaments in the plays of W. B. Yeats, Gabriele D'Annunzio, and Luigi Pirandello, focusing on unorthodox representations of gender and power performance. She is also founding member of Modernist Studies Ireland.

Claire Bracken is an associate professor in the English Department at Union College, New York. She is co-editor (with Susan Cahill) of *Anne Enright* (Irish Academic Press, 2011) and (with Emma Radley) *Viewpoints: Theoretical Perspectives on Irish Visual Texts* (Cork University Press, 2013). Her book *Irish Feminist Futures* was published by Routledge in 2016. In 2017 she co-edited, with Tara Harney-Mahajan, a double special issue of the journal *LIT*, entitled *Recessionary Imaginings: Post-Celtic Tiger Ireland and Contemporary Women's Writing*.

Alex Bubb is a senior lecturer in English at Roehampton University in London. His book *Meeting Without Knowing It: Kipling and Yeats at the Fin de Siècle* (Oxford University Press, 2016) is a comparative study of Yeats and his antagonistic contemporary in the 1890s. It won the University English Book Prize in 2017.

Rob Doggett is Professor and Chair of English at the State University of New York (SUNY), Geneseo. He is the author of *Deep-Rooted Things: Empire and Nation in the Poetry and Drama of William Butler Yeats* (University of Notre Dame Press, 2005) and is editor of two editions of Yeats's early writings from Penguin Press.

Rosie Lavan is an assistant professor at Trinity College, Dublin. Her monograph Seamus Heaney and Society is forthcoming with Oxford University Press in 2019. Her articles on Heaney have been published in The Irish Review, Essays in Criticism, and Seamus Heaney in Context. She is the author of "Violence, Politics, and Irish Poetry" for the forthcoming *Irish Literature in Transition* volume 5 (with Cambridge University Press). Her current research project is "Representing Derry, 1968–2003."

NEIL MANN has written extensively on Yeats's esoteric interests, particularly *A Vision*, in essays, on the website YeatsVision.com, and most recently in *A Reader's Guide to Yeats's* A Vision (Clemson University Press, 2019). Based in Spain, he works as an editor, translator, and teacher.

CARRIE PRESTON is the Arvind and Chandan Nandlal Kilachand Professor and Director of Kilachand Honors College at Boston University. She is the author of *Modernism's Mythic Pose: Gender, Genre, & Solo Performance* (Oxford University Press, 2011) and *Learning to Kneel: Noh, Modernism, & Journeys in Teaching* (Columbia University Press, 2016). She is currently working on a new book entitled *Participate! Race and Gender in the Audience for Interactive Theater*, a critical examination of the political and pedagogical work of audience participation.

JUSTIN QUINN is an associate professor at the University of West Bohemia in Pilsen, Czech Republic. His most recent monograph is *Between Two Fires: Transnationalism and Cold War Poetry* (2015). At present he is editing a book (with Gabriela Klečková) on the role of literature in Second Language Teacher Education, which is based on the new program in the English Department of the Faculty of Education at the University of West Bohemia.

MALCOLM SEN is an assistant professor in the Department of English at the University of Massachusetts, Amherst. He is the editor (with Lucienne Loh) of *Postcolonial Studies and the Challenges of the New Millennium* (Routledge, 2016) and *The Cambridge History of Irish Literature and the Environment* (forthcoming, Cambridge University Press, 2020). He is completing his monograph study, *Unnatural Disasters: Literature, Climate Change and Sovereignty*. His article, "Risk and Refuge: Contemplating Precarity in Contemporary Irish Fiction," was recently published in the *Irish University Review*.

KELLY SULLIVAN is a clinical associate professor at Glucksman Ireland House, New York University. Her work is published or forthcoming in *Modernism/modernity*, *Eire-Ireland*, *Irish University Review*, the *Public Domain Review*, and elsewhere. Her poetry chapbook, *Fell Year*, was published by Green Bottle Press in 2016.

TOM WALKER is the Ussher Assistant Professor of Irish Writing at Trinity College, Dublin. He is the author of *Louis MacNeice and the Irish Poetry of his Time* (Oxford University Press, 2015). He recently co-edited a special issue of *Modernist Cultures* on "Collaborative Poetics." He is currently trying to write a book about Yeats and art writing.